HMH SCIENCE DIMENSIONS.
EARTH & HUMAN ACTIVITY

Module G

This Write-In Book belongs to

Sarah Quevedo

Teacher/Room

Garvey / 201

Houghton Mifflin Harcourt.

Consulting Authors

Michael A. DiSpezio

Global Educator
North Falmouth,
Massachusetts

Michael DiSpezio has authored many HMH instructional programs for Science and Mathematics. He has also authored numerous trade books and multimedia programs on various topics and hosted dozens of studio and location broadcasts for various organizations in the United States and worldwide. Most recently, he has been working with educators to provide strategies for implementing the Next Generation Science Standards, particularly the Science and Engineering Practices, Crosscutting Concepts, and the use of Evidence Notebooks. To all his projects, he brings his extensive background in science, his expertise in classroom teaching at the elementary, middle, and high school levels, and his deep experience in producing interactive and engaging instructional materials.

Marjorie Frank

Science Writer and Content-
Area Reading Specialist
Brooklyn, New York

An educator and linguist by training, a writer and poet by nature, Marjorie Frank has authored and designed a generation of instructional materials in all subject areas, including past HMH Science programs. Her other credits include authoring science issues of an award-winning children's magazine, writing game-based digital assessments, developing blended learning materials for young children, and serving as instructional designer and coauthor of pioneering school-to-work software. In addition, she has served on the adjunct faculty of Hunter, Manhattan, and Brooklyn Colleges, teaching courses in science methods, literacy, and writing. For *HMH Science Dimensions™,* she has guided the development of our K–2 strands and our approach to making connections between NGSS and Common Core ELA/literacy standards.

Acknowledgments for Covers

Cover credits: (plant) ©HMH; (Earth at night) ©Nastco/iStock/Getty Images Plus/Getty Images.

Section Header Master Art: (rivers on top of Greenland ice sheet) ©Maria-José Viñas, NASA Earth Science News Team.

Printed in the U.S.A.

ISBN   978-0-544-86100-8

12   0928   25 24 23 22

4500844123   C D E F G

Michael R. Heithaus, PhD

Dean, College of Arts, Sciences & Education
Professor, Department of Biological Sciences
Florida International University
Miami, Florida

Mike Heithaus joined the FIU Biology Department in 2003 and has served as Director of the Marine Sciences Program and Executive Director of the School of Environment, Arts, and Society, which brings together the natural and social sciences and humanities to develop solutions to today's environmental challenges. He now serves as Dean of the College of Arts, Sciences & Education. His research focuses on predator-prey interactions and the ecological importance of large marine species. He has helped to guide the development of Life Science content in *HMH Science Dimensions™*, with a focus on strategies for teaching challenging content as well as the science and engineering practices of analyzing data and using computational thinking.

Cary I. Sneider, PhD

Associate Research Professor
Portland State University
Portland, Oregon

While studying astrophysics at Harvard, Cary Sneider volunteered to teach in an Upward Bound program and discovered his real calling as a science teacher. After teaching middle and high school science in Maine, California, Costa Rica, and Micronesia, he settled for nearly three decades at Lawrence Hall of Science in Berkeley, California, where he developed skills in curriculum development and teacher education. Over his career, Cary directed more than 20 federal, state, and foundation grant projects and was a writing team leader for the Next Generation Science Standards. He has been instrumental in ensuring *HMH Science Dimensions™* meets the high expectations of the NGSS and provides an effective three-dimensional learning experience for all students.

Program Advisors

Paul D. Asimow, PhD
Eleanor and John R. McMillan Professor of Geology and Geochemistry
California Institute of Technology
Pasadena, California

Joanne Bourgeois
Professor Emerita
Earth & Space Sciences
University of Washington
Seattle, WA

Dr. Eileen Cashman
Professor
Humboldt State University
Arcata, California

Elizabeth A. De Stasio, PhD
Raymond J. Herzog Professor of Science
Lawrence University
Appleton, Wisconsin

Perry Donham, PhD
Lecturer
Boston University
Boston, Massachusetts

Shila Garg, PhD
Emerita Professor of Physics
Former Dean of Faculty & Provost
The College of Wooster
Wooster, Ohio

Tatiana A. Krivosheev, PhD
Professor of Physics
Clayton State University
Morrow, Georgia

Mark B. Moldwin, PhD
Professor of Space Sciences and Engineering
University of Michigan
Ann Arbor, Michigan

Ross H. Nehm
Stony Brook University (SUNY)
Stony Brook, NY

Kelly Y. Neiles, PhD
Assistant Professor of Chemistry
St. Mary's College of Maryland
St. Mary's City, Maryland

John Nielsen-Gammon, PhD
Regents Professor
Department of Atmospheric Sciences
Texas A&M University
College Station, Texas

Dr. Sten Odenwald
Astronomer
NASA Goddard Spaceflight Center
Greenbelt, Maryland

Bruce W. Schafer
Executive Director
Oregon Robotics Tournament & Outreach Program
Beaverton, Oregon

Barry A. Van Deman
President and CEO
Museum of Life and Science
Durham, North Carolina

Kim Withers, PhD
Assistant Professor
Texas A&M University-Corpus Christi
Corpus Christi, Texas

Adam D. Woods, PhD
Professor
California State University, Fullerton
Fullerton, California

Classroom Reviewers

Cynthia Book, PhD
John Barrett Middle School
Carmichael, California

Katherine Carter, MEd
Fremont Unified School District
Fremont, California

Theresa Hollenbeck, MEd
Winston Churchill Middle School
Carmichael, California

Kathryn S. King
Science and AVID Teacher
Norwood Jr. High School
Sacramento, California

Donna Lee
Science/STEM Teacher
Junction Ave. K8
Livermore, California

Rebecca S. Lewis
Science Teacher
North Rockford Middle School
Rockford, Michigan

Bryce McCourt
*8th Grade Science Teacher/Middle
School Curriculum Chair*
Cudahy Middle School
Cudahy, Wisconsin

Sarah Mrozinski
Teacher
St. Sebastian School
Milwaukee, Wisconsin

Raymond Pietersen
Science Program Specialist
Elk Grove Unified School District
Elk Grove, California

You are a scientist!
You are naturally curious.

Have you ever wondered . . .

- why is it difficult to catch a fly?
- how a new island can appear in an ocean?
- how to design a great tree house?
- how a spacecraft can send messages across the solar system?

HMH SCIENCE DIMENSIONS™

will *SPARK* your curiosity!

AND prepare you for

✓	tomorrow
✓	next year
✓	college or career
✓	life!

Where do you see yourself in 15 years?

Observe

Collect Data

Be a scientist.
Work like real scientists work.

Analyze

Be an engineer.
Solve problems like engineers do.

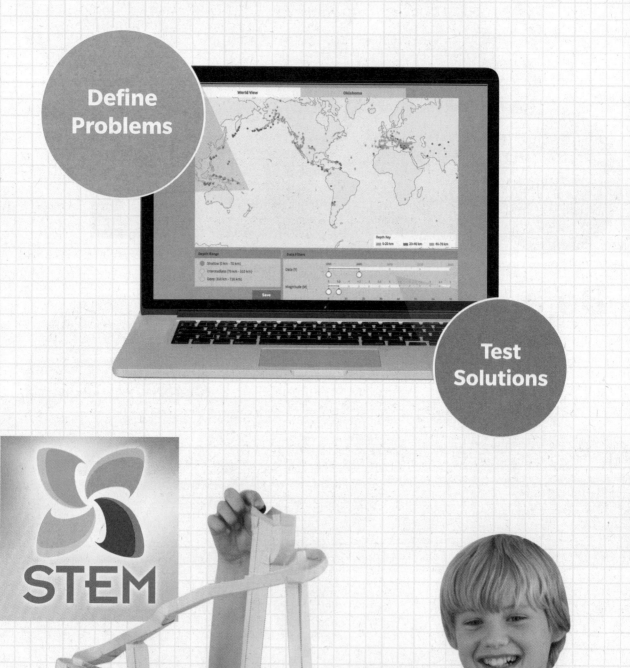

Define Problems

Test Solutions

STEM

Gather Information

Think Critically

Explain your world.

Start by asking questions.

Conduct Investigations

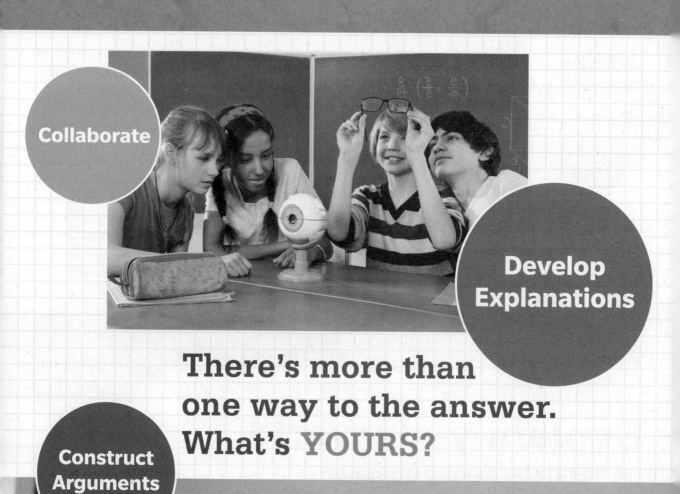

Collaborate

Develop Explanations

Construct Arguments

There's more than one way to the answer. What's YOURS?

YOUR Program

Write-In Book:

- a brand-new and innovative textbook that will guide you through your next generation curriculum, including your hands-on lab program

Interactive Online Student Edition:

- a complete online version of your textbook enriched with videos, interactivities, animations, simulations, and room to enter data, draw, and store your work

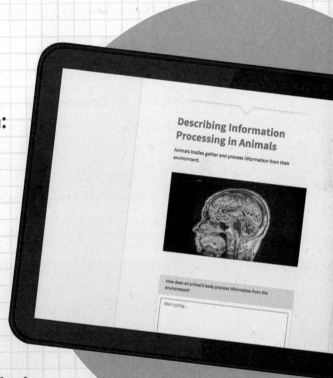

More tools are available online to help you practice and learn science, including:

- Hands-On Labs
- Science and Engineering Practices Handbook
- Crosscutting Concepts Handbook
- English Language Arts Handbook
- Math Handbook

UNIT 1

1

Earth's Natural Hazards

Lesson 1
Natural Hazards 4

 Hands-On Lab Assess Building Sites Near a Volcano 15

Lesson 2
Natural Hazard Prediction 26

Hands-On Lab Predict a Landslide 30

Lesson 3
Engineer It: Reducing the Effects of Natural Hazards 48

Hands-On Lab Develop and Evaluate a Flood Solution 58

Careers in Engineering Geotechnical Engineer 61

Unit Review 67

ENGINEER IT **Unit Performance Task** 71

Mount Vesuvius, on the coast of Italy, has produced eight
major volcanic eruptions within the last 17,000 years.

UNIT 2   73

Resources in Earth Systems

Lesson 1
Natural Resources. 76

 Hands-On Lab   Explore Replacement of a Natural Resource 86

     Careers in Engineering   Biomass Engineer 91

Lesson 2
The Distribution of Natural Resources. 96

Hands-On Lab   Model Recharge and Withdrawal in an Aquifer. 109

Unit Review 117

Unit Performance Task 121

Fish are a resource humans use for food and plant fertilizer.

UNIT 3

Using Resources

Lesson 1
Human Population and Resource Use 126

 Hands-On Lab Model Resource Use 135

Hands-On Lab Model Factors in Resource Use 138

Careers in Science Conservation Scientist 143

Lesson 2
Resource Use and Earth's Systems 148

Hands-On Lab Analyze Your Impact 160

Unit Review 171

Unit Performance Task 175

The water lilies and other living things in and around this lake depend on its water.

UNIT 4

Human Impacts on Earth Systems

Lesson 1
Human Impacts on the Environment 180

 Hands-On Lab Model Ocean Pollution from Land 186

Lesson 2
Engineer It: Reducing Human Impacts on the Environment 200

Hands-On Lab Design a Method to Monitor Solid Waste from a School 209

Hands-On Lab Evaluate a Method to Reduce the Impact of Solid Waste on
the Environment 217

Lesson 3
Climate Change 224

Hands-On Lab Model the Greenhouse Effect 228

Careers in Science Geeta G. Persad, Postdoctoral Research Scientist 241

Unit Review 247

Unit Performance Task 251

Deforestation is the removal of trees and other plants
from an area, such as the forest shown in this photo.

Whether you are in the lab or in the field, you are responsible for your own safety and the safety of others. To fulfill these responsibilities and avoid accidents, be aware of the safety of your classmates as well as your own safety at all times. Take your lab work and fieldwork seriously, and behave appropriately. Elements of safety to keep in mind are shown below and on the following pages.

Safety in the Lab

- [ ] Be sure you understand the materials, your procedure, and the safety rules before you start an investigation in the lab.

- [ ] Know where to find and how to use fire extinguishers, eyewash stations, shower stations, and emergency power shutoffs.

- [ ] Use proper safety equipment. Always wear personal protective equipment, such as eye protection and gloves, when setting up labs, during labs, and when cleaning up.

- [ ] Do not begin until your teacher has told you to start. Follow directions.

- [ ] Keep the lab neat and uncluttered. Clean up when you are finished. Report all spills to your teacher immediately. Watch for slip/fall and trip/fall hazards.

- [ ] If you or another student are injured in any way, tell your teacher immediately, even if the injury seems minor.

- [ ] Do not take any food or drink into the lab. Never take any chemicals out of the lab.

Safety in the Field

- [ ] Be sure you understand the goal of your fieldwork and the proper way to carry out the investigation before you begin fieldwork.

- [ ] Use proper safety equipment and personal protective equipment, such as eye protection, that suits the terrain and the weather.

- [ ] Follow directions, including appropriate safety procedures as provided by your teacher.

- [ ] Do not approach or touch wild animals. Do not touch plants unless instructed by your teacher to do so. Leave natural areas as you found them.

- [ ] Stay with your group.

- [ ] Use proper accident procedures, and let your teacher know about a hazard in the environment or an accident immediately, even if the hazard or accident seems minor.

Safety Symbols

To highlight specific types of precautions, the following symbols are used throughout the lab program. Remember that no matter what safety symbols you see within each lab, all safety rules should be followed at all times.

Dress Code

- Wear safety goggles (or safety glasses as appropriate for the activity) at all times in the lab as directed. If chemicals get into your eye, flush your eyes immediately for a minimum of 15 minutes.
- Do not wear contact lenses in the lab.
- Do not look directly at the sun or any intense light source or laser.
- Wear appropriate protective non-latex gloves as directed.
- Wear an apron or lab coat at all times in the lab as directed.
- Tie back long hair, secure loose clothing, and remove loose jewelry. Remove acrylic nails when working with active flames.
- Do not wear open-toed shoes, sandals, or canvas shoes in the lab.

Glassware and Sharp Object Safety

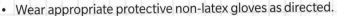
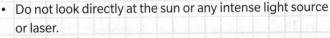

- Do not use chipped or cracked glassware.
- Use heat-resistant glassware for heating or storing hot materials.
- Notify your teacher immediately if a piece of glass breaks.
- Use extreme care when handling any sharp or pointed instruments.
- Do not cut an object while holding the object unsupported in your hands. Place the object on a suitable cutting surface, and always cut in a direction away from your body.

Chemical Safety

- If a chemical gets on your skin, on your clothing, or in your eyes, rinse it immediately for a minimum of 15 minutes (using the shower, faucet, or eyewash station), and alert your teacher.
- Do not clean up spilled chemicals unless your teacher directs you to do so.
- Do not inhale any gas or vapor unless directed to do so by your teacher. If you are instructed to note the odor of a substance, wave the fumes toward your nose with your hand. This is called wafting. Never put your nose close to the source of the odor.
- Handle materials that emit vapors or gases in a well-ventilated area.
- Keep your hands away from your face while you are working on any activity.

Safety Symbols, continued

Electrical Safety

- Do not use equipment with frayed electrical cords or loose plugs.
- Do not use electrical equipment near water or when clothing or hands are wet.
- Hold the plug housing when you plug in or unplug equipment. Do not pull on the cord.
- Use only GFI-protected electrical receptacles.

Heating and Fire Safety

- Be aware of any source of flames, sparks, or heat (such as flames, heating coils, or hot plates) before working with any flammable substances.
- Know the location of the lab's fire extinguisher and fire-safety blankets.
- Know your school's fire-evacuation routes.
- If your clothing catches on fire, walk to the lab shower to put out the fire. Do not run.
- Never leave a hot plate unattended while it is turned on or while it is cooling.
- Use tongs or appropriately insulated holders when handling heated objects.
- Allow all equipment to cool before storing it.

Plant and Animal Safety

- Do not eat any part of a plant.
- Do not pick any wild plant unless your teacher instructs you to do so.
- Handle animals only as your teacher directs.
- Treat animals carefully and respectfully.
- Wash your hands throughly with soap and water after handling any plant or animal.

Cleanup

- Clean all work surfaces and protective equipment as directed by your teacher.
- Dispose of hazardous materials or sharp objects only as directed by your teacher.
- Wash your hands throughly with soap and water before you leave the lab or after any activity.

Student Safety Quiz

Circle the letter of the BEST answer.

1. Before starting an investigation or lab procedure, you should
   A. try an experiment of your own
   B. open all containers and packages
   C. read all directions and make sure you understand them
   D. handle all the equipment to become familiar with it

2. At the end of any activity you should
   A. wash your hands thoroughly with soap and water before leaving the lab
   B. cover your face with your hands
   C. put on your safety goggles
   D. leave hot plates switched on

3. If you get hurt or injured in any way, you should
   A. tell your teacher immediately
   B. find bandages or a first aid kit
   C. go to your principal's office
   D. get help after you finish the lab

4. If your glassware is chipped or broken, you should
   A. use it only for solid materials
   B. give it to your teacher for recycling or disposal
   C. put it back into the storage cabinet
   D. increase the damage so that it is obvious

5. If you have unused chemicals after finishing a procedure, you should
   A. pour them down a sink or drain
   B. mix them all together in a bucket
   C. put them back into their original containers
   D. dispose of them as directed by your teacher

6. If electrical equipment has a frayed cord, you should
   A. unplug the equipment by pulling the cord
   B. let the cord hang over the side of a counter or table
   C. tell your teacher about the problem immediately
   D. wrap tape around the cord to repair it

7. If you need to determine the odor of a chemical or a solution, you should
   A. use your hand to bring fumes from the container to your nose
   B. bring the container under your nose and inhale deeply
   C. tell your teacher immediately
   D. use odor-sensing equipment

8. When working with materials that might fly into the air and hurt someone's eye, you should wear
   A. goggles
   B. an apron
   C. gloves
   D. a hat

9. Before doing experiments involving a heat source, you should know the location of the
   A. door
   B. window
   C. fire extinguisher
   D. overhead lights

10. If you get chemicals in your eye you should
    A. wash your hands immediately
    B. put the lid back on the chemical container
    C. wait to see if your eye becomes irritated
    D. use the eyewash station right away, for a minimum of 15 minutes

Go online to view the Lab Safety Handbook for additional information.

Earth's Natural Hazards

Lesson 1 Natural Hazards 4

Lesson 2 Natural Hazard Prediction 26

Lesson 3 Engineer It: Reducing the
Effects of Natural Hazards 48

Unit Review 67

Unit Performance Task 71

Wildfires, such as this one in the Rocky Mountains, are a type of natural hazard. These destructive events can destroy thousands of acres of forest and can threaten cities and homes.

Natural hazards can occur at any time. Fires, earthquakes, floods, tornadoes, hurricanes, and tsunamis are all events that may cause destruction, injury, and death. Scientists and engineers are studying these events and developing technologies that will help to better predict when these events will occur. Scientists and community planners are constantly working on ways to reduce the effects of these events and save human lives. In this unit you will explore different types of natural hazards and how they can affect people.

Why It Matters

Here are some questions to consider as you work through the unit. Can you answer any of the questions now? Revisit these questions at the end of the unit to apply what you discover.

Questions	Notes
What types of natural hazards are likely where you live?	
How could the natural hazards you listed above cause damage or injury?	
What is a natural disaster?	
What types of monitoring and communication networks alert you to possible natural hazards?	
How could your home and school be affected by a natural hazard?	
How can the effects of a natural disaster be reduced?	

Unit Starter: Analyzing the Frequency of Hurricanes

Hurricanes develop in the Atlantic Ocean most years. Depending on how much energy they have when they strike land, they can become natural disasters and cause destruction of natural land and human communities.

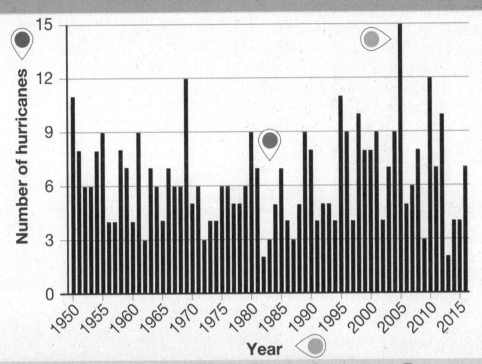

The y-axis shows how many hurricanes happen in the North Atlantic Basin each year.

The x-axis shows the year when the hurricanes occurred.

1982 and 2013 were the years with the fewest hurricanes recorded from 1950 to 2105.

In 2005, 15 hurricanes developed in the North Atlantic Basin.

1. From 1950 to 1983, there were 9 or more hurricanes in two / four / five different years. From 1984 to 2016, there were 9 or more hurricanes in two / nine / twelve different years.

Go online to download the Unit Project Worksheet to help you plan your project.

Unit Project

Natural Hazard Planning

There are many different types of natural hazards. How do people prepare for them? How do people respond when a disaster strikes? Choose a natural hazard to research, and create a plan to minimize the effects of that hazard.

Natural Hazards

In 2015, this wildfire near Clear Lake, California, destroyed property and devastated the environment.

By the end of this lesson . . .

you will be able to analyze and interpret data to describe natural hazards.

Go online to view the digital version of the Hands-On Lab for this lesson and to download additional lab resources.

CAN YOU EXPLAIN IT?

How was this city suddenly buried without warning?

In the 1700s, scientists in Italy discovered a city that had been buried for over 1,900 years. As they dug down to see more and more of the city, they discovered that the buildings and other structures were still standing. And it appeared that the city had been buried very suddenly. There were cavities in the ground in the shapes of people and animals all over the city. The city's inhabitants had been buried suddenly, and over hundreds of years the bodies had decayed. Scientists began filling the cavities with plaster or cement and letting it dry. Then they carefully removed the material around the cement so they could see the shape of the cavity. One of these cement casts is shown in the photo.

1. What could have buried this city and its people so suddenly?

EVIDENCE NOTEBOOK As you explore this lesson, gather evidence to help explain what could have suddenly buried this ancient city.

Describing Natural Hazards and Natural Disasters

A naturally occurring event that can have a negative effect on humans or the environment is called a **natural hazard**. Natural hazards include floods, storms, droughts, avalanches, wildfires, earthquakes, tsunamis, hurricanes, tornadoes, and volcanic eruptions. Natural hazards also include the spread of disease and space-related hazards such as meteorite impacts. Humans cannot control the causes of natural hazards. However, understanding these events can help humans find ways to make these events less destructive. Humans can identify areas where natural hazards are likely to occur and find ways to prepare for these events.

Natural Hazard Risk in the United States

This map shows where the risk is greatest for tornadoes, hurricanes, and earthquakes.

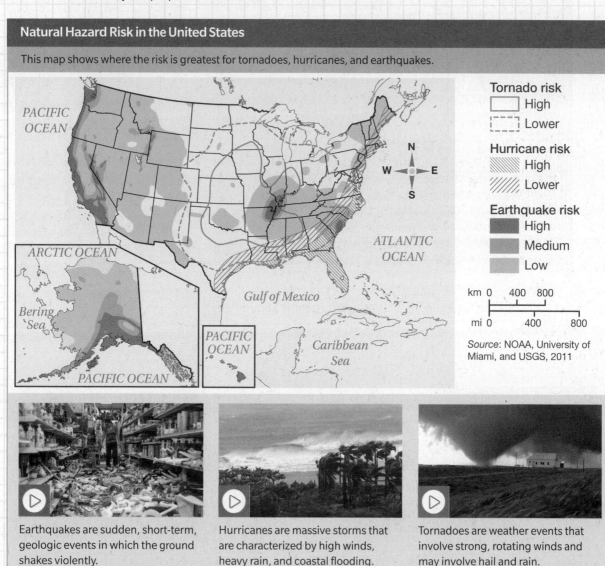

Earthquakes are sudden, short-term, geologic events in which the ground shakes violently.

Hurricanes are massive storms that are characterized by high winds, heavy rain, and coastal flooding.

Tornadoes are weather events that involve strong, rotating winds and may involve hail and rain.

2. **Discuss** Do any of the natural hazards shown on the map occur where you live? Do you know why or why not? Discuss your ideas with a partner.

Natural Hazards and Natural Disasters

Any natural hazard can become a **natural disaster** if it causes widespread injury, death, or property damage. A natural disaster may occur in only one small area, or it may cover large areas—even several countries. As the human population increases, the number of natural disasters increases as well. Whenever a natural hazard affects a heavily populated area, the chance of it becoming a natural disaster increases.

3. Label each photo to show whether it is a natural hazard or a natural disaster.

Sometimes, hurricanes occur over the ocean and never reach land. This satellite image shows several large hurricanes. Hawaii is in the middle of the image.

Hurricanes with strong winds and heavy rain can cause flooding and structural damage if they reach land. This photo shows Hurricane Isaac when it struck Gulfport, Mississippi in 2012.

Types of Natural Hazards

There are many types of natural hazards. Weather hazards include thunderstorms, tropical storms, lightning, and tornadoes. Too much rain can cause floods, erosion, and landslides. Too little rain can cause droughts, which are climate hazards. Geologic hazards include earthquakes and volcanic eruptions. Earthquakes can cause ground shaking, landslides, and tsunamis. Volcanic eruptions can bring molten rock, hot gases, and volcanic ash to Earth's surface. Other types of natural hazards include wildfires, space-related hazards such as asteroid impacts, and widespread diseases. Sometimes natural hazards are related to each other. For example, an area is more likely to have wildfires during a drought. Earthquakes can cause tsunamis that rapidly flood coastal areas.

Worldwide Natural Disasters, (1995–2015)		
Natural hazard type	Number of occurrences	Percentage of total (%)
Flood	3,062	43
Storm	2,018	28
Earthquake	562	8
Extreme temperature	405	6
Landslide	387	5
Drought	334	5
Wildfire	251	3
Volcanic eruption	111	2

Source: The Centre for Research on the Epidemiology of Disasters, United Nations Office for Disaster Risk Reduction, *The Human Cost of Weather Related Disasters, 1995–2015*

4. **Draw** Create a circle graph or another type of graphic to show what percentage of all worldwide natural disasters each hazard type represents.

Geologic Hazards

Geologic hazards are caused by geologic processes such as plate motion. Some geologic hazards, such as landslides, earthquakes, tsunamis, and volcanic eruptions, can happen quickly or without warning.

When groundwater dissolves rock below the surface, the ground can suddenly collapse to form a *sinkhole*.

Earthquakes occur when slabs of Earth's crust move and release energy, causing violent shaking.

A *tsunami* is a powerful wave caused by movement of ocean water after an earthquake, a landslide, or an eruption.

Weather and Climate Hazards

Weather describes the conditions in the atmosphere at any given time. *Climate* describes long-term weather patterns. Weather and climate hazards include droughts, hurricanes, tornadoes, blizzards, severe thunderstorms, and floods. Severe storms can have heavy rain, lightning, high winds, and hail, and they can lead to tornadoes and floods.

When heavy rain cannot soak into the ground it runs over Earth's surface and causes a *flood*.

During a *drought*, too little rain causes the land to dry out, and plants are unable to get the water they need.

Very cold temperatures and strong winds combined with extreme amounts of snowfall cause a *blizzard*.

EVIDENCE NOTEBOOK

5. What kinds of natural hazards could suddenly bury a city and the people who live there? Record your evidence.

Natural Hazard Data

Historical data from past natural hazards help us understand the causes and effects of natural hazards and allow us to see patterns in hazard occurrences. Depending on the natural hazard, data could include location, time, and duration. It may also include *frequency*, or how often events occur, and *magnitude*, or how large events are. Current conditions are also monitored to learn about natural hazards. For example, weather instruments collect data on current atmospheric conditions. Meteorologists analyze these data to determine when and where a storm might occur.

6. Look at the data in the two maps. Is there a correlation between historic earthquake locations and earthquake hazard level? Explain.

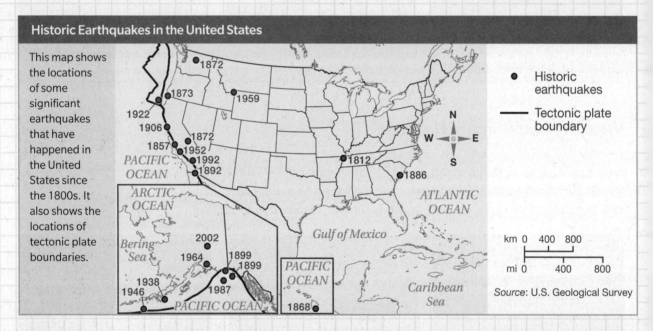

Historic Earthquakes in the United States

This map shows the locations of some significant earthquakes that have happened in the United States since the 1800s. It also shows the locations of tectonic plate boundaries.

- Historic earthquakes
— Tectonic plate boundary

Source: U.S. Geological Survey

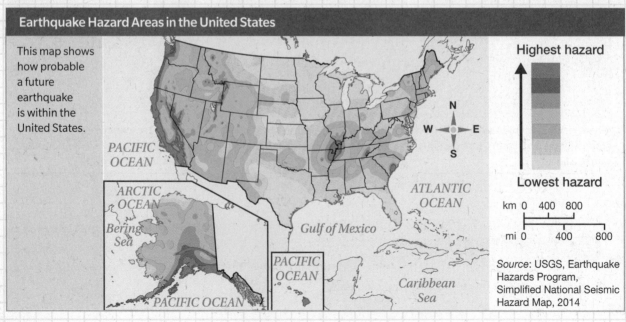

Earthquake Hazard Areas in the United States

This map shows how probable a future earthquake is within the United States.

Highest hazard

Lowest hazard

Source: USGS, Earthquake Hazards Program, Simplified National Seismic Hazard Map, 2014

Do the Math
Interpret Natural Disaster Data

The table shows the number of people affected by weather and climate disasters.

Effects of Weather and Climate Disasters Worldwide, (1995–2015)	
Natural hazard type	Number of people affected (excluding deaths)
Flood	2,300,000,000
Drought	1,100,000,000
Storm	660,000,000
Extreme temperatures	94,000,000
Landslide and wildfire	8,000,000

Source: The Centre for Research on the Epidemiology of Disasters, United Nations Office for Disaster Risk Reduction, *The Human Cost of Weather Related Disasters, 1995–2015*

7. One researcher claimed, "Between 1995 and 2015, more than twice as many people were affected by floods as were affected by droughts and extreme temperatures."

    STEP 1 Use the variables to write an expression to find out if the researcher's claim is true. You can divide the number of people affected by floods by the total number of people affected by droughts and extreme temperatures.

    $$\frac{number\ affected\ by\ floods}{(number\ affected\ by\ droughts\ +\ number\ affected\ by\ extreme\ temperatures)} = \underline{\hspace{3cm}}$$

    f = number affected by floods
    d = number affected by droughts
    e = number affected by extreme temperatures

    STEP 2 Simplify the expression by dividing. Round to the nearest hundredth.

    STEP 3 Do the data support the researcher's claim? Explain.

8. Based on your results, do you think the researcher should reword the claim? Explain.

Interpreting Patterns in Volcanic Data

A *volcano* is a place where molten rock and gases can rise from Earth's interior to the surface. Volcanoes are located on continents and at the bottom of the ocean. Some volcanoes are tall mountains, while others are just cracks in Earth's surface. A *volcanic eruption* is a geologic hazard in which molten rock—called *magma* or *lava*—gases, ash, and other materials are released onto Earth's surface and into the atmosphere.

9. Match these terms to the photos: explosive, quiet.

▷ *Explore ONLINE!*

A. During _____ eruptions, lava oozes downhill.

B. During _____ eruptions, lava, ash, and gases shoot into the air.

Volcanic Eruptions

When a volcano erupts, molten rock reaches Earth's surface. Once at the surface, the molten rock is called *lava*. Not all volcanic eruptions are the same. Some are explosive, forcefully throwing hot lava, ash, and gases into the air. Volcanic eruptions may also be quiet or slow, with lava oozing out and flowing downhill.

Volcanoes erupt on Earth every day, but most eruptions are small or far from human populations. Only some of Earth's volcanoes have erupted in the past 10,000 years. These are considered *active volcanoes*. Those that have not erupted in the past 10,000 years are considered *dormant volcanoes*. If geologists agree that a volcano is not likely to erupt ever again, it is considered an *extinct volcano*.

Volcano Classification and Volcanic Hazards

Volcanic eruptions are natural disasters when they occur near populated areas and cause property damage, injury, or death. Lava flows can burn down structures and start wildfires. Gases can cause breathing issues. Hot ash over 1,000 °C can flow along the ground. This is called a *pyroclastic flow*. Heat from volcanoes can melt ice and snow and form a mudflow called a *lahar*. Both pyroclastic flows and lahars move rapidly downhill and destroy things in their paths. Ash from explosive eruptions can be spread by wind in the atmosphere and partially block sunlight, lowering Earth's temperature over a period of months to years. Volcanic ash can also contaminate water supplies. Large eruptions may cause earthquakes and tsunamis. Shaking from earthquakes can damage buildings and roads. *Tsunamis* are powerful ocean waves that can flood coastal areas.

Volcanic Explosivity Index (VEI)			
VEI number	Type of eruption	Minimum volume of material erupted (cubic kilometers, km^3)	Eruption cloud height (km)
0	nonexplosive	0.000001	<0.1
1	gentle	0.00001	0.1–1
2	explosive	0.001	1–5
3	severe	0.01	3–15
4	cataclysmic	0.1	10–25
5	paroxysmal	1	>25
6	colossal	10	>25
7	super-colossal	100	>25
8	mega-colossal	1,000	>25

Scientists compare the magnitudes of volcanic eruptions by using the Volcanic Explosivity Index (VEI). The scale starts at 0 and has no upper limit. The largest known eruption had a magnitude of 8.

Source: USGS Volcano Hazards Program

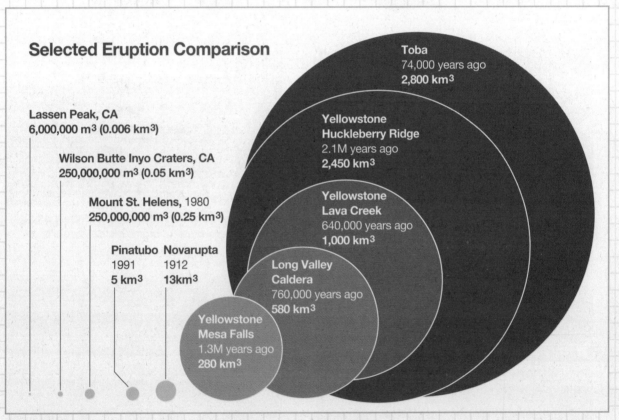

Selected Eruption Comparison

Lassen Peak, CA
6,000,000 m^3 (0.006 km^3)

Wilson Butte Inyo Craters, CA
250,000,000 m^3 (0.05 km^3)

Mount St. Helens, 1980
250,000,000 m^3 (0.25 km^3)

Pinatubo   Novarupta
1991   1912
5 km^3 13km^3

Yellowstone Mesa Falls
1.3M years ago
280 km^3

Long Valley Caldera
760,000 years ago
580 km^3

Yellowstone Lava Creek
640,000 years ago
1,000 km^3

Yellowstone Huckleberry Ridge
2.1M years ago
2,450 km^3

Toba
74,000 years ago
2,800 km^3

Source: USGS, Yellowstone Volcano Observatory, "How Much Magma Erupts?" 2015

10. Mount Pinatubo erupted in 1991, as a(n) _____ on the VEI and is therefore categorized as a(n) _____ eruption.

Volcanic Hazards

The diagram and photos illustrate some of the hazards associated with a volcanic eruption.

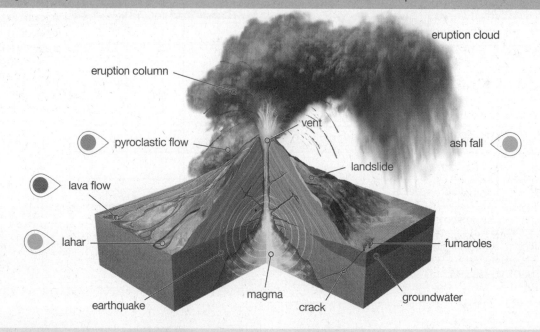

eruption cloud

eruption column

vent

pyroclastic flow

ash fall

lava flow

landslide

lahar

fumaroles

earthquake

magma

crack

groundwater

A *pyroclastic flow* can destroy buildings, forests, and croplands and can kill living things. Pyroclastic flows can travel at speeds of up to 700 km/h.

A *lahar* is a mudslide that is like a flood of concrete. A lahar can travel at speeds up to 200 km/h and can crush or carry away everything in its path.

Lava can surround and cover objects in its path. When lava cools, the objects are buried under hardened rock. Lava can flow at speeds up to 60 km/h and can also trigger wildfires.

As volcanic ash falls from the sky for hours to weeks after an eruption, it can bury everything, including buildings, homes, forests, and crops.

EVIDENCE NOTEBOOK

11. Could a volcanic eruption suddenly bury a city and its inhabitants? Record your evidence.

Hands-On Lab
Assess Building Sites Near a Volcano

You will assess potential building sites near an active volcano.

Kilauea (kee•low•AY•uh) volcano, located on the Big Island of Hawaii, has been erupting constantly since 1983. Lava has been continually flowing out of vents, or cracks, on the side of the volcano. Depending on where the lava is flowing from and the shape of the land it flows over, the direction of the lava flow changes. The volume of lava can also change.

Lava Flows on Kilauea

This map shows the locations of all the lava flows on Kilauea from 1983 to 2016. Much of the area is tropical rainforest. The white areas represent roads and communities.

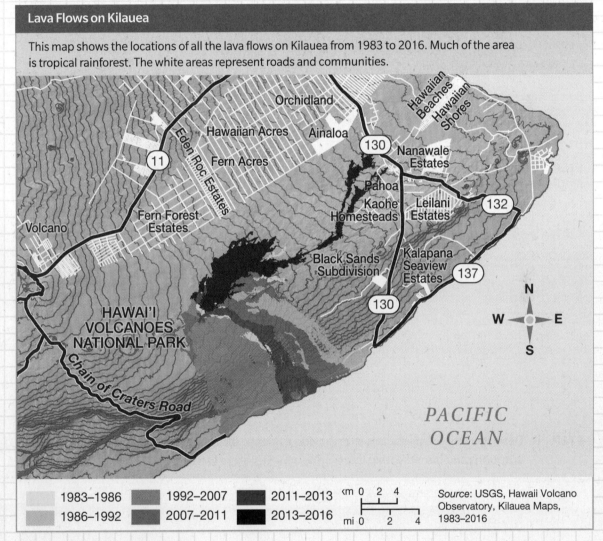

1983–1986	1992–2007	2011–2013
1986–1992	2007–2011	2013–2016

km 0 2 4
mi 0 2 4

Source: USGS, Hawaii Volcano Observatory, Kilauea Maps, 1983–2016

Procedure and Analysis

STEP 1 Use the map to identify where and when past lava flows occurred.

STEP 2 In the past, Kilauea has had many devastating and deadly eruptions. Today the eruption of Kilauea is quiet rather than explosive. Hazards associated with the current type of eruption of Kilauea include poisonous _____ around the crater, _____ that burn vegetation and structures, and _____ that flows downhill.

WORD BANK
- wildfires
- lava
- gases

Engineer It

STEP 3 Imagine that a developer wants to build a hotel near the national park. What factors should the developer consider when deciding where to build? How would these factors affect where the hotel is built?

These homes near the town of Pahoa were destroyed by lava flowing from Kilauea in 2014.

STEP 4 Use the map to identify the best places to build the hotel. Select a building site that would be at a relatively low risk from the hazards of the volcano. Describe its location on the map.

STEP 5 Describe why you chose this site. Provide evidence from your knowledge of eruptions and from the map to describe why this site is the best choice.

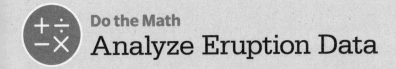

Do the Math

Analyze Eruption Data

Although every volcanic eruption is different, scientists can compare the explosiveness, frequency, and size of volcanic eruptions. The table compares eruption size to eruption frequency and provides examples of volcanoes that fall into each category.

Mount Vesuvius, on the coast of Italy, has produced eight major eruptions within the last 17,000 years. These eruptions included lava, pyroclastic flows, and ash clouds.

Volcanic Eruption Frequency and Size		
Eruption size (km³)	Eruption frequency (approximate)	Volcano example(s)
<0.001	Daily	Kilauea, Stromboli
0.001–0.01	Weekly to monthly	Etna
0.01–0.1	Annually	St. Helens (1980)
1–10	Once every 10 to 100 years	Pinatubo (1991), Vesuvius (79)
10–100	Once every 100 to 1,000 years	Krakatau (1883), Katmai (1912)
100–1,000	Once every 1,000 to 10,000 years	Tambora (1815)
> 1,000	Once or twice every 100,000 years	Yellowstone, Toba

Source: Oregon State University, "How Big Are Eruptions?" 2017

12. Look at the table. Eruption size is the volume of material erupted. Eruption frequency is approximately how often an eruption of that size occurs. Is there a relationship between eruption size and eruption frequency?

_____

_____

_____

_____

_____

_____

Interpreting Patterns in Tornado Data

A *tornado* is a rapidly spinning column of air extending from a storm cloud to the ground. Tornadoes are weather hazards that are most common in spring and summer. This time of year is sometimes referred to as "tornado season."

This mobile Doppler radar truck was used to collect data from a storm in Nebraska that caused several tornadoes like the one shown in the inset. These data help scientists better understand how, when, and where tornadoes form and end.

Tornadoes

Severe thunderstorms can bring heavy rain, hail, high winds—and tornadoes. Tornadoes can develop when rotating thunderstorms, called *supercells*, occur. However, not all supercells form tornadoes. A combination of factors must be present for a tornado to form. A body of warm, moist air must collide with a body of cooler, drier air. As a result, winds at different altitudes blow at different speeds and cause a column of air in the thunderstorm to spin. Because the air pressure is low in the middle of the spinning column, air in the middle of the column rises. The result is that the spinning column of air rotates in a vertical direction and drops below the thunderstorm to form a funnel cloud. When the funnel cloud touches the ground, it becomes a tornado.

A tornado can last anywhere from a few seconds to more than an hour. Most tornadoes last less than ten minutes. More than 1,000 tornadoes occur in the United States each year, but they are not evenly distributed across the country. Most tornadoes occur in the middle of continents. In the United States, the area where most tornadoes happen is called "Tornado Alley." You can find out about the average number of tornadoes per year in each state by studying the map.

EVIDENCE NOTEBOOK

13. As you explore this section, think about whether a tornado could suddenly bury a city and its inhabitants. Record your evidence.

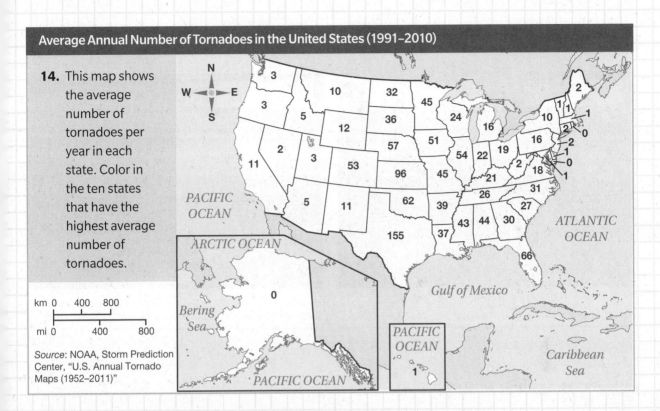

Average Annual Number of Tornadoes in the United States (1991–2010)

14. This map shows the average number of tornadoes per year in each state. Color in the ten states that have the highest average number of tornadoes.

km 0   400   800

mi 0   400   800

Source: NOAA, Storm Prediction Center, "U.S. Annual Tornado Maps (1952–2011)"

Tornado Classification and Hazards

When a tornado strikes a populated area and is strong enough, it can cause damage, injury, or death. Its strong winds destroy many objects in its path, including buildings, roads, trees, crops, and sometimes people and other animals. A tornado that causes these types of damage is considered a natural disaster.

Meteorologists collect tornado data, such as a tornado's path, wind speeds, duration, and temperatures. These data are organized into tables, graphs, and maps and then analyzed to help us understand the causes of tornadoes and their effects on people and the environment. Tornado data are also analyzed to identify areas at risk for tornado hazards and to make predictions about when and where tornadoes might occur. The Enhanced Fujita (foo•JEE•tuh) Scale, also known as the EF Scale, describes tornado damage.

The Enhanced Fujita Scale		
EF rating	**Wind speeds (km/hr)**	**Expected damage**
EF-0	105–137	Chimneys damaged; tree branches broken; shallow-rooted trees toppled.
EF-1	142–177	Roof surfaces peeled off; windows broken; some tree trunks snapped; garages may be destroyed.
EF-2	179–217	Roofs damaged; manufactured homes destroyed; trees snapped or uprooted; debris entered air.
EF-3	219–265	Roofs and walls torn from buildings; some small buildings destroyed; most forest trees uprooted.
EF-4	267–322	Well-built homes destroyed; cars lifted and blown some distance; large debris flew through the air.
EF-5	Over 322	Strong houses lifted, concrete structures damaged; very large debris flew through the air; trees debarked.

Source: NOAA

15. These photos show different places where a tornado occurred. How would you rate the damage caused by each tornado based on the Enhanced Fujita (EF) Scale?

This tornado uprooted a few shallow-rooted trees and damaged many chimneys in the neighborhood.

This tornado damaged all of the homes in this community and tossed large debris and several cars through the air.

Compare Tornado Data

16. A researcher wants to collect tornado data from the three states where tornado risk is highest. Where and when should the researcher collect data? Support your claim by citing evidence from this graph and from the map of tornadoes in the United States.

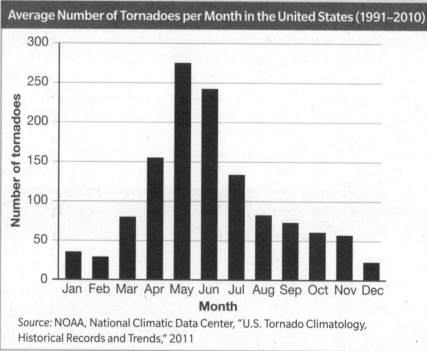

Average Number of Tornadoes per Month in the United States (1991–2010)

Source: NOAA, National Climatic Data Center, "U.S. Tornado Climatology, Historical Records and Trends," 2011

Continue Your Exploration

Name: _____ Date: _____

Check out the path below or go online to choose one of the other paths shown.

| The Cost of Natural Disasters | • Hands-On Labs ✋
 • Forest Fires
 • Propose Your Own Path | *Go online to choose one of these other paths.* |

Natural disasters can destroy homes, buildings, crops, and sources of clean water. They can also cause injury and death. It costs money to repair the damage caused by a natural disaster. The cost can be determined by considering many factors, such as

- What was damaged or destroyed?
- Do the inhabitants of the area need to have those objects or systems repaired or replaced?
- What can be repaired and what must be replaced?
- What materials and labor are needed to repair or replace objects or systems?

Once the necessary work is identified, someone will have to pay for it. The costs are paid by insurance companies; local, state, and federal agencies; government disaster relief programs; and the individuals who live in the area.

Natural Disasters in the United States

Natural disasters can be very costly. In 2015, the most expensive type of natural disaster in the United States was a tropical cyclone. *Tropical cyclone* is a term used by scientists to refer to any rotating, organized storm that starts over tropical waters. "Hurricane," "cyclone," and "typhoon" are all regional names for tropical cyclones.

These storms cause massive and widespread destruction by bringing high winds, heavy rains, and possible tornadoes and flooding to large areas. The wind and flooding from *tropical cyclones* can affect people in populated areas by damaging buildings, roads, dams, sea walls, and other structures along coastlines and waterways.

This man used a kayak to travel flooded roads in South Carolina after heavy rains fell during a tropical cyclone.

Continue Your Exploration

Billion-Dollar Weather and Climate Disasters in the United States (1980–2016)		
Disaster type	Number of events	Cost of damage (in billions of dollars)
Tropical cyclone	35	560.1
Drought/heat wave	24	223.8
Severe local storm	83	180.1
Nontropical flood	26	110.7
Winter storm	14	41.3
Wildfire	14	33.0
Freeze	7	25.3

Source: NOAA National Centers for Environmental Information (NCEI), U.S. Billion-Dollar Weather and Climate Disasters, January 2017

1. Compare the cost of damage caused by tropical cyclones and by severe local storms, and compare the number of each of those events. Was the average cost of damage per event higher for tropical cyclones or for severe local storms?

2. How could you explain this?

3. Circle all the costs that would be associated with a severe freeze in an apple orchard.

    A. recovering from the cost of a loss of apples

    B. replacing damaged or destroyed trees

    C. repairing irrigation lines that burst when they froze

    D. buying new harvesting equipment

4. Collaborate With a partner, discuss ways that volunteers could reduce the cost of recovering from a natural hazard.

Can You Explain It?

Name: _____   Date: _____

How was this city suddenly buried without warning?

 EVIDENCE NOTEBOOK

Refer to the notes in your Evidence Notebook to help you construct an explanation for what could have suddenly buried this city.

1. State your claim. Make sure your claim fully explains what could have suddenly buried this city and its people and why the people were unable to escape.

2. Summarize the evidence you have gathered to support your claim and explain your reasoning.

Checkpoints

Answer the following questions to check your understanding of the lesson.

3. After a volcanic eruption, where would you expect to find lahar deposits?

    A. on the side of the volcano

    B. in the crater of the volcano

    C. in a valley leading away from the volcano

    D. on the hilltops surrounding the volcano

Use the photo to answer Question 4.

4. Which of the following natural hazards could have caused the ash damage in this photo? Select all that apply.

    A. flood

    B. hurricane

    C. volcanic eruption

    D. earthquake

    E. wildfire

Use the graph to answer Questions 5–6.

5. Which of the following statements is true?

    A. The number of tornadoes per year remains about the same.

    B. The number of tornadoes per year varies from year to year.

    C. The number of tornadoes per year is increasing each year.

    D. The number of tornadoes per year is decreasing each year.

6. Which of the following periods had the fewest tornadoes?

    A. 1960–1964

    B. 1970–1974

    C. 1985–1989

    D. 2005–2009

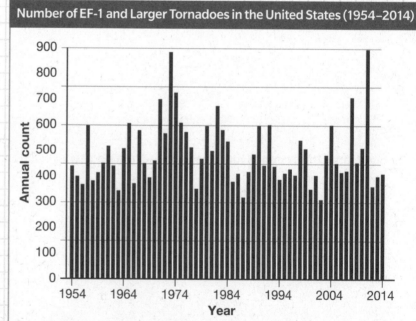

Source: NOAA, National Weather Service Storm Prediction Center, "U.S. Annual Count of EF-1+ Tornadoes, 1954 through 2014"

Interactive Review

Complete this section to review the main concepts of the lesson.

Natural hazards are naturally occurring events such as wildfires, earthquakes, and hurricanes. Natural disasters are natural hazards that negatively affect humans.

A. Explain the difference between a natural hazard and a natural disaster. Provide two examples of natural hazards that are not natural disasters.

A volcanic eruption is a geologic hazard. Any type of volcanic eruption can become a natural disaster.

B. Describe a volcanic hazard and explain how it could become a natural disaster.

A tornado is a weather hazard that forms quickly and with little warning. A tornado can become a natural disaster.

C. Describe how the terms "Tornado Alley" and "tornado season" are related to the analysis of data about tornadoes.

Natural Hazard Prediction

This flood in New Jersey was caused by the melting of snow and ice after a major snowstorm. Understanding weather patterns can help people forecast natural hazards like floods.

By the end of this lesson . . .

you should be able to analyze natural hazard data to forecast the likelihood of future events.

Go online to view the digital version of the Hands-On Lab for this lesson and to download additional lab resources.

CAN YOU EXPLAIN IT?

Why is there a tsunami hazard warning sign on this calm beach?

This beach on the east coast of New Zealand is a popular recreation spot.

1. Some coastal areas are at a higher risk for tsunamis than others are. How do we know which coastal areas are more likely to be affected by tsunamis?

EVIDENCE NOTEBOOK As you explore this lesson, gather evidence to help explain how we know which coastal areas are at risk for tsunamis.

Predicting Natural Hazards

If the sky is full of dark clouds, you might predict that rain is about to fall. Making predictions is an important part of science. Natural hazard predictions can prevent natural disasters because warnings can be issued to help people prepare.

2. People living near this stream think that if heavy rains continue, the stream will overflow and flood their homes. What information might these people be using to make this prediction?

When it rains, water runs downhill and collects along the lowest elevations in an area, such as this stream.

Natural Hazard Predictions

Natural hazard predictions are efforts to forecast the occurrence, intensity, and effects of natural hazards. Some natural hazards are not predictable. Other hazards follow known patterns or are preceded by precursor events. If precursor events or patterns can be detected far enough in advance, a prediction may be made. For example, a precursor event to a flood may be heavy rainfall over a short period of time. Natural hazard predictions can help people reduce the effects of a natural hazard or even prevent some natural disasters.

Natural hazard predictions involve some uncertainty. Uncertainties can include a hazard's exact location, timing, magnitude, and whether it will actually happen. Certainty generally increases as the time of the predicted event gets closer. Natural hazard predictions are improved by gaining a scientific understanding of hazards, collecting and analyzing data, and using monitoring technology. Advances in science and technology can help improve natural hazard predictions. These advances can help us prepare for the effects of natural hazards. Societal needs, such as keeping people safe, drive development of these advances.

Scientific Understanding

A natural hazard prediction can be improved by gaining scientific understanding of a natural hazard. To gain scientific understanding, you can start by asking questions that can be answered by using scientific methods. For example, if you wanted to understand more about avalanches, you might ask: On which slopes are avalanches most common? What weather conditions are related to avalanches? What types of snow are related to avalanches? To answer these kinds of questions, you can collect and analyze data, use models, or conduct experiments. These practices help scientists better understand natural hazards.

Scientists analyze the snow conditions on slopes to determine how likely an avalanche is to occur.

Historical Data

Historical data are used to evaluate the likelihood that a natural hazard will happen in a given place. Historical data can include the locations of past events as well as their frequency, magnitude, and effects on the environment or people. Some hazards, such as volcanic eruptions, landslides, and earthquakes, tend to occur in specific areas. However, these hazards can happen at any time of the year. Hazards such as hurricanes and tornadoes tend to happen in specific places and during specific times of the year.

Historic Hurricane and Tropical Cyclone Paths

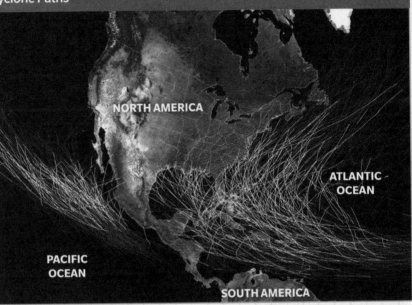

The lines on this map show the paths of past hurricanes and tropical cyclones. These data help us identify where hurricanes are likely to occur in the future.

Hurricane Paths

— Hurricane

— Tropical cyclone (intensity below major hurricane)

Atlantic Ocean data: 1851–2013
Pacific Ocean data: 1949–2013

Source: NOAA, Major Hurricane History of the U.S., 2013

Data from Monitoring

Scientists use technology to monitor conditions that relate to the occurrence of natural hazards. For example, satellites orbit Earth and collect weather data. These data go into computer models that help scientists predict weather-related hazards. For hazards that are likely to occur in specific locations, monitoring technology may be designed for and placed in those areas. For example, underwater earthquakes, landslides, and volcanic eruptions can be precursor events to tsunamis. So, scientists monitor ocean water movement after those events in order to predict tsunamis. Tsunami sensors might be put on buoys or on the sea floor to detect water movement in areas at high risk of tsunamis.

This tsunami in Miyako City, Japan was caused by an earthquake on the ocean floor. The waves arrived less than one hour after the earthquake. Luckily, many people received warnings before the waves struck thanks to monitoring data.

 EVIDENCE NOTEBOOK

3. How might scientific understanding, historical data, and monitoring help to determine where tsunami hazard signs should be placed? Record your evidence.

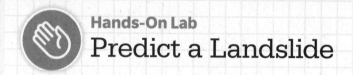

Hands-On Lab
Predict a Landslide

You will model the relationship between rainfall, hill slope, and landslides.
Heavy rain is forecast for Pineville. Historical data for this area show that heavy rains increase the chance of landslides. Landslides occur when soil and rock slide down a slope and can travel fast and threaten lives and property.

MATERIALS
- duct tape
- gutter, vinyl, U-shaped, 60 cm section (chute)
- plastic scoop
- plastic tub, shallow
- potting soil, saturated
- protractor
- spray bottle

Procedure

STEP 1 Look at the slopes on the map and the slope angles in the table. On which slopes do you predict landslides are likely to occur?

STEP 2 One at a time, model Slopes 1, 2, 3, and 4. Place the chute so one end is at the edge of the plastic tub and tape it to the inside wall of the tub. The other end of the chute should be inside the tub.

STEP 3 To model Slope 1, rest the chute on the edge of the tub. Use the scoop to fill the top $\frac{1}{3}$ of the chute with damp soil.

STEP 4 Outside of the tub and under the chute, set up the protractor to measure the angle between the table and the bottom edge of the chute. Have a partner slowly tilt the chute until the angle is about 10 degrees.

STEP 5 Spray the slope to simulate rainfall until the soil is saturated. Record your observations in the table.

STEP 6 Model Slopes 2, 3, and 4 by repeating STEPS 3–5. Why should you use the same amount of soil and spray the water in a consistent way for all of the trials?

Landslide Model Data	
Slope angle (degrees)	Results
Slope 1: 10°	
Slope 2: 15°	
Slope 3: 35°	
Slope 4: 55°	

Landslide Study Area for Pineville

This map shows how the Pineville area is surrounded by hillsides. The hillsides are generally made up of the same type of soil and have little vegetation. Rainfall amounts are even across the area.

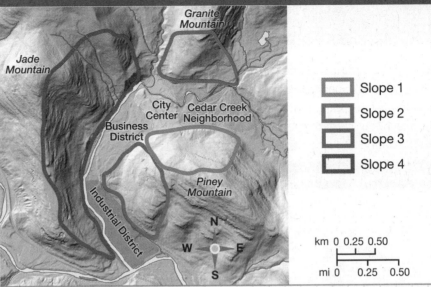

Analysis

STEP 7 Soil on steeper slopes requires less / more rain to result in a landslide than the soil on flatter slopes does.

STEP 8 Compare your prediction to your results. Was your prediction correct?

STEP 9 Based on your model, are any areas in Pineville at risk of damage from a landslide? Explain why or why not.

STEP 10 Evaluate your model. What did your model represent well? What could be changed or added to improve your model?

Engineer It

Determine a Safe Building Site

4. What criteria and constraints might you consider when choosing a site on which to build new homes in Pineville? Where would you build new homes in Pineville?

_____

_____

_____

_____

_____

Predicting Geologic Hazards

Geologic hazards include volcanoes, earthquakes, tsunamis, sinkholes, and landslides. Different areas experience different geologic hazards. For example, areas near tectonic plate boundaries experience more earthquakes than areas far from plate boundaries. The likelihood of a geologic hazard occurring in a specific location can be determined. But the timing and magnitude of geologic hazards are difficult to predict.

Worldwide Distribution of Earthquakes and Volcanoes

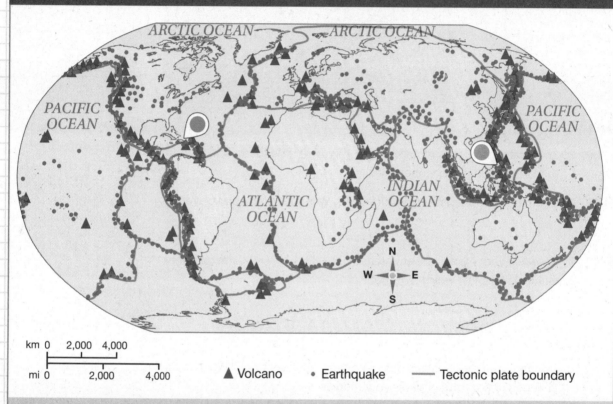

km 0   2,000   4,000

mi 0   2,000   4,000

▲ Volcano   • Earthquake   ── Tectonic plate boundary

In 2010, a major earthquake shook the ground and toppled buildings in Haiti. Earthquakes happen suddenly and currently cannot be predicted.

Scientists predicted the eruption of Mount Pinatubo in 1991. The predictions helped thousands of people evacuate before falling ash and lahars destroyed villages.

5. **Discuss** Look at the photo of the effects of the Mount Pinatubo eruption. Predicting volcanic eruptions such as this one can save lives and prevent injuries. How do you think scientists predicted this eruption?

Predictions of Volcanic Eruptions

Predictions of volcanic eruptions usually include the likelihood of an eruption within a given time frame. They might also identify possible hazardous effects or related hazards, such as lava flows or wildfires. To determine the likelihood of a volcanic eruption, scientists analyze data, such as the locations of active volcanoes or a certain volcano's past eruptions. Eruption predictions are not always certain because most volcanoes do not erupt on regular schedules. Before some eruptions, specific conditions or precursor events can be identified. Therefore, scientists monitor some volcanoes to watch for changes in conditions and precursor events. Data from monitoring help scientists predict the likelihood of an eruption. However, precursor events and changes in a volcano's conditions may occur without ending in an eruption.

Scientific Understanding

Scientists study the causes and effects of volcanic eruptions. Scientists know that before an eruption, molten rock in Earth's interior, called *magma*, moves closer to the surface. The movement of the magma cracks the surrounding rock and causes swarms of small earthquakes. The moving magma also releases gases into the air and causes the ground surface to change shape.

Scientists study volcanoes to determine whether a volcano is active. They also see whether an eruption could result in a natural disaster. Because scientists have identified where active volcanoes exist around the world, they can identify areas that are at risk for eruption-related natural disasters. For example, the map shows that there are many active volcanoes along the west coasts of North and South America.

This lava flowed over 20 km downhill from the Kilauea volcano. It stopped just outside the town of Pahoa, Hawaii.

Data from Past Eruptions

Past eruption data for a volcano can include eruption timing, precursor events, and eruption types. For example, volcanic rocks and ash layers from past eruptions can tell how often and how explosively a volcano has erupted in the past. This helps scientists determine whether a volcano is active and what type of eruption, if any, is likely to happen in the future. For example, a volcano that explosively erupted and made large amounts of ash in the past most likely will have a similar eruption in the future.

Mauna Loa is an active volcano located on the Big Island of Hawaii. It is a *shield volcano*. This means that it is a broad dome with gently sloping sides. Shield volcanoes often have steady lava flows rather than explosive eruptions. Many eruptions of Mauna Loa have been witnessed by people living in Hawaii. For safety, scientists monitor many active volcanoes near populated areas.

Mauna Loa Eruption Data 1832–2004	
General Information	**Eruption History**
Location: Mauna Loa, Hawaii	1832, 1843, 1849, 1851, 1852, 1855–1856, 1859, 1865–1866, 1870 (?)*, 1871, 1872, 1873, 1873–1874, 1875, 1876, 1877, 1879, 1880, 1880–1881, 1887, 1892, 1896, 1899, 1903, 1907, 1914–1915, 1916, 1919, 1926, 1933, 1935–1936, 1940, 1950, 1975, 1984
Type and Elevation: Shield volcano, 4,170 m (13,681 ft)	
Eruption Style: Nonexplosive, with steady lava flows	

*The question mark indicates that the exact year of the eruption is not known.
Source: USGS, Hawaii Volcano Observatory, "Summary of Historical Eruptions, 1843–Present", 2004

6. Mauna Loa erupted on average once every four years between 1832 and 1984. From 1870 to 1880, the number of eruptions was *greater / fewer* than average. Beginning in 1940, eruptions were *more / less* frequent than average.

Monitoring Volcanoes

Scientists monitor volcanoes by using technology that detects slight changes in the ground and air around a volcano. They use GPS instruments and thermal imaging sensors set on planes and satellites. These instruments show if magma is moving or if the ground is changing shape. They use *seismometers*, which detect vibrations in the ground, to monitor earthquake activity. Increases in local earthquakes can show movements of magma before a volcanic eruption. Scientists also use *tiltmeters* to monitor changes in the volcano's shape that are related to pressure changes inside the volcano. They also measure the concentration of gases around volcanic vents because the volcano may release more of these gases just before an eruption.

Scientists use tiltmeters to see if a volcano is expanding or shrinking. They use GPS stations to see how much the surface of a volcano is moving.

Change in Distance Across Mauna Loa's Summit Crater (2010–2015)

GPS units measure the change in distance between Stations 1 and 2.

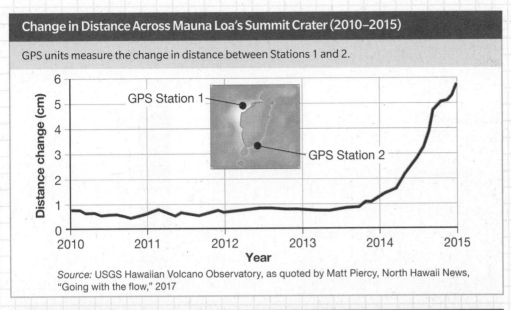

Source: USGS Hawaiian Volcano Observatory, as quoted by Matt Piercy, North Hawaii News, "Going with the flow," 2017

Mauna Loa's Earthquake Activity (2010–2015)

This graph shows the frequency of earthquakes on Mauna Loa.

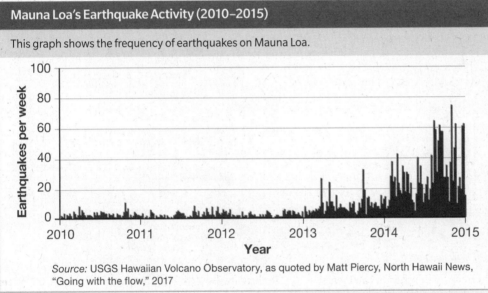

Source: USGS Hawaiian Volcano Observatory, as quoted by Matt Piercy, North Hawaii News, "Going with the flow," 2017

7. The graphs show that Mauna Loa's crater expanded / shrank and the number of earthquakes increased / decreased. The data appear to be correlated.

Earthquake Prediction

Earthquakes can become natural disasters because the shaking can damage structures. Earthquakes can also cause tsunamis, fires, and landslides. Scientists are able to identify areas where earthquakes are likely to happen and cause damage. But they can't predict the timing of an earthquake. Scientists use historical data, seismograph data, and GPS data to make earthquake risk maps. These maps show the relative likelihood of an earthquake of a specific size happening in a given area within a given time frame.

EVIDENCE NOTEBOOK

8. What kinds of data might scientists collect in order to identify where tsunamis are likely to occur? How can scientists predict when tsunamis are likely to occur? Record your evidence.

A magnitude 7.0 earthquake is a large earthquake that could cause major damage, injury, or death.

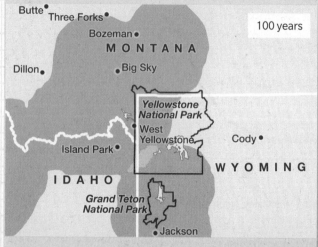

Probability of a 7.0 earthquake within the next 100 years.

PROBABILITY (%)

Source: USGS, Geologic Hazards Science Center, National Seismic Hazard Mapping Project, 2009

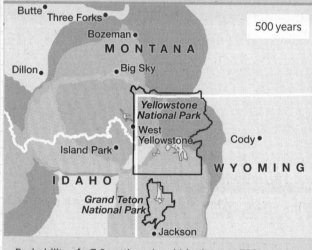

Probability of a 7.0 earthquake within the next 500 years.

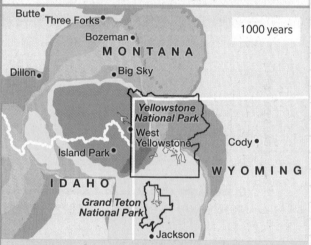

Probability of a 7.0 earthquake within the next 1,000 years.

9. The probability of a magnitude 7.0 earthquake happening in Bozeman, Montana in the next 100 years is 0–1% / 1–10% / 10–20%.

Do the Math

Explain Earthquake Probability

10. Choose Big Sky, Island Park, or Jackson. Use the key to explain how the chance of a magnitude 7.0 earthquake relates to the length of time for which the projection is made for the town you have chosen.

_____

_____

_____

_____

_____

Predicting Weather and Climate Hazards

Weather hazards include thunderstorms, snowstorms, tornadoes, and floods. These hazards occur in locations where the atmosphere, ocean, and land interact to create specific conditions. Weather predictions describe what the weather is likely to be on a particular day. A weather-hazard prediction indicates when and where dangerous weather conditions are likely to develop. Warnings about weather hazards are issued only minutes to days before a potential event.

   Climate hazards are large-scale phenomena that are related to long-term weather patterns. Climate hazards include droughts, sea-level changes, and wildfires.

Worldwide Tornado Risk

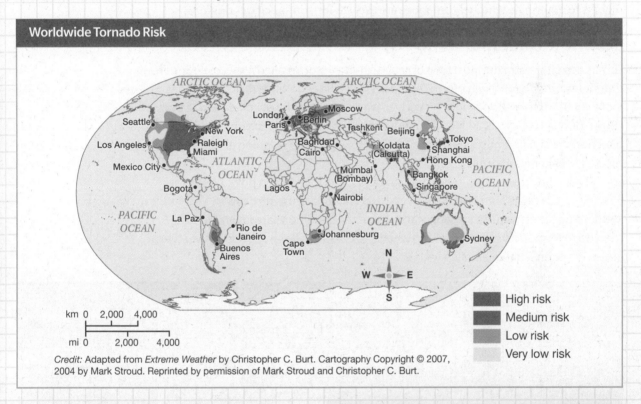

High risk
Medium risk
Low risk
Very low risk

Credit: Adapted from *Extreme Weather* by Christopher C. Burt. Cartography Copyright © 2007, 2004 by Mark Stroud. Reprinted by permission of Mark Stroud and Christopher C. Burt.

11. Look at the map and the photo. We know where tornado risk is high, but do you think we can prevent tornadoes from causing damage and injury? Explain.

In 2011, a tornado destroyed this house in North Carolina. A tornado warning was issued about 24 minutes before the tornado struck the area.

Predicting Tornadoes

Tornadoes are rapidly spinning columns of air that extend from storm clouds to the ground. Their winds can travel at almost 500 kilometers per hour. They can destroy neighborhoods or entire towns in seconds, sometimes causing fatalities. Their path of destruction can be more than 1 kilometer wide and 100 kilometers long.

Tornadoes are difficult to predict with any certainty. Thus, tornado forecasts are usually made for large areas and do not specify exact timing. However, predictions of actual tornado events can be made only minutes or seconds before a tornado strikes. Agencies such as the National Oceanic and Atmospheric Administration (NOAA) and the National Weather Service (NWS) collect weather data that are used by meteorologists to predict tornadoes. Data are collected by weather satellites, weather stations, and weather balloons and from reports from trained weather observers. Data are used in computer models to determine whether tornadoes are likely to form in specific conditions.

Scientific Understanding

Tornadoes often form during a type of severe thunderstorm called a *supercell*. Supercell thunderstorms do not always form tornadoes. Specific conditions make tornadoes more likely. For a tornado to form, a body of warm, moist air must collide with a body of cooler, drier air. As winds at different altitudes within the thunderstorm blow in various directions or at different speeds, the air begins to spin. If the spinning air reaches the ground, it becomes a tornado.

By analyzing data from supercell thunderstorms that do and do not form tornadoes, scientists learn more about which conditions cause tornadoes. Meteorologists can issue a tornado watch when the conditions are favorable for a tornado to form. They issue a warning when a tornado has been spotted by weather observers or on radar or satellite images.

This armored vehicle is designed to be driven into a tornado to gather important weather data.

Historical Data

Meteorologists analyze historical data to determine when and where tornadoes are most common. In the United States, tornadoes tend to strike during late afternoons and evenings during spring, summer, and fall. However, tornadoes have struck in the morning and in winter. Scientists also analyze historical data, such as this map of tornado tracks in the United States, to determine where tornadoes are most common.

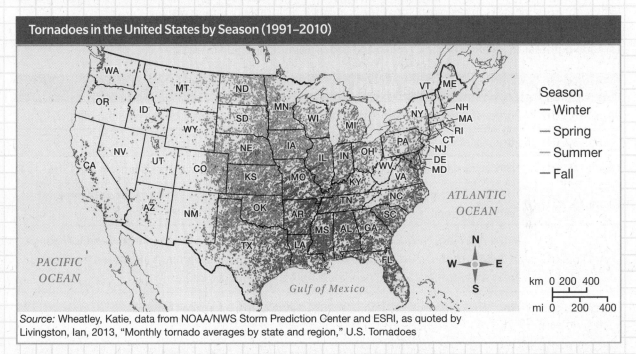

Tornadoes in the United States by Season (1991–2010)

Season
— Winter
— Spring
-- Summer
— Fall

Source: Wheatley, Katie, data from NOAA/NWS Storm Prediction Center and ESRI, as quoted by Livingston, Ian, 2013, "Monthly tornado averages by state and region," U.S. Tornadoes

12. The tornado data on this map show a pattern. In the northernmost states where tornadoes occur, most tornadoes occur in the
winter / spring / summer / fall. In the southeastern United States, most tornadoes occur in the winter / spring / summer / fall.

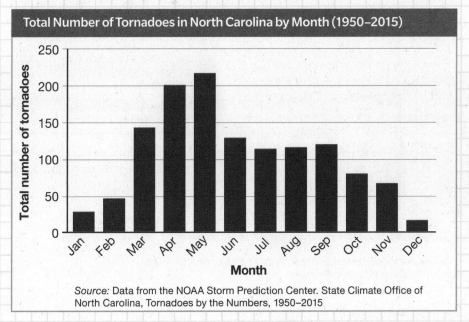

Total Number of Tornadoes in North Carolina by Month (1950–2015)

Source: Data from the NOAA Storm Prediction Center. State Climate Office of North Carolina, Tornadoes by the Numbers, 1950–2015

13. These historical data show that tornadoes are least likely to occur in North Carolina in May / December.

Monitoring

Weather conditions are monitored during supercell thunderstorms to determine the likelihood of a tornado. Several types of monitoring technologies are used. For example, Doppler radar uses radio waves to identify direction and intensity of precipitation, wind direction and speed, and the locations of boundaries between large air masses. Meteorologists look at wind patterns in supercell thunderstorms that show rotation. Where the rotation is strong enough, tornadoes can form. This table and map were made from weather monitoring data. The data were gathered before and during a tornado outbreak in Raleigh, North Carolina and the surrounding region in 2011.

Weather Forecasts for Raleigh, NC, from April 12 to April 16, 2011	
April 12, 2011	Forecast mentions a likely threat of upcoming severe weather on the evening of April 15th.
April 13, 2011	Forecast of severe weather is shifted to the daytime of April 16th.
April 14, 2011	NWS issues a prediction of a 30% chance of a major severe weather event on the 16th.
April 15, 2011	The likelihood of a severe weather event is increased to 45% and tornadoes are deemed "likely" to occur.
April 16, 2011	In the morning, NWS issues a warning for afternoon severe thunderstorms and tornadoes. In the afternoon, more than 30 tornadoes strike. Tornado warnings are issued for specific areas an average of 20–30 minutes before the tornadoes strike.

Source: National Weather Service, Raleigh, NC, "April 16, 2011, North Carolina Tornado Outbreak Event Summary," 2012

NOAA Storm Prediction Center Outlooks and Confirmed Tornado Tracks

In the late afternoon on April 16th, 2011, several tornadoes were confirmed and a prediction of more tornadoes was issued.

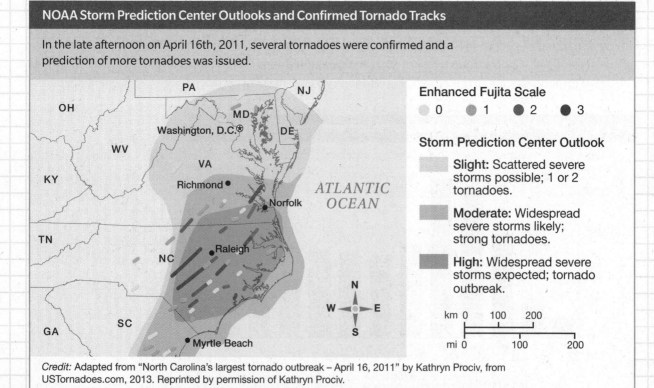

Credit: Adapted from "North Carolina's largest tornado outbreak – April 16, 2011" by Kathryn Prociv, from USTornadoes.com, 2013. Reprinted by permission of Kathryn Prociv.

14. Discuss How did the information available in the weather forecasts change in the days leading up to April 16th? Do you think these forecasts gave people enough time to prepare for the tornadoes? Explain.

Predicting Floods

Natural hazards such as thunderstorms and hurricanes can cause flooding. Flooding happens when land that is normally dry is covered by water. Floodwaters can sweep away objects and injure people. There are three main types of floods: flash floods, overbank floods, and coastal floods. Flash floods occur suddenly as very fast moving water from excessive rainfall runs over land. Overbank floods happen slowly when rain or melting snow makes river or lake levels rise. Coastal floods happen when high winds or storms push ocean water onto shore.

To predict floods, scientists monitor amounts of rainfall and snow melt, as well as water levels in lakes, streams, and oceans. Scientists also consider how much water the ground can absorb and how water flow is affected by an area's landforms.

Worldwide Locations of Floods and Their Causes, 1985–2002

This map shows the types of conditions that cause floods around the world.

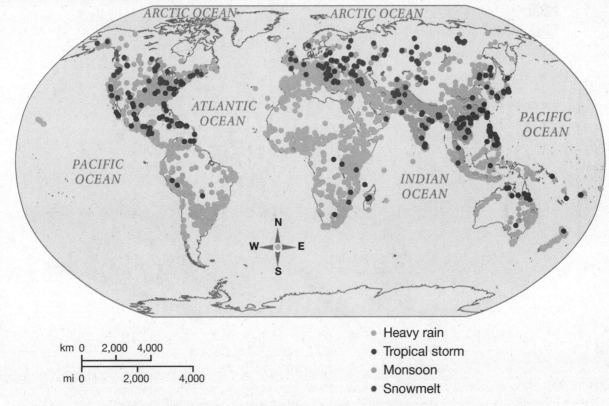

- Heavy rain
- Tropical storm
- Monsoon
- Snowmelt

Credit: Adapted from the World Atlas of Large Flood Events 1985-2002, Dartmouth Flood Observatory. Reprinted by permission of Prof. Robert Brakenridge.

15. The most widespread cause of flooding in the world is
heavy rain / tropical storm / monsoon / snowmelt.
The type of flooding that mainly affects only the Northern Hemisphere is
heavy rain / tropical storm / monsoon / snowmelt.
The region most affected by monsoonal rains is
North America / South America / Europe / Africa / Asia.

Use Flood Maps

Historical data are used to create flood-risk maps to show how likely areas are to flood under certain conditions. When locations that can flood are identified, the effect of the floods on people can be predicted. It is important that people know safe routes to get out of flood-prone areas. Evacuation routes connect evacuation zones, or areas to be evacuated, to evacuation centers, where people can go to be safe during a flood event.

Flood Risk in New York City

This flood-risk map of New York City shows the evacuation zones for the areas that flood.

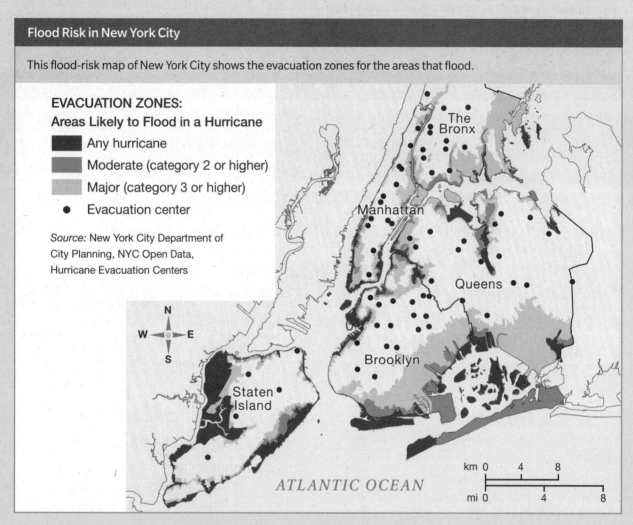

EVACUATION ZONES:
Areas Likely to Flood in a Hurricane

- Any hurricane
- Moderate (category 2 or higher)
- Major (category 3 or higher)
- Evacuation center

Source: New York City Department of City Planning, NYC Open Data, Hurricane Evacuation Centers

16. A moderate hurricane in the Atlantic Ocean is heading toward New York City. Based on the map, identify the areas that have a high chance of flooding during and after this storm. Suggest which areas people should evacuate based on the coming storm, and support your claim with evidence and reasoning.

_____

_____

_____

_____

_____

_____

_____

Continue Your Exploration

Name: _____   Date: _____

Check out the path below or go online to choose one of the other paths shown.

| Predicting Asteroid Impacts | • **Hands-On Labs** ✋
• **Technology for Hurricane Forecasts**
• **Propose Your Own Path** | *Go online to choose one of these other paths.* |

An *asteroid* is a large, rocky body that orbits the sun. Tens of thousands of asteroids orbit the sun between Mars and Jupiter. However, some asteroids pass close to Earth, and some even cross Earth's orbit. At times, small fragments of asteroids approach Earth, but most burn up as they travel through the atmosphere. People call these bright streaks of light "shooting stars." Scientists call them meteors. Some small fragments do not burn up entirely and they strike Earth, causing little to no damage. A larger asteroid impact could be a worldwide catastrophe, but this type of event is extremely rare. A large asteroid strikes Earth about once every 10,000 years.

Potentially Hazardous Asteroids

Scientists use monitoring technology, such as telescopes, to locate asteroids that orbit close to Earth. Automated systems are used to determine whether these asteroids could pose a threat to Earth. As monitoring technology continues to improve, new asteroids are continually identified. Some of these asteroids pass very close to Earth.

A *potentially hazardous asteroid* (PHA) is one that orbits close enough to Earth to pose a threat. A PHA must be large enough to survive the trip through the atmosphere and hit Earth's surface. Identified PHAs will not necessarily strike Earth's surface, but because an impact is possible, PHAs are continuously monitored. This ongoing monitoring helps scientists better predict whether a PHA poses a threat. The National Aeronautics and Space Administration (NASA) currently monitors more than 1,700 PHAs. As of 2017, no asteroids were categorized as an immediate threat to Earth in the near future.

The Barringer Crater in Arizona is the result of an asteroid impact about 50,000 years ago. The asteroid was about 50 meters wide.

Continue Your Exploration

1. Based on the timeline, how likely is a large asteroid impact in your lifetime? Explain.

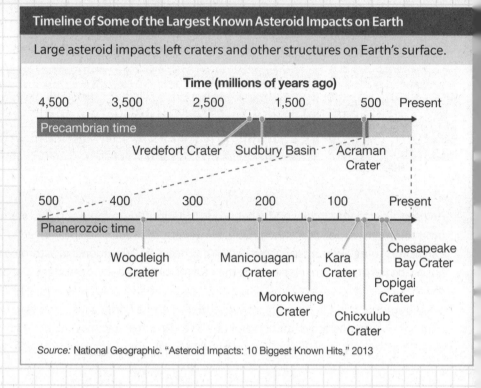

Timeline of Some of the Largest Known Asteroid Impacts on Earth

Large asteroid impacts left craters and other structures on Earth's surface.

Source: National Geographic. "Asteroid Impacts: 10 Biggest Known Hits," 2013

2. Why are new PHAs continually discovered?

3. An asteroid over 100 meters in diameter could affect an entire country. Scientists predict that there is a 1% chance that an asteroid of this size could strike Earth in the next 100 years. What factors could cause the calculation of this probability to increase or decrease?

4. **Collaborate** Conduct research to evaluate the following statement: "The chances of a small asteroid affecting humans are greater than the chances of a large asteroid affecting humans." Cite evidence to support your evaluation.

Can You Explain It?

Name: **Date:**

Why is there a tsunami hazard warning sign on this calm beach?

TSUNAMI HAZARD ZONE

IN CASE OF A TSUNAMI ALERT GO TO HIGH GROUND OR ASSEMBLY AREA

Far North District Council

EVIDENCE NOTEBOOK

Refer to the notes in your Evidence Notebook to help you construct an explanation for how we know which coastal areas are at risk for tsunamis.

1. State your claim. Make sure your claim fully explains why there is a tsunami hazard warning sign on a calm beach.

2. Summarize the evidence you have gathered to support your claim and explain your reasoning.

Checkpoints

Answer the following questions to check your understanding of the lesson.

Use the map to answer Questions 3–4.

3. At which locations have tsunamis struck in the past? Select all that apply.

   A. along the southern coast of Alaska

   B. along the western coast of Canada

   C. in the middle of the Pacific Ocean

   D. along the western coast of Alaska

   E. along the western coast of the United~States

   F. on many islands off the coast of the continent

Past Tsunamis and Tsunami Detector Locations

- Past tsunami
- Tsunami detector

Source: NOAA Natural Hazards Viewer

4. Which statements are true of tsunami detectors? Choose all that apply.

   A. They are on land.

   B. They are placed to stop tsunamis from occurring.

   C. They are placed to detect future tsunamis.

   D. They are in the ocean.

Use the table to answer Question 5.

Eruption History of Mt. Etna, Italy, 2002–2015										
2002	2003	2005	2006	2008	2009	2010	2011	2013	2014	2015

Source: Smithsonian Institute National Museum of Natural History Global Volcanism Program

5. Mt. Etna is an active / extinct volcano. Scientists should occasionally / continuously monitor changes in the shape of the volcano that may signal a volcanic eruption by using seismometers / tiltmeters.

6. How does a better scientific understanding of Earth's atmosphere and oceans help scientists predict natural hazards? Choose all that apply.

   A. Changes in the atmosphere and oceans trigger geologic hazards such as earthquakes and volcanic eruptions.

   B. The atmosphere and oceans are primarily responsible for weather and climate patterns that could lead to hazards such as hurricanes or tornadoes.

   C. Understanding the atmosphere and oceans can help scientists develop new technologies to monitor conditions that could lead to hazardous events.

Interactive Review

Complete this page to review the main concepts of the lesson.

Scientists gather natural hazard data to improve scientific understanding, analyze historical occurrences, and monitor conditions to better predict natural hazards.

A. How can analyzing historical data and monitoring hazardous events help scientists improve their predictions of natural hazards?

Geologic hazards are natural hazards caused by geologic processes at or below Earth's surface, such as erosion and the movement of magma.

B. Identify two geologic hazards that are related and explain their relationship.

Weather and climate hazards result from the movement of air and water in the atmosphere and the oceans.

C. How do scientific understanding, historical data, and monitoring help scientists predict weather and climate hazards?

Reducing the Effects of Natural Hazards

This "dome home" in Pensacola Beach, Florida, located directly on the Gulf of Mexico, has unique features designed to help it withstand the wind and waves of a hurricane.

By the end of this lesson . . .

you will be able to define an engineering problem and evaluate solutions to reduce the effects of a natural hazard.

CAN YOU EXPLAIN IT?

How can we reduce the harmful effects of a flood?

During a flood, water flows into low areas, damaging homes and blocking transportation.

1. How could some of the harmful effects of flooding be reduced in a community like the one shown above?

 EVIDENCE NOTEBOOK As you explore this lesson, gather evidence to determine how people can reduce the harmful effects of flooding.

Describing Natural Hazard Mitigation

Natural hazards such as floods, earthquakes, and severe storms are dangerous events. These events may cause harm to people and property and, sometimes, they happen without warning. Scientists, engineers, and community officials work together to prepare for and minimize the damage caused by natural hazards.

2. **Discuss** With a partner, discuss how a house could be designed to protect it from the strong winds, flooding, and erosion that happen during a hurricane. Record the key points from your discussion.

We cannot stop hurricanes, but we can build houses, like this one, that minimize the potential damage caused by this type of hazard.

Natural Hazard Mitigation

Hazard **mitigation** describes efforts to prevent or reduce property damage or loss of life caused by a natural disaster. Although people cannot prevent natural disasters, a good mitigation plan can help keep people safe and reduce damage to property and the environment when a disaster does occur. Mitigation plans are specific to different types of natural hazards and to different locations and communities.

Hazard mitigation requires an understanding of the problems involved. Scientists collect and analyze data about natural hazards and disasters. These data help scientists understand the causes and possible effects of these events. Scientists also use these data to determine if an area is at risk for a natural hazard. Scientists work with engineers to apply what they have learned from the data. They design solutions and develop ways to predict and, if possible, to control the hazard or its effects. Engineers and planners use data to develop mitigation strategies. Different strategies are used before, during, and after a natural hazard. Before the event, engineers focus on preparation. After a disaster, their focus shifts to response to the disaster and recovery from its effects.

3. What types of data might be useful in mitigation efforts for an area that experiences frequent floods? Choose all that apply.

   A. historic information on rainfall patterns

   B. elevation mapping of the area

   C. average income of residents of the area

   D. location of population centers in the region

Preparation

Preparation is an important mitigation strategy. People prepare for disasters at many different levels. For example, mitigation planning is performed by individuals, families, communities, and local or federal governments.

Governments and other agencies develop and test plans in advance for how to respond to and recover from disastrous events. They work with scientists and engineers to develop technologies to monitor conditions, to make predictions, and to communicate with the public. They monitor conditions and share information before, during, and after natural hazards. Emergency management agencies find good locations for shelters and collect supplies to help people affected by a disaster.

Governments and communities can prepare by setting standards, also called *building codes*. These codes require structures to be likely to survive hazardous events and to protect people during these events. Architects and engineers design and build structures to meet these standards.

Preparation includes education so that people know what to expect, what to do, and where to go. If you know what hazards exist in your area and pay attention to predictions, you can prepare for the effects of natural hazards. Then, when you need to act, you will know what to do and you will have the things that you need in order to face the emergency.

If you are prepared, you are less likely to be severely affected by an event. If you learn what to expect during and after a natural hazard, you can identify what supplies you will need in case a disaster occurs. You can build an emergency kit as part of your preparations. Many kits include flashlights and batteries, blankets, first-aid supplies, fresh water, and other necessary items.

Being prepared helps people avoid some of the harmful effects of natural hazards. It also helps them recover after an event.

Scientists monitor conditions that lead to volcanic mudflows, called *lahars*, at Mount St. Helens. They use the data to predict lahars and warn people before a disaster occurs.

Television, radio, and emergency websites communicate information about weather hazards before, during, and after an event, such as a hurricane.

Preparation includes actions to prevent disasters. Restored wetlands help control water flow and reduce flooding.

4. A mitigation plan may define how people can be notified about the time and location of potential hazards. Weather forecasts provide information that communities need to prepare for / respond to natural hazards such as severe storms. During the emergency, governments and residents must be ready to prepare for / respond to changing local conditions.

Response

Natural hazard mitigation continues after the event begins. Appropriate and timely response helps reduce the negative effects of the hazard. Governments, relief agencies, and individuals can all respond to natural hazards. Responding to a natural hazard event means providing people with information and services as an event occurs and later. For example, during a flood, some responders rescue people whose homes or cars are surrounded by water. Others provide first aid and transportation to people who are injured or stranded.

Technology plays an important role in disaster response. Some technologies are used to monitor changing conditions. Other technologies, such as radios and phones, are essential for communication. Modern mapping technology helps responders reach affected locations as quickly as possible. Portable medical equipment and temporary shelters are used by doctors and nurses to provide care wherever or whenever it is needed.

Explore ONLINE!

Firefighters respond to a wildfire by using water and other chemicals to keep the fire from spreading.

Recovery

Emergency preparation and response efforts reduce damage and injury but they cannot prevent all damage or loss. Recovery is the final part of a mitigation plan. Recovery generally occurs after a disaster, but planning for recovery takes place long before it is needed. In some cases, recovery efforts may start before the event is over.

Recovering from a natural disaster may involve providing temporary shelter and services until permanent repairs can be made. Recovery involves providing supplies such as food, water, and medical supplies wherever they are needed as quickly as possible. Recovery also involves rebuilding and repairing damaged structures. The final step of recovery involves reviewing and revising mitigation plans for greater success in the future. Recovery is performed by government agencies, volunteer organizations, and members of a community.

Professionals and volunteers work together to help a community recover from a natural disaster.

EVIDENCE NOTEBOOK

5. Explain how preparation, response, and recovery can help people deal with a flood and minimize its effects. Record your evidence.

Scientific Knowledge and Engineering Design Principles

Natural hazard mitigation relies on science and engineering for success. Scientists study the causes and effects of natural hazards. They apply what they learn to explain how, where, and why hazardous events may occur. This information is then used to mitigate the events' effects. For example, scientists study the conditions in the atmosphere that may lead to the formation of tornadoes. They use this information to decide which conditions to monitor in order to predict tornadoes. Scientists and engineers can then develop instruments such as satellites and radar systems to monitor the atmosphere. They design computer models to analyze the collected data. When the conditions are right for tornadoes to form, scientists issue warnings that tornadoes may happen.

Mitigation plans are developed using the engineering design process. Scientists and engineers identify a problem that needs to be solved. Problems may include how to evacuate areas at risk of a disaster or how to get emergency supplies to people affected by a disaster. Once engineers identify a problem or need, they conduct research and more clearly define the problem. They then propose, evaluate, and test solutions to the problem. Solutions related to mitigating natural hazards could involve new tools or equipment. Other solutions could include new systems or processes.

Compare Stages of Earthquake Mitigation

WORD BANK
- preparation
- recovery
- response

6. These photos show three different parts of earthquake mitigation. Examine each photo and its caption. Then use the words from the word bank to label each photo with the stage of mitigation that is illustrated.

Students practice ways to protect themselves from falling objects during an earthquake.

Teams of volunteers and professionals search through rubble to rescue survivors of an earthquake.

Volunteers travel to areas affected by earthquakes to help residents rebuild homes and infrastructure.

7. Choose one of the examples from the photos. Suggest another mitigation activity that could be performed during that phase of hazard mitigation.

_____

_____

_____

_____

_____

_____

Developing a Natural Hazard Mitigation Plan

Identify a Need

To develop a mitigation plan using the engineering design process, you must first identify a need. Needs may vary, depending on the type of hazard and the place being affected. For example, the effects of a flood on a farm are different from the effects of an earthquake in a city. The need also varies with the stage of mitigation. For example, preparation for an earthquake may involve developing technology to reduce the amount of shaking a building experiences. However, response to an earthquake requires designing processes that people can follow to stay safe during the shaking. Recovery requires determining how best to repair damage caused by the shaking.

Tornado Effects Differ by Location

Tornadoes move quickly through a region, but can leave behind a lot of damage.

This farm raises animals and crops in large fields.

This city has many people in tall buildings in a small area.

This neighborhood has many homes on separate lots.

8. Examine the images. Describe at least one need that people in each location may have if a tornado was approaching.

Define the Engineering Problem

After the mitigation need is identified, scientists and engineers define an engineering problem. An engineering problem is more precise than a statement of the need. It is a statement that defines the type of solution that is required to address the need. To find a solution that works, the problem must be defined precisely using criteria and constraints.

Criteria and Constraints

Criteria are the conditions, requirements, or standards that a solution should meet. They provide specific information about the need and how it must be addressed. For example, a specific need for protecting people in a city may be a shelter to provide tornado protection to students in a middle school. To address this need, one criterion might be that the shelter is large enough to hold everyone at the school. Another criterion might be that the shelter is easy to get to from any part of the building. A final criterion may be that the walls and roof are strong enough to withstand a tornado with 200 km/h winds.

Constraints are conditions that limit the design solution or that could prevent the solution from being accomplished. They could include factors such as cost, time, size, availability of materials, limits on technology, the laws of physics, or current scientific understanding. If the school sets the cost as a constraint on the shelter, then the design must not cost more than the budget for the project. Engineers will study the problem and suggest solutions that meet the criteria while staying within the constraints.

Scientists and engineers will combine an understanding of the need with the criteria and constraints to state a specific engineering design problem. For example, one engineering problem could be, "Design a tornado shelter for a school that can fit 400 people, can be reached quickly from anywhere in the school, can withstand 200 km/h winds, and does not cost more than $1 million."

9. Look at this list of criteria and constraints for a barn area to protect livestock during a tornado. Identify each item on the list as a criterion or a constraint.

   A. criterion / constraint   should have room for 50 cows

   B. criterion / constraint   must cost less than $100,000 to build

   C. criterion / constraint   should have a door at least 7 meters wide

   D. criterion / constraint   must not extend into current milking areas

   E. criterion / constraint   must use current basic building framework

Propose Solutions

Before proposing solutions, scientists and engineers may perform research. For example, they may need to know how tornadoes cause damage and what building designs and materials can withstand high winds. A proposed solution must meet the most important criteria and all of the constraints of the engineering problem. However, when choosing a solution, sometimes tradeoffs must be made. A tradeoff is giving up one thing in return for another. In these cases, criteria can be modified, and the problem is then redefined. For example, imagine that, after researching the problem, engineers find that there is no way that a single room can fit everyone at the school and be able to withstand 200 km/h winds. Engineers may change the criteria to allow for several smaller rooms or for protection against a lower wind speed.

10. Language SmArts Complete the table by identifying criteria and constraints and stating the design problem for each location.

Tornado Engineering Problems

Location	Mitigation Need	Criteria and Constraints	Precisely Stated Engineering Problem
	Protect cattle from a tornado	must protect 50 cows, must work with existing barn design, must cost less than $100,000, must withstand a medium-strength tornado	Reinforce an existing barn to protect 50 cows from a medium-strength tornado without spending more than $100,000.
	Protect people in a city skyscraper from the effects of a tornado.		
	Protect a family in a home during a tornado.		

Brainstorming

Brainstorming is a way to generate ideas for solving the engineering problem. Although brainstorming can be done several times during the process, it commonly follows the identification of criteria and constraints and research.

Brainstorming is used after the problem is defined to come up with a list of possible solutions. Many different ideas may be suggested. For example, consider designing a safe place in a home during a tornado. An engineer or team may suggest a large room with concrete walls and ceiling, a room in the basement, an underground cellar outside the house, or an interior room without any modifications. Some of these ideas might not meet the criteria or constraints. One or more of these ideas may be better than the others. However, during brainstorming, ideas are not evaluated or compared.

Evaluate and Choose Solutions

After research and brainstorming, the suggested solutions are evaluated. Solutions that appear to meet most of the criteria and all of the constraints are compared to one another. Engineers decide which criteria are most important and use that information to evaluate the proposed solutions. Criteria may be sorted into "necessary" and "desirable" elements. Necessary criteria must be met. Desirable criteria allow a solution to go "above-and-beyond" what is required. Solutions that include all necessary features, plus some desirable features, may be considered better than other solutions.

A decision-making tool such as a decision matrix may help during evaluation. Using the matrix, solutions can be ranked with a number value to determine which solutions best meet the criteria of the problem.

Potential solutions can be modeled and tested before choosing a final solution. The engineering design process does not end with a test of the model or even with enacting the solution. The process allows for continual improvement. Solutions must be evaluated for their effectiveness and can be adjusted to increase future success.

Decision Matrix for Evaluating Tornado Shelter Solutions

Rankings		Solutions			
Criteria	Criterion Rating (1-5)	Concrete room	Basement room	Cellar outside house	Unmodified interior room
Protects from high winds	5	5	5	5	1
Not expensive	3	1	3	1	3
No change to living area	2	1	2	2	2
Easy to get to quickly	4	4	3	1	4
Totals					

 Criteria are listed for the design problem. The next column rates their importance. Protection from wind is the most important criterion with a maximum value of 5. Expense is less important with a maximum value of 3.

 Possible solutions are added to the table. Each solution is evaluated based on how well it meets each criterion. The criterion rating is the highest number that can be assigned for each solution for that criterion.

 For a given solution, the ratings for all of the criteria can be added together. This total number shows how well the solution meets the whole set of criteria. Then, solutions can be ranked by their totals and compared.

 11. Do the Math Find the total value for each of the solutions in the table by adding the columns. Then circle the correct answers in the paragraph below.

Of the proposed solutions, the highest overall evaluation score was for the concrete / basement / cellar / interior room.

The solution with the lowest criterion rating for protection from the wind was the concrete / basement / cellar / interior room.

Based on this decision matrix, the two options for the safe room that best fit the criteria are the concrete and basement / cellar and interior rooms.

Hands-On Lab
Develop and Evaluate a Flood Solution

You will use the engineering design process to design and model a structure that will withstand the effects of a flood in a warm, moist climate. Keep in mind that the effects of flooding include damage due to water even after floodwaters recede.

   The village you are assisting is located near a river that frequently overflows its banks after heavy rains. The river level rises slowly and then gradually drops. The floodwaters move slowly but many homes are still destroyed during a flood.

Procedure

STEP 1 Identify a Need What mitigation need or needs must be addressed by this design solution?

STEP 2 Define the Engineering Problem Precisely state the problem you will address based on the mitigation need and include criteria and constraints. Review the images and consider the needs of the villagers and the limits that result from the location, the design problem, and the materials. Rank the criteria in order of importance.

STEP 3 Brainstorm Solutions As a group, brainstorm ideas for a building design that will solve the engineering problem. Remember that you are not evaluating the ideas at this time, so list all ideas, even if they do not seem to meet the criteria.

STEP 4 Evaluate Solutions As a group, evaluate the possible solutions generated during brainstorming. Solutions not meeting the constraints should be eliminated. You may want to use a decision matrix to help in your evaluation.

MATERIALS

- aluminum foil (model for corrugated iron)
- building blocks, small, plastic (model for bricks)
- craft sticks (model for lumber)
- drink stirrers, tubular plastic (model for bamboo)
- glue
- plaster of Paris (model for concrete)
- soil or mud
- straw
- tape
- water

Building Materials and Their Characteristics

Concrete

very strong, expensive, locally sourced, requires long preparation time, does not rot, heavy

Bamboo

strong, inexpensive, locally sourced, quick to install, resistant to rot when damp, lightweight

Hardwood lumber

strong, expensive, locally sourced, quick to install, tends to rot when damp for long periods, heavy

Mud

weak unless reinforced, inexpensive, locally sourced, requires time to dry, does not rot, heavy

Corrugated iron

strong, expensive, not locally sourced, quick to install, resistant to rot but can rust, lightweight

Clay bricks

very strong, expensive, not locally sourced, requires long installation time, does not rot, heavy

STEP 5 Choose and Test Solutions Choose a design to test and explain how you will test it. Build the model, then test and record your results.

Analysis

STEP 6 Discuss the results of your test with your group and record your evaluation of the design. How well does your design meet the criteria and constraints of the engineering problem? Is the building likely to survive a flood?

STEP 7 With your group, brainstorm possible improvements to your solution. If the model did not pass your test, how could you change it so that it could pass? If it did pass the test, how could you improve the design to make it better?

The Role of Technology in Mitigation Planning

Technology is important at all stages of natural hazard mitigation. It is useful in identifying hazard probability, in developing mitigation plans, in testing solutions, in response and recovery, and in evaluating the success of mitigation activities after a hazard. Sometimes, solutions involve developing new technologies, such as equipment or processes, or redesigning existing technologies. The uses of technologies are driven by the needs of the people in an area and the hazards they face. However, the availability of technology may be limited by location or by the economic conditions of a community or region.

EVIDENCE NOTEBOOK

12. What are some ways that the engineering design process can be used to reduce the impact of floods? Record your evidence.

Evaluate Mitigation Technologies

Tsunamis are giant waves that can be caused by an earthquake at the bottom of the ocean. Tsunami waves travel outward in all directions from the source. When the waves reach a shore, they can cause massive damage and loss of life. Scientists and engineers work to mitigate the hazards of tsunamis by developing ways to predict when one will occur and to issue timely warnings.

13. Use the word bank to fill in the table to show which needs are met by the technologies that are shown. Some needs may be used more than once. Others may not be used at all.

> **WORD BANK**
> - saving lives
> - preventing damage
> - communication
> - data collection
> - environment cleanup

	Technology	Meets Needs
	Scientists use seismographs to detect and record earthquakes. When an undersea earthquake occurs, scientists model the earthquake's effects to predict whether tsunamis may occur.	
	Evacuation plans are in place long before a tsunami occurs. Evacuation signs direct people to safe areas.	
	When data indicate that an earthquake has generated a tsunami, scientists use computers to determine where it is likely to strike. Then, scientists issue warnings to affected areas.	

Continue Your Exploration

Name: _____   Date: _____

Check out the path below or go online to choose one of the other paths shown.

Careers in Engineering

- **Hands-On Labs** 🔬
- **Climate Change Mitigation**
- **Propose Your Own Path**

Go online to choose one of these other paths.

Geotechnical Engineer

Buildings, bridges, dams, walls, and roads are all held up by solid ground. At least it looks solid. Geotechnical engineers study soil and rock and how these materials support human structures and activities. This research is done before foundations are designed and built in order to ensure the safety of these structures.

Geotechnical engineering is a type of civil engineering, and it is part of any form of construction. Geotechnical engineers assess a building site based on the properties of soil and rock. Different types of rock have different properties. If a structure such as a large building, a bridge, or a dock for large ships is not sufficiently supported, a failure could occur. This could cause a lot of property damage and even lead to injury or death. Architects and builders rely on geotechnical engineers to determine how these structures should be supported. Before any construction starts, geotechnical engineers investigate the site, assess the risk of geologic hazards, and confirm that the rock underground is strong enough for the project.

Geotechnical engineers are involved in all parts of hazard mitigation. They assess locations for structures that must withstand earthquakes, floods, or landslides. They lead efforts to stabilize slopes and assess the safety of structures during response and recovery efforts. And they work with government officials and agencies to review and improve mitigation plans after hazards occur.

A geotechnical engineer monitors flood control wells that help control water flow at the base of a levee, an embankment to prevent flooding.

Continue Your Exploration

At 41.6 kilometers, the Qingdao Haiwan Bridge is the longest sea bridge in the world. Below the water of the bay, a tunnel passes under the bridge. The bridge has more than 5,000 support pillars that extend into the rock beneath the bay.

Qingdao Haiwan Bridge

The Qingdao Haiwan Bridge crosses a bay in eastern China. Because of natural hazards and human activity, the bridge has to be very strong. It is designed to survive powerful magnitude 8 earthquakes, tropical cyclones, and even a collision with a 300,000 ton cargo ship.

1. What are some possible criteria or constraints that engineers needed to consider when designing and constructing the Qingdao Haiwan Bridge?

2. Which part(s) of the design of the Qingdao Haiwan Bridge would involve a geotechnical engineer?

3. How might a geotechnical engineer help a repair team during the response phase after an underwater landslide that may have affected one of the bridge supports?

4. **Collaborate** With your group, discuss how a geotechnical engineer would use the engineering design process while designing supports for a large bridge. List your ideas and share them with the class.

Can You Explain It?

Name: _____   Date: _____

How can we reduce the harmful effects of a flood?

EVIDENCE NOTEBOOK

Refer to the notes in your Evidence Notebook to help you construct an explanation for ways that harmful effects of flooding can be reduced.

1. State your claim. Make sure your claim fully explains how the harmful effects of flooding can be reduced.

2. Summarize the evidence you have gathered to support your claim and explain your reasoning.

Checkpoints

Answer the following questions to check your understanding of the lesson.

Use the photograph to answer Question 3.

3. Which process would be an important part of preparation for a hurricane that is about to strike the city shown in the photograph?

   A. Build buildings farther from the coastline.

   B. Determine how to keep traffic moving during an emergency.

   C. Use boats to move emergency responders to the island if bridges are closed.

   D. Clean up the area so people can return as soon as possible.

Use the photograph to answer Questions 4–5.

4. Which of these actions would likely be part of a hazard mitigation plan to reduce the negative impacts of a blizzard? Select all that apply.

   A. warning about a blizzard before it arrives

   B. clearing snow from the street as quickly as possible after the storm

   C. having emergency response personnel available when the snow begins

   D. assigning work crews to repair damage caused by the weight of the snow

5. Many cities do not allow parking on the street when a blizzard has been predicted. How might parked cars interfere with hazard mitigation?

   A. People cannot get the cars out of the parking spaces to drive to work.

   B. Parked cars force traffic to move slower.

   C. Snow-covered cars on the street slow down emergency responders.

   D. The cars make the snow appear worse than it actually is.

6. A town is designing a flood-response plan. The town wants to close roads as soon as they are not passable. One of the *criteria / constraints* of the plan is to deploy warning signs as soon as flooding starts. The number of road crew employees working at a particular time is limited, which is one of the *criteria / constraints* of the plan. After writing a plan, the team will pretend that there is a flood to find out how quickly the crew can respond. This is a way to *brainstorm / test* the solution before an actual flood.

Interactive Review

Complete this section to review the main concepts of the lesson.

There are three parts to natural hazard mitigation: preparation, response, and recovery.

A. How does a hazard mitigation plan help a community deal with a disaster?

The engineering design process helps find a workable solution to a need.

B. How would the engineering design process be used to develop a mitigation plan for a geologic hazard, such as a landslide or a sinkhole?

Lesson 3 Engineer It: Reducing the Effects of Natural Hazards **65**

Choose one of the activities to explore how this unit connects to other topics.

☐ Life Science Connection

Ecological Succession When natural hazards occur, the habitats for living things may be affected. Wildfires, floods, and volcanic eruptions can cause plants and animals to relocate or face possible death. But after the event, living things move back into the area. This process is called ecological succession.

Research the process of ecological succession that has occurred after a natural disaster, such as the eruption of Mount St. Helens in 1980. Summarize your research in a report. Your report should identify the natural disaster and include diagrams or graphs that show how the natural disaster affected the natural surroundings.

Thick layers of ash covered the ground after the eruption of Mount St. Helens in 1980.

☐ Literature Connection

The Great Flood of 1913 In 1913, a massive flood devastated Ohio and Indiana and brought widespread damage to 12 other states. In his book, *Washed Away: How the Great Flood of 1913, America's Most Widespread Natural Disaster, Terrorized a Nation and Changed It Forever*, Geoff Williams wrote about the devastation of the flood.

Research the Great Flood of 1913, using sources such as Williams's book, other similar books, original newspaper stories, and reputable websites about the disaster. Write an analysis of what happened, and construct an explanation for how this flood led to such devastation. Design a solution that could have helped ease the destruction caused by this disaster.

☐ Health Connection

Natural Disasters and Disease When natural disasters happen, many people lose access to resources such as fresh water and services such as proper sanitation. Without the ability to stay clean and get rid of wastes, the chances of becoming sick greatly increase.

Research how natural disasters can affect the quality of life. Using Hurricane Katrina as a case study, analyze how natural disasters can lead to disease outbreaks. Identify ways that this effect of natural hazards could be mitigated. Prepare a multimedia presentation to summarize your findings.

Name: _____

Date: _____

Complete this review to check your understanding of the unit.

Use the photo to answer Questions 1–2.

1. Which weather conditions can help scientists predict the likelihood of a snow avalanche? Select all that apply.

   A. The temperature rises a few degrees over several days.

   B. A snowstorm results in 12 inches of snow in less than 24 hours.

   C. Strong winds have been blowing in the same direction for several days.

   D. Temperatures have remained steady and no snowmelt has been observed.

2. To decrease deaths caused by snow avalanches, engineers should focus their monitoring efforts on areas in higher / lower elevations.

Use the information provided in the graph to answer Questions 3–4.

3. Between 1900 and 1995, the amount of property damage caused by hurricanes has increased / decreased and the number of deaths caused by hurricanes has increased / decreased.

4. Which of these factors most likely account for the trends in hurricane damage and deaths over time? Circle all that apply.

   A. decrease in human population in hurricane-prone areas

   B. increase in number of structures in hurricane paths

   C. change in the locations where hurricanes happen

   D. change in the conditions that cause hurricanes

   E. changes in monitoring and forecasting technology

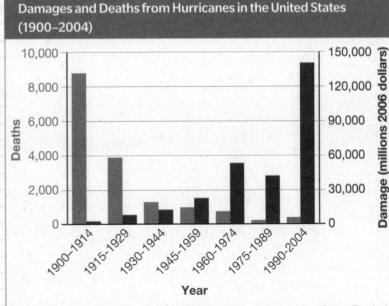

Damages and Deaths from Hurricanes in the United States (1900–2004)

Source: Blake et al., *The Deadliest, Costliest, and Most Intense United States Tropical Cyclones from 1851 to 2006 (and Other Frequently Requested Hurricane Facts)*, NOAA Technical Memorandum NWS TPC-5, updated April 2007

5. Complete the table by providing descriptions of how these hazards relate to each big concept.

Hazard	Method of Prediction	Cause	Effect
Floods	Rainfall, snowmelt, and water levels in streams, rivers, and lakes are monitored to predict floods.		
Tornadoes			
Volcanic Eruptions			

Name: _____   Date: _____

Use the map to answer Questions 6–9.

6. Which regions of Florida have the most sinkholes?

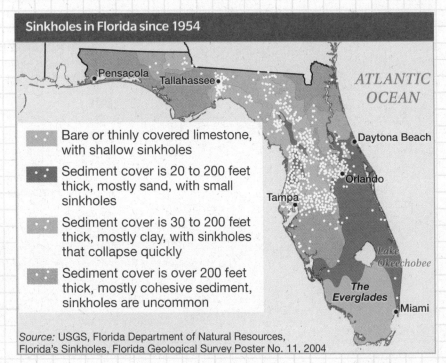

Sinkholes in Florida since 1954

- Bare or thinly covered limestone, with shallow sinkholes
- Sediment cover is 20 to 200 feet thick, mostly sand, with small sinkholes
- Sediment cover is 30 to 200 feet thick, mostly clay, with sinkholes that collapse quickly
- Sediment cover is over 200 feet thick, mostly cohesive sediment, sinkholes are uncommon

Source: USGS, Florida Department of Natural Resources, Florida's Sinkholes, Florida Geological Survey Poster No. 11, 2004

7. What types of sinkholes form most often in each type of rock or soil?

8. What types of monitoring technology and/or precursor events (if any) could be used to forecast sinkhole formation?

9. What would people in Florida need to know in order to develop mitigation protocols for the type of sinkholes that form in a given area? How might mitigation plans differ for people in Pensacola and Orlando?

Use the map to answer Questions 10–13.

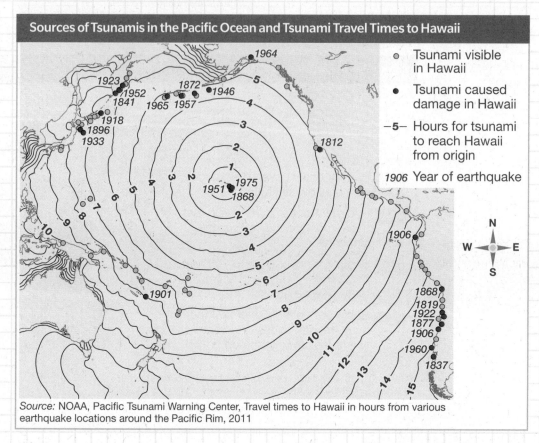

Sources of Tsunamis in the Pacific Ocean and Tsunami Travel Times to Hawaii

Legend:
- ○ Tsunami visible in Hawaii
- ● Tsunami caused damage in Hawaii
- —5— Hours for tsunami to reach Hawaii from origin
- *1906* Year of earthquake

Source: NOAA, Pacific Tsunami Warning Center, Travel times to Hawaii in hours from various earthquake locations around the Pacific Rim, 2011

10. Based on this map, do all tsunamis that reach Hawaii cause natural disasters? Explain your reasoning.

11. Where do most damaging tsunamis in Hawaii originate (from which directions)?

12. Which point of origin for damaging tsunamis would allow the most time for warnings to be issued to people in Hawaii?

13. Based on this map, how would you rate the tsunami risk in Hawaii? Use evidence and reasoning to support your claim.

Name: _____   Date: _____

What is the best plan to improve a park?

Imagine you are on a task force making plans to improve a park near Halls Bayou in Houston, Texas. (A bayou is a sluggish stream or river.) You want to add features to an existing park for people to enjoy, such as picnic pavilions, playgrounds, soccer fields, a stage, and walking and jogging trails. However, the area is at risk of seasonal flooding. Analyze information about the risk of flooding and use that information to develop a map of your proposed park improvements and a plan for minimizing any flood damage.

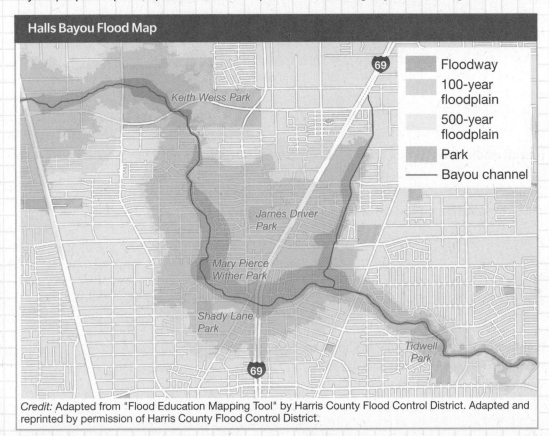

Halls Bayou Flood Map

Legend:
- Floodway
- 100-year floodplain
- 500-year floodplain
- Park
- Bayou channel

Keith Weiss Park
James Driver Park
Mary Pierce Wither Park
Shady Lane Park
Tidwell Park

Credit: Adapted from "Flood Education Mapping Tool" by Harris County Flood Control District. Adapted and reprinted by permission of Harris County Flood Control District.

The steps below will help guide your research and will help you propose a map of the new park features and a plan to mitigate the effects of flooding.

Engineer It

1. **Ask a Question** What questions are important to ask in order to develop your plan?

Engineer It

2. **Conduct Research** Research the meaning of the different zones on the map: *channel, floodway, 100-year floodplain,* and *500-year floodplain.*

3. **Analyze and Interpret Data** Using past data on floods in this area, determine which areas are more or less likely to flood. Choose one of the existing parks in the area to develop by adding your proposed features.

4. **Design a Solution** Consider how each of your park features will respond to flooding. Create a map of your park plan that includes the proposed park features. Include flood zone information in the map, and identify ways to reduce the effects of a flood on the park's features.

5. **Communicate** Present your map and park plan to the class. Explain how you chose the placement of your park's features and how your park is designed to minimize the effects of flooding.

✓ **Self-Check**

	I conducted research about what different flood risk zones mean.
	I analyzed and interpreted data about flood risk, topography, and construction constraints.
	I designed a solution for building park structures in a flood-prone area.
	I clearly communicated my solution to others.

Resources in Earth Systems

Lesson 1 Natural Resources 76

Lesson 2 The Distribution of Natural Resources 96

Unit Review 117

Unit Performance Task 121

The Strokkur geyser in Iceland brings hot groundwater to the surface. Because much of Iceland's rock and groundwater are heated by Earth processes, geothermal energy is a popular option for heat and electricity.

Everything people need to live can be found at or near Earth's surface. This includes all of the materials we use to make products, develop new technologies, and generate electrical energy. In this unit, you will discover what natural resources are and how they are distributed on and near Earth's surface.

Why It Matters

Here are some questions to consider as you work through the unit. Can you answer any of the questions now? Revisit these questions at the end of the unit to apply what you discover.

Questions	Notes
What are natural resources?	
What natural resources do you use every day?	
Why are natural resources more common in some places than in others?	
How do organisms depend on natural resources from their environment?	
How do people locate and acquire natural resources?	

Unit Starter: Analyzing Patterns in Resource Distribution

Bauxite (BAWK•syt) ore, which is rich in aluminum oxide, is the world's primary source of aluminum. Bauxite forms deep in the soil when warm rainwater soaks into the ground and removes some minerals and chemicals from the soil. This leaves behind concentrated aluminum. The map shows the climates and locations of the largest bauxite producers.

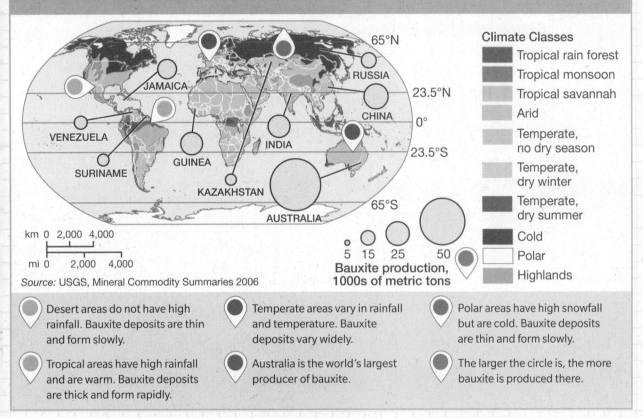

Source: USGS, Mineral Commodity Summaries 2006

Desert areas do not have high rainfall. Bauxite deposits are thin and form slowly.

Temperate areas vary in rainfall and temperature. Bauxite deposits vary widely.

Polar areas have high snowfall but are cold. Bauxite deposits are thin and form slowly.

Tropical areas have high rainfall and are warm. Bauxite deposits are thick and form rapidly.

Australia is the world's largest producer of bauxite.

The larger the circle is, the more bauxite is produced there.

1. Most of the large bauxite producers are located within tropical / polar regions. This is related to cold / warm temperatures and high / low rainfall amounts.

2. If you were interested in establishing a new bauxite mining operation, where is the best place to look for concentrated aluminum?

   A. cold areas near the oceans

   B. areas near a tropical rain forest

   C. areas with dry conditions

   D. areas with a temperate climate and dry winters

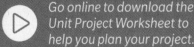

Go online to download the Unit Project Worksheet to help you plan your project.

Unit Project

Natural Resource Distribution

Natural resources are not evenly distributed around the globe. What caused this uneven distribution? Choose a natural resource, and research its distribution on Earth. Prepare a booklet that describes how your resource forms, how much of it is left, and where it is distributed and why.

Natural Resources

This photo of Iceland's Godafoss waterfall shows many of Earth's natural resources, such as rocks, water, plants, and energy from the sun.

By the end of this lesson . . .

you will be able to explain the effects of human use of natural resources on resource availability, on people, and on the environment.

Go **online** to view the digital version of the Hands-On Lab for this lesson and to download additional lab resources.

CAN YOU EXPLAIN IT?

Why are trees a renewable resource but coal, which comes from plants, is not?

Coal and trees are both natural resources that humans use.

1. Have you ever seen a tree grow? How long do you think it takes a tree to grow to full size?

2. Have you ever seen coal form? How do you think coal forms from plants?

3. What do you think the word *renewable* means? How might it relate to human use of coal and trees?

EVIDENCE NOTEBOOK As you explore the lesson, gather evidence to help explain why trees are a renewable resource but coal is not.

Exploring the Ways We Use Natural Resources

Plants, animals, and other organisms live in many places on Earth. Yet, they need the same basic things to survive, no matter where they are.

Compared to Earth's green and brown landmasses and blue oceans, the surface of the moon looks gray and dry.

4. **Discuss** Think about the basic things you need every day. What resources would you need to survive on the moon?

Natural Resources

You breathe air, drink water, and use energy from the sun. Air, water, and energy from the sun are all natural resources. **Natural resources** are used by humans for survival and to improve the quality of their lives. Natural resources are obtained from the natural world and can be matter or energy. Natural resources can be living or nonliving things.

Natural resources can come from the Earth system or from outside the Earth system. The four parts of the Earth system are the atmosphere (air), biosphere (living things), geosphere (rocks, minerals, soil), and hydrosphere (water). One example of a resource that comes from outside the Earth system is energy from the sun.

Fish are a biosphere resource humans use for food and as plant fertilizer.

5. Name one material you use from each part of the Earth system. Give an example of how it might be used.

Material Resources

We harvest and use resources from all over Earth. *Material resources* are natural resources humans use to make objects or to eat as food. For example:

- *Minerals*, such as iron or table salt, are naturally occurring inorganic solids. Minerals are used in manufacturing and construction.

- *Rocks* are solid mixtures of minerals and organic matter. Rocks are often used as building materials.

- *Soil* is a loose mixture of rock pieces, organic material, water, and air. It can be used to grow plants or used for building.

- Earth's atmosphere is mostly nitrogen and oxygen and also contains other substances. The atmosphere provides the air we breathe.

- Freshwater lakes and rivers provide us with food to eat, such as fish, and water for drinking and cleaning. Oceans contain materials such as salt, fish, and seaweed.

- Plants and animals are used for food and to make materials such as clothing.

- Fossil fuels include coal, petroleum—commonly called *oil*—and natural gas. They formed from the buried remains of plants and animals. These resources are used to generate electrical energy and to make materials such as plastic and carbon air filters.

Examples of Material Resources

6. Write the name of the material from the word bank in the box that matches the natural resource it comes from.

- drinking water
- food
- air in a balloon
- ~~charcoal in air filters~~
- garden beds
- buildings

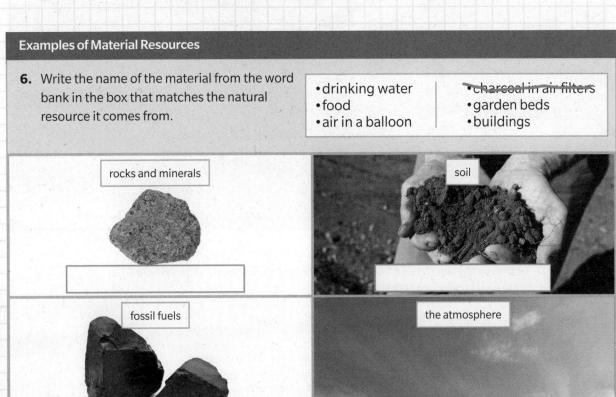

rocks and minerals

soil

fossil fuels

charcoal in air filters

the atmosphere

plants and animals

water

7. A house is made from many material resources. Write the name of each material resource in the correct box to identify that resource and to show which parts of the house each resource is used to construct.

clay	sand
~~limestone~~	trees
oil	

limestone

8. **Draw** Think about different types of transportation, such as a bicycle, a car, a plane, or a bus. Draw one of the vehicles. Label at least three materials used in the vehicle, and identify the natural resource it came from.

9. The sun is an important natural resource. How do you think people use the sun as a natural resource?

Energy from the sun radiates through space into the Earth system.

Energy Resources

Natural resources that people use for energy are called *energy resources*. People use energy resources for things such as heating, cooling, lighting, industry, transportation, communication, and entertainment. Energy exists in many different forms, and it can change from one form to another. However, energy cannot be created or destroyed.

The most commonly used energy resources are fossil fuels such as coal, natural gas, and petroleum. Fossil fuels release energy when they are burned. Other sources of energy include wind, sunlight, moving water, geothermal energy, biomass materials, and nuclear materials. Geothermal energy is thermal energy that comes from deep within Earth. Biomass is plant matter, such as wood or crop waste, that is burned for heat or made into fuel called *biofuel*. Uranium is a nuclear material.

Plant matter is burned to heat the pot and cook the food inside the pot.

10. Match each type of energy resource with an example of how it is used. Write the energy resource from the word bank in the correct box of the table.

WORD BANK
- ~~biomass~~
- solar
- wind
- nuclear
- fossil fuel
- moving water

Type of energy resource	Example of how the resource is used
biomass	Wood is burned to generate energy as heat and light.
	Water flows through a hydroelectric dam to turn the blades of a turbine and generate electrical energy.
	Atoms of uranium are split apart to release energy.
	Natural gas is burned to generate energy as heat and light.
	Energy from the sun is absorbed and converted to electrical energy.
	A windmill uses moving air to turn the blades of a turbine and generate electrical energy.

Energy Resource Use

Most of the energy that people use comes from fossil fuels. The graph shows the sources of energy used in the United States. A total of 81% of the energy used in the United States in 2014 was from fossil fuel energy.

Wind and sunlight can be used to generate energy without mining, processing, or transportation. Most fossil fuels have to be mined or drilled, transported, and processed in order to be used to generate energy.

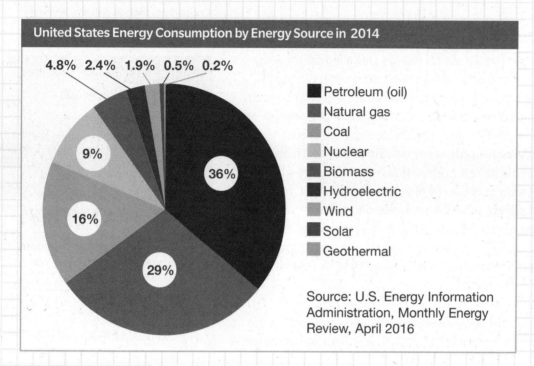

United States Energy Consumption by Energy Source in 2014

4.8% 2.4% 1.9% 0.5% 0.2%

36%
29%
16%
9%

■ Petroleum (oil)
■ Natural gas
■ Coal
■ Nuclear
■ Biomass
■ Hydroelectric
■ Wind
■ Solar
■ Geothermal

Source: U.S. Energy Information Administration, Monthly Energy Review, April 2016

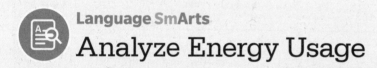

Language SmArts

Analyze Energy Usage

Use the circle graph and the information you have read to answer the questions.

11. Use evidence from the graph to support the statement that 81% of the energy used in the United States in 2014 was fossil fuel energy.

12. Use evidence from the graph to explain whether the following statement is true.

In the United States, more energy was generated in 2014 from coal than from wind, solar, and hydroelectric sources combined.

13. Think about all the ways corn can be used. Is corn a material resource or an energy resource or both? Explain your answer.

Corn is harvested and processed to make animal feed, fuel, plastics, and human food products such as sweeteners and cereals.

Some Resources Are Both Material and Energy Resources

A single natural resource can be both a material resource and an energy resource. Resources such as wheat, corn, and soybeans are food. They can also be made into biofuel. Petroleum is processed for use as a fuel. It is also used to make paint, crayons, candles, and plastic.

EVIDENCE NOTEBOOK

14. Describe and categorize trees and coal as natural resources. Record your evidence.

Analyze Outcomes

15. Suppose a new invention allows tractors to run on fuel made from potatoes. If potato fuel is found to be a good replacement for fossil fuels, how might that affect the supply of potatoes for food?

_____

_____

_____

_____

_____

_____

16. Which of these are possible positive outcomes of the use of potatoes for fuel? Circle all that apply.

A. The cost of potato food products will increase.

B. Potato farmers will have more options for selling their crops.

C. Potato fuel will significantly cut the use of fossil fuels throughout the world.

Comparing Renewable and Nonrenewable Resources

Imagine that you and a friend take a long bike ride. You fill your water bottles and start out on your ride. The day is hot, and you both drink all of your water sooner than expected. You can drink as much water as you want when you get home. But right now your water supply is gone.

17. **Discuss** Think about everything you use in a day. What are some things that affect how quickly you are able to replace the materials you used?

This bike rider has used up his supply of water to drink.

The Availability of Natural Resources

The more a resource is used, the sooner it will be used up, unless it can be replaced. As people use a resource, its supply decreases. The ability to replace a resource depends on how much of it can be found, grown, mined, or processed. When some resources are used up, no more is available. Other resources are easily replaced. Resources can be categorized by how quickly they can be replaced.

18. Look at the list below. Think about how each resource grows or forms. Determine whether it could be replaced within a human lifetime (quickly) or whether it would take many human lifetimes (slowly).
Write quickly or slowly to describe how fast each resource can be replaced.

   A. soil _____

   B. cotton ___quickly____

   C. petroleum _____

   D. fish _____

   E. trees _____

   F. coal _____

Crop resources, such as the cotton shown here, can be replaced quickly. Quickly may mean a time period as short as a growing season or as long as a human lifetime.

19. The following conditions occurred at a town one summer. Which could negatively affect the replacement rate of the town's water resources? Circle all that apply.

A. The town put a limit on how often people could water their lawns.

B. More rain fell than normal.

C. Temperatures were higher than normal.

D. Twice as many tourists visited the town than normal.

Nonrenewable Resources

A **nonrenewable resource** is a natural resource that cannot be replaced as quickly as it is used. Rocks and minerals form beneath Earth's surface over millions of years. Coal, petroleum, natural gas, and uranium do not form as quickly as they are used. People cannot control or speed up the geologic processes that form rocks, minerals, or fossil fuels. Therefore, these resources are nonrenewable.

Renewable Resources

A **renewable resource** is a natural resource that can be replaced at the same rate it is used, or faster. Hydroelectric energy, wind energy, solar energy, and biomass are renewable energy resources. Air, water, fish, animals, and plants are renewable material resources. These resources can be managed so they do not run out. For example, some commercial fishers used to catch as many fish as possible, causing some species of fish to near extinction. To become *extinct* means to die out completely. Today in some places, conservation limits fish catches. These limits are designed to allow the populations of those species of fish to be maintained.

Water can be a renewable resource. But it must be managed so that it is not polluted or used more quickly than it can be replaced. Water, biomass, and animals are examples of renewable resources that could be used up. They are called *potentially renewable resources* because they are only renewable if they are not used too quickly. If they are used too quickly, they may not be able to be replaced. For example, passenger pigeons, such as the one in the photo, were hunted to extinction.

Some renewable resources cannot be used up by human activity. They are considered to be *inexhaustible*. Wind and solar energy are inexhaustible renewable resources because the supply of these resources is not affected by human use.

Cassiterite, the main ore of tin, forms in veins of rock.

The passenger pigeon was once the most common bird in North America, numbering 3–5 billion pigeons. Mass hunting led to extinction within 300 years. In 1914, the last passenger pigeon died in the Cincinnati Zoo.

Hands-On Lab
Explore Replacement of a Natural Resource

You will model and explore the rates of water use and replacement.

Procedure and Analysis

STEP 1 On the inside of each cup, measure 8 cm up from the bottom. Mark the cups with the marker. The marks should be horizontal and about 2 cm long. Label the outside of the cups Cup 1, Cup 2, and Cup 3.

STEP 2 Start with Cup 1. Using the skewer, carefully make two holes through the bottom of the cup from the inside toward the outside of the cup.

STEP 3 Hold Cup 1 over the tray. Pour water at a steady rate up to the mark. Continue to add water to keep the amount of water up to but not over the black mark. Record your observations in the table.

STEP 4 Circle the correct word(s) to complete each sentence.

In the model, the water flowing out of the holes represents the
replacement rate / use of a resource.

The water being poured in the cup represents the
replacement rate / use of a resource.

STEP 5 Decide how you could use Cups 2 and 3 to model two other water use and replacement scenarios that are different from the situation shown by what you did with Cup 1. Describe your plans for Cups 2 and 3 in the table.

STEP 6 Use a liter of water to model your scenarios with Cup 2 and Cup 3. Record your observations in the table.

Cup	Plan	Observations
1	2 medium-sized holes, pour water to keep it at the level of the black mark	
2		
3		

STEP 7 Describe the water use and replacement scenario you modeled using Cup 1.

STEP 8 Describe the water use and replacement scenario you modeled using Cup 2 and Cup 3. Compare these models to the model made using Cup 1.

EVIDENCE NOTEBOOK

20. Describe how the availability of trees and coal is affected by their formation. In what conditions does each resource form? How quickly does each resource form? Record your evidence.

Do the Math

Compare Rates of Renewal

Pine trees are harvested as building material after growing for about 40 years. About 14 acres of pine are needed to build a 1,000 ft² house. About 2 acres of bamboo are needed for the same size house. A bamboo stand regrows and is ready for harvesting in about 5 years.

Complete the equation. Then solve it.

21. About how many times as many acres of pine are needed to produce the same amount of building material as using bamboo?

$x =$ _____ ÷ _____

$x =$ _____

About _____ times as many acres of pine are needed to produce the same amount of building material as using bamboo.

22. About how many harvests of bamboo can be collected during the time it takes to fully grow one pine tree?

$y =$ _____ ÷ _____

$y =$ _____

About _____ harvests of bamboo can be collected in the same time it takes to fully grow one pine tree.

Bamboo is a fast-growing alternative to wood. It can be used as a building and flooring material.

Evaluating the Effects of Using Natural Resources

A *consequence* is a result that follows naturally from the actions of a person or group. Consequences may be good or bad. They can occur immediately or over a long time. Here is an example: You choose to ignore the alarm clock one morning. You get more sleep, but you arrive late to school and get detention. These are immediate consequences of your decision to sleep later than usual.

23. **Discuss** Marisol earns ten dollars for babysitting. She decides to go to the movies with her friends, and she spends all her money on the ticket. What is a positive consequence of Marisol's decision? What is a negative consequence of her decision?

Consequences of Using Natural Resources

Human use of resources results in consequences for people and the environment. Imagine a paper factory near a forest and a river. The paper is made using trees from the forest and water from the river. Paper is an important resource, but the processes used to make it pollute the river, forest, and the air. Also, using river water and trees can degrade and destroy habitats. These negative effects can be reduced by using less paper, recycling paper, using less-polluting processes in the factory, and by replanting trees.

The extraction of resources can negatively affect other resources. For example, offshore drilling for oil can pollute marine environments, which are resources for food and medicine.

Positive and Negative Consequences

Our use of resources has positive and negative effects on people and on the environment. For example, nuclear power plants provide energy and do not pollute the air. But they produce radioactive wastes that must be handled and stored safely for thousands of years or more.

Management of resources can help reduce negative consequences. For example, clear-cutting is a way of harvesting trees in which every tree in an area is cut down and removed. It destroys forests and increases soil erosion. But selective cutting

Resources can be protected. For example, The Pacific Remote Islands Marine National Monument is an area that is protected from practices such as offshore drilling.

and replanting allows trees to be used while still conserving forest resources. New energy technologies, such as those that use solar or wind power, reduce human use of nonrenewable fossil fuels.

Consequences of Resource Use

Wind is an energy resource that does not pollute the environment. It also reduces dependence on fossil fuels.

Road construction cuts through a natural ecosystem. This can interrupt migration patterns and cause animals to cross dangerous roads.

Because resource use can have both positive and negative consequences, choices have to be made about how to use them. A *tradeoff* is a situation that involves giving something up in return for gaining something else. For example, crude oil can be processed into gasoline. The tradeoff is that we gain gasoline so that people can travel, but we lose air quality because the processing and the burning of the gasoline sends pollutants into the air.

24. Give an example of how using soil, trees, or air might result in a tradeoff.

Short-Term and Long-Term Consequences

Our use of resources has both short- and long-term effects on people and on the environment. A short-term effect would last a human lifetime or less. A long-term effect would last longer than a human lifetime. Burning of fossil fuels introduces pollutants to the air, including greenhouse gases and chemicals that cause acid rain and affect human health. In the short-term, these pollutants affect air quality and may affect people with asthma and other respiratory conditions. In the long-term, acid rain may cause damage to structures and environments. Greenhouse gases cause warming of Earth's atmosphere that can last for centuries.

Wetlands are areas with standing water that covers the soil. Wetlands filter pollutants from water before they reach rivers and streams. Many wetlands have been drained or filled in so that crops can be grown or structures can be built. Short-term consequences of wetland loss include increased erosion and chemical pollution of rivers. Fish populations also decrease because wetlands are fish nurseries. Long-term consequences of wetland loss include habitat loss, extinction of organisms, and increased vulnerability of the area to severe weather and climate events.

Examples of Short-Term and Long-Term Consequences

Oil spills from deep-sea drilling can have short-term, negative consequences for wildlife. For example, oil from an oil spill coated this bird's feathers, preventing it from flying. Rescuers washed the bird with dish soap to remove the oil.

Mountaintop removal mining has long-term, negative consequences for the environment. For example, explosives are used to remove rock and soil above this coal deposit. This practice destroys habitats and leaves behind pollutants.

25. Write S to label the event as a *short-term* effect or write L to label the event as a *long-term* effect.

_____ A large, fast-flowing river is cloudy and muddy for a few days after 2 tons of soil is spilled by a barge.

_____ People who live near an oil refinery are advised to avoid outdoor activity for a week after a smokestack filter malfunctions and releases toxic chemicals.

_____ A nuclear energy accident results in immediate and permanent evacuation of a 20-mile radius because of radioactive contamination.

_____ An oil spill in the ocean coats penguins' feathers with oil until volunteers can clean them up.

Engineer It

Identify the Effects of an Engineering Solution

An engineering team has developed an idea for a drinking straw that filters out parasites from polluted water.

26. Identify at least one way this engineered solution might affect the health of people in a positive way or a negative way. Explain.

_____

_____

_____

_____

27. Identify at least one way this engineered solution might affect the health of the environment in a positive way or a negative way. Explain.

_____

_____

_____

_____

Continue Your Exploration

Name: _____   Date: _____

Check out the path below or go online to choose one of the other paths shown.

Careers in Engineering

- **Hands-On Labs** ✋
- **Desalination**
- **Propose Your Own Path**

Go online to choose one of these other paths.

Biomass Engineer

Biomass is organic matter that can be processed to make fuel. Biomass engineers apply engineering practices to process biomass into biofuel. Some biomass engineers focus on ensuring that the source of the biomass remains a renewable resource.

Biomass engineers and biologists work together in teams. These teams develop and test cost-efficient ways to make biofuels. They conduct research and use technology to find ways to turn plant waste into biofuel sources. They come up with environmentally safe ways to get rid of or use biomass waste. Biomass engineers also help design machines that use biofuel. Biomass engineers need at least a bachelor's degree in engineering or a related science field.

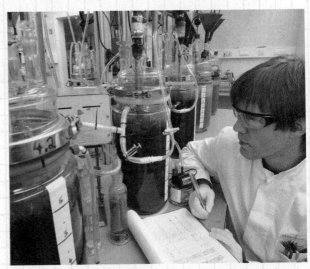

This biomass engineer investigates the quality of biofuel made from algae, a type of organism that grows in many parts of the world.

Making Biofuel

Using biomass for fuel began when humans first built fires with wood. Wood is still the largest biomass energy resource worldwide.

Many types of biomass can be used to produce biofuel. For example, used vegetable oils and animal fats can be turned into biodiesel fuel to run a school bus. Any plant matter—such as wood shavings, grass, leaves, algae, wheat straw, and corncobs—can be turned into biofuel. Some common biofuel sources include soybeans, corn, and waste products from wood production. In the future, biomass engineers hope to find new ways to make fuel, plastics, chemicals, and other products from plant matter.

Farmers used to grow and harvest soybeans only for food. Now they harvest the soybeans and the rest of the plant matter too. Stalks, stems, and leaves are used to produce biofuel.

archive/Alamy; (b) ©sima/Fotolia;

Continue Your Exploration

Use the circle graph to answer Questions 1 and 2.

1. What can you conclude from the information shown in the graph?

   A. Used cooking oil is used more than canola oil to produce biofuels in the United States.

   B. People in the United States use twice as much animal fat for biofuel as they do soybean oil.

   C. More corn oil is used for biofuel in the United States than was used in the past.

   D. More people in the United States would use corn oil if there were no canola oil.

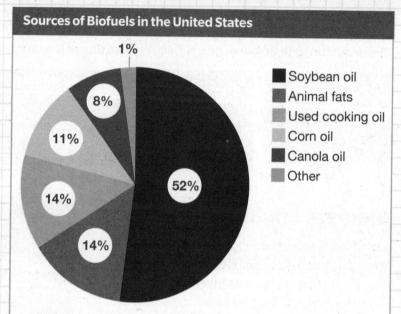

Sources of Biofuels in the United States

1%
8%
11%
14%
14%
52%

- Soybean oil
- Animal fats
- Used cooking oil
- Corn oil
- Canola oil
- Other

Source: U.S. Energy Information Administration, Monthly Biodiesel Production Report with data for December 2015, February 2016

2. A biomass engineering team is developing a new way to power lawnmowers by using biofuel. What might influence their decision about which oil to use? Circle all that apply.

   A. Soybean oil is the most common source of biofuels in United States.

   B. A new opportunity for using used cooking oil might encourage people to recycle.

   C. Canola oil is one of the least common sources of biofuels in the United States.

   D. Engineers would not want to use a type of biofuel that is already in use.

3. Which of these is a positive consequence of using biomass as an energy resource?

   A. No burning is required.

   B. More new machines are designed.

   C. It is potentially renewable.

   D. No waste is produced.

4. **Collaborate** Biofuel can be made from wood, grass clippings, leaves, crops, or crop waste. Methane can be collected from rotting garbage and community landfills to produce biofuel. Ethanol can be made from fruit or other crops, such as corn. These energy resources can be used to do the same work as fossil fuels.

   Together with a partner, come up with an idea to power a household item with a biofuel. Draw and label a cartoon to show your idea. Present your cartoon to the class, along with any new or different ideas you and your partner had about promoting biomass energy.

Can You Explain It?

Name: _____   Date: _____

Why are trees a renewable resource, but coal, which comes from plants, is not?

EVIDENCE NOTEBOOK

Refer to the notes in your Evidence Notebook to help you construct an explanation for why trees are renewable resources and coal is not.

1. State your claim. Make sure your claim fully explains why trees are renewable resources and coal is not a renewable resource.

2. Summarize the evidence you have gathered to support your claim and explain your reasoning.

Checkpoints

Answer the following questions to check your understanding of the lesson.

Use the photo to answer Question 3.

3. What positive effect might the car in the photo have on the environment?

   A. A solar-powered car will go faster than a car powered by fossil fuel.

   B. A solar-powered car will take up more space than a car powered by fossil fuel.

   C. A renewable energy resource is being used to replace a nonrenewable energy resource.

   D. A renewable water resource is being used to replace a nonrenewable fossil fuel resource.

Use the photo to answer Questions 4 and 5.

4. Which of these is shown by the photo? Circle all that apply.

   A. harvesting a nonrenewable material resource

   B. harvesting a nonrenewable energy resource

   C. harvesting a renewable energy resource

   D. harvesting a renewable material resource

5. Harvesting wood from trees results in
   a gain / a loss of animal habitat and
   a gain / a loss of land for growing
   crops. Harvesting wood also results in a
   greater / lesser chance of soil erosion and in
   more / less wood to use for building homes.

6. Are plants and animals potentially renewable natural resources?

   A. Yes, because plants and animals are resources that can be replaced at the same rate they are used, if managed well.

   B. No, because it is not possible for humans to use plant and animal resources at a faster rate than they can be replaced.

   C. No, because plants and animals are inexhaustible resources.

   D. Yes, because we use plant resources at the same rate as we use animal resources.

Interactive Review

Complete this section to review the main concepts of the lesson.

Natural resources can be classified as energy or material resources.

A. What is the difference between energy resources and material resources? Include examples in your answer.

Natural resources can be classified as renewable or nonrenewable.

B. What is the difference between a renewable resource and a nonrenewable resource?

Human use of natural resources affects the environment and people in many ways.

C. Provide an example of a consequence from using a natural resource. Explain whether it is a short-term or long-term consequence. Explain whether the consequence has a positive or negative effect on people or the environment.

The Distribution of Natural Resources

The water in the Ladybower Reservoir in England is used to generate electrical energy and to provide drinking water for people in several cities.

By the end of this lesson . . .

you will be able to explain why natural resources are unevenly distributed on Earth.

Go online to view the digital version of the Hands-On Lab for this lesson and to download additional lab resources.

CAN YOU EXPLAIN IT?

What determines where gold is found in nature?

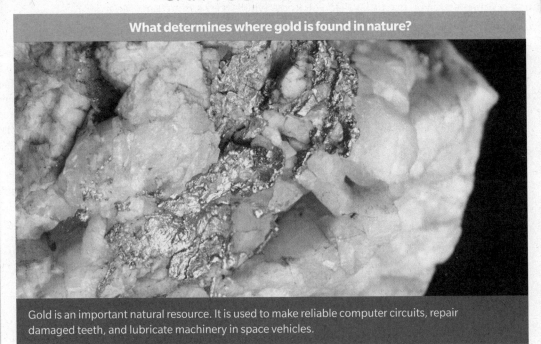

Gold is an important natural resource. It is used to make reliable computer circuits, repair damaged teeth, and lubricate machinery in space vehicles.

Gold deposits that are worth mining exist only in certain places in the world. In the United States, major gold deposits are found in Alaska, California, Colorado, and Nevada. The United States is among the top gold-producing countries in the world, which also include China, Australia, Russia, and Canada.

1. Why do you think gold deposits are found in the places listed above? Do you think natural processes, human processes, or both have an impact on these places?

EVIDENCE NOTEBOOK As you explore the lesson, gather evidence to help explain where gold is found in nature.

Explaining Patterns in Natural Resource Distribution

What natural resources did you use today? Do you know where they came from? Most resources, including minerals and fossil fuels, are found in specific places on Earth.

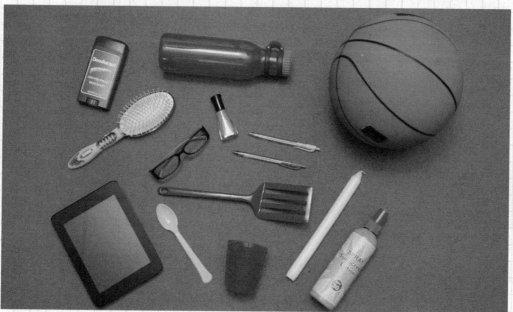

Oil, also called petroleum, is a nonrenewable resource found in specific locations beneath Earth's surface. Oil is processed to make paint, plastics, gasoline, cosmetics, technological products, and clothing.

2. **Discuss** Oil is used to generate electrical energy and make many products. The amount of oil on Earth is limited. How might this affect the search for oil in the future?

Natural Resource Distribution

Earth's many natural resources, including oil, water, soil, minerals, wind, and sunlight, are unevenly distributed on Earth's surface. In other words, resources are concentrated in specific places because of the processes by which they form. For example, fossil fuels found today were formed by different geologic processes. Each process took place in a certain location under specific conditions. For example, most of the coal we use today formed where tropical swamps existed millions of years ago. However, salt deposits formed where seawater entered a shallow bay. As the water evaporated, dissolved materials were left behind and layers of minerals, such as salt, formed. Because many geologic processes occur over millions of years, resources formed in these ways tend to be nonrenewable. Some resources, such as wind and sunlight, are renewable. However, these resources are also limited in their distribution.

Geologic processes can also move and change resources. Therefore, not all natural resources are found where they first formed. For example, rocks containing gold can be uplifted and exposed at Earth's surface. Weathering breaks rock down into small pieces of sediment, and erosion carries the sediment away. As a result, gold can be found in streams downhill from the rock where it came from. Geologic processes can also change resources. For example, calcite, a mineral used in medicine and building materials, can be dissolved by water and then deposited in a new form in a different location.

3. Mineral resources, such as gold deposits, may take millions of years to form. The same is true for oil, coal, and natural gas. Because of these timescales, these resources are ~~renewable~~ / nonrenewable. In other words, humans use the resources more ~~slowly~~ / quickly than the resources form.

Soil

Soil is an essential part of the Earth system. Soil is important to the biosphere because it provides a place for plants, animals, and other organisms to live. Plants use nutrients and water from soil to grow and survive. Humans use soil to grow food. Soil even plays an important role in storing water, which helps prevent flooding.

Soil takes hundreds or even thousands of years to form. The conditions required for soil to form do not exist everywhere on Earth, so soil distribution is not uniform. The rate of soil formation and the type of soil that forms depend on factors such as rock type, climate, and the presence of organisms. Soil forms on land where rock is broken down by chemical and physical weathering processes. Wind, water, plant roots, and animals all weather rock. The type of soil that forms depends in part on the characteristics, such as color and composition, of the parent rock that breaks down into sediment. Therefore, different soils are found in different places on Earth.

Some soils are more fertile than others. Soil fertility depends on how much organic matter and other nutrients the soil has. Organic matter in the soil comes from dead organisms and animal waste. Bacteria and fungi break down organic matter and release chemical byproducts that mix with the top layer of soil. These materials are the nutrients that make the soil better able to support plant life.

The shape of the land also affects soil distribution. The tops and sides of hills and mountains often have less soil than valleys have because wind and water erode materials on hillsides. Eroded materials are deposited in valleys.

4. Is healthy, nutrient-rich soil a renewable or nonrenewable resource? Use evidence and scientific reasoning to support your claim.

Steps in Soil Formation

parent rock

Rock is broken down into smaller and smaller pieces. These fragments of rock are called *sediment*.

young soil

Over time, sediment mixes with air, water, and organic matter present in the ground. The soil can now support some plant life.

mature soil

More organic matter is added as organisms die and decompose. This process makes a nutrient-rich layer of soil at the surface called *topsoil*.

Nonrenewable Energy Resources

Nonrenewable energy resources include fossil fuels such as oil, coal, and natural gas. Fossil fuels are burned to turn turbines that generate electrical energy. Natural gas is used to heat homes and to cook. Oil is also used to make plastics and gasoline.

Fossil fuels are nonrenewable because the processes that form them take place over millions of years. That is much longer than one thousand human lifetimes. The processes that formed fossil fuels millions of years ago still occur today. So, millions of years in the future, there will be new deposits of fossil fuels that are forming right now.

Look at the map. Each fossil fuel is found in specific places because it forms by specific geologic processes. For example, coal and oil form by different processes and from different materials. The diagram shows the processes by which oil deposits form.

Fossil Fuel Deposits in the United States

Source: U.S. Geological Survey, Open File Report OF 96-92.

Oil formed where dead marine life collected on the sea floor and was buried by sediment. Heat and pressure turned the organic remains to oil.

Oil and natural gas form by similar processes, so these resources are commonly found together in permeable rock.

Natural gas formed by a process similar to oil formation. This gas tends to rise toward Earth's surface to form deposits in permeable rock.

Most coal formed in ancient swamps where dead plants piled up to form peat. When peat is buried, heat and pressure turn the peat into coal.

Steps in Oil Formation

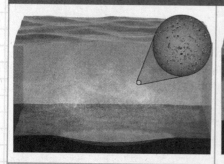

In some parts of Earth's ancient seas, large numbers of microscopic marine organisms died and collected in layers on the ocean floor.

Sediment collected in layers over the organisms. The weight of the sediment increased pressure on the remains of the organisms. Over time, the sediment turned to rock.

Increased pressure and heat caused a chemical reaction that changed carbon, hydrogen, and oxygen in the remains of the organisms into a thick liquid—oil.

5. Locate one area where oil is found on the fossil fuel distribution map. Describe the likely geologic history of that region. Explain the reasoning behind your description.

Renewable Energy Resources

Like nonrenewable energy resources, alternative energy resources are distributed unevenly on Earth's surface. These resources include sunlight, wind, water, and biomass. *Biomass* is plant matter that can be burned for heat or used to make other fuels. Crops, plant waste, and trees are all types of biomass. These resources are considered renewable because they can be replenished more rapidly than they are used by humans.

Worldwide Distribution of Solar Energy

6. Label the map using the numbers 1 through 5 to help a solar energy company decide where to install new solar panels. The number 1 represents the most desirable location and 5 represents the least desirable location.

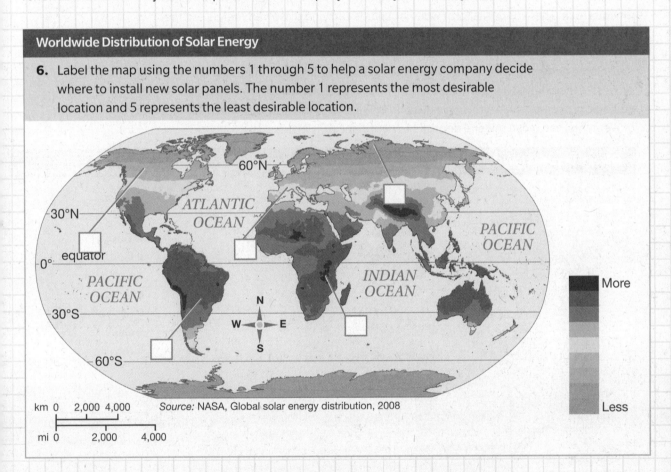

Source: NASA, Global solar energy distribution, 2008

Places that receive a lot of sunlight are the best for using solar energy. Sunlight is unevenly distributed across the globe. Near the equator, daytime and nighttime hours are roughly equal throughout the year. Near Earth's poles, daytime is long in summer and short in winter. However, closer to the poles, sunlight is less intense than it is near the equator throughout the year. Some places, such as coastal cities, experience frequent cloud cover, which can reduce solar energy availability.

Wind and water resources are also unevenly distributed. Wind can be harnessed to generate electrical energy where wind blows consistently and in a predictable direction. Hydroelectric energy is usually generated by harnessing large amounts of moving river water. Dams are built to control the flow of water in some rivers, but not every river has enough water or a strong enough flow for a hydroelectric dam.

Mineral Resources

Minerals are mined and processed for a wide range of uses. Minerals are used for making buildings and roads, for making electronics, and even for making cosmetics. Mineral deposits may take millions of years to form and tend to be nonrenewable. Not all minerals are found in their pure form. Most often, a mineral is mixed with several other minerals in rock. A deposit that has a high enough concentration of a specific mineral to be worth mining is called an *ore*. For example, an iron ore is a rock that has a high amount of iron. Ores are processed to separate the desired mineral from the other materials in the rock. The processing method varies based on the minerals in the ore.

Minerals form by various processes and from different chemical building blocks. Therefore, mineral resources are unevenly distributed on Earth. The location of mineral deposits depends on the processes by which the minerals and deposits formed. For example, metals such as gold and silver are commonly found in and nearby intrusive igneous rock. These deposits form when hot fluids carrying dissolved metals escape from cooling magma, or molten rock, inside Earth. As the fluids cool and the dissolved substances solidify, the metals are deposited in the surrounding rock.

Some geologic processes change existing minerals into new minerals. These processes include dissolution, evaporation, and contact with molten rock. Other geologic processes, such as erosion by wind or water and uplift by tectonic plate movements, can move mineral deposits to new places.

Mineral Deposits in North America

Minerals are unevenly distributed across North America.

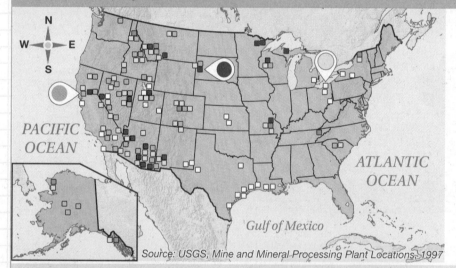

- Cobalt
- Copper
- Gold
- Iron ore
- Lead
- Molybdenum
- Salt
- Silver

PACIFIC OCEAN

ATLANTIC OCEAN

Gulf of Mexico

km 0   400   800
mi 0   400   800

Alaska is shown at a smaller scale

Source: USGS, Mine and Mineral Processing Plant Locations, 1997

Gold is found in and around intrusive igneous rocks below ground, or above ground where it has been uplifted by geologic processes. Some gold is also found in stream bottoms.

Most iron ore is found where oceans existed millions of years ago. Limonite is one type of iron ore mined today.

Table salt is made from a mineral called *halite*. It forms when salt water evaporates. Halite is forming today in the Great Salt Lake in Utah and in other places around the globe.

EVIDENCE NOTEBOOK

7. How can gold deposits form? How could gold be moved from its original location to a new location? Record your evidence.

Freshwater Resources

Humans use fresh water for drinking water, agriculture, and manufacturing processes, including the generation of electrical energy. However, the supply of fresh water is limited and unevenly distributed around Earth. Only about 2.5% of Earth's water is fresh water. And much of that fresh water is frozen in glaciers and icecaps.

Fresh surface water is distributed based on both past and present Earth processes, such as climate patterns and the shape of the land. For example, landforms such as mountains and valleys form slowly by geologic processes. The locations of freshwater resources depend on where the ground surface was uplifted, how the ground was eroded to form valleys or depressions, and how sediment was deposited in basins and plains. After heavy rains, water flows downhill through valleys to form streams and rivers. Eventually, some of the flowing water collects in depressions to form ponds or lakes, and some enters the ocean and becomes salt water.

Climate and latitude also affect the distribution of fresh water on Earth's surface. At both of Earth's poles, large amounts of fresh water are stored as ice in icecaps and sea ice. In polar regions, some water is also stored as ice in frozen soil called *permafrost*. At high elevations, fresh water may also be stored as glaciers or permanent snowpacks. In dry, desert regions, surface water is rare because it quickly evaporates into the dry air.

Some fresh water exists underground, because some water seeps down into soil and rock and fills small spaces in these materials. This water is known as *groundwater*. Groundwater is stored in layers of rock called *aquifers*. Aquifers exist beneath the surface almost everywhere on Earth, including under mountains, plains, forests, and even deserts. Groundwater can flow hundreds of miles under the surface through an aquifer and then rise to the surface at a distant location. So, groundwater may flow under the driest desert, and it may reach the surface at a spring, oasis, or well.

The Huacachina Oasis near Ica, Peru, formed in the desert where groundwater rises to Earth's surface.

Groundwater and Surface Water Distribution

Aquifers are found in many places on Earth. Aquifers are connected to surface water in springs, lakes, streams, and rivers. Water can flow back and forth between these reservoirs.

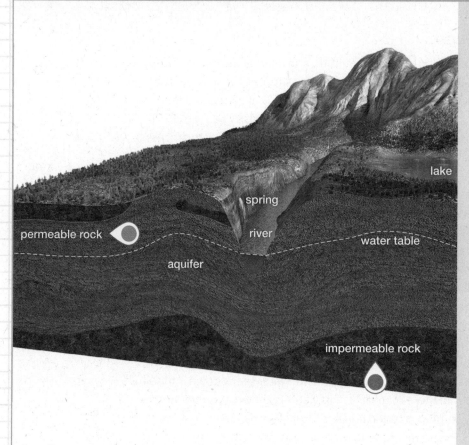

Aquifers consist of permeable rocks that hold groundwater. Like a sponge, permeable rocks allow liquid or gas to pass into and through them.

Water and other fluids cannot flow through impermeable rock. Impermeable layers prevent groundwater from entering or leaving aquifers.

Groundwater is not always accessible from the surface because the types of rocks that the water collects in and flows through are unevenly distributed within Earth's crust. Water flows through pore spaces and cracks in permeable rocks. Impermeable rocks do not allow water to flow through and act as barriers to the movement of groundwater.

Both surface water and groundwater resources are replenished as part of the water cycle. As rain falls or snow and ice melt, the water flows over Earth's surface and seeps into the ground. The process by which water enters an aquifer is called *recharge*. Groundwater collects and flows through rock layers very slowly. So, the time it takes to recharge an aquifer can vary from a few hours to thousands of years.

Locate Oil

8. Use words from the word bank to complete the passage.
   A geologist looks for a new place to drill for oil. She knows the
   remains of _____ organisms formed oil and finds
   areas that were once ancient _____. She uses
   special equipment that can show data about rock beneath the
   surface to tell if there is _____ rock that might
   hold oil.

WORD BANK
- sea floors
- volcanoes
- impermeable
- marine
- land
- permeable

Explaining Human Impact on Natural Resource Distribution

As humans use more resources, the availability of these resources may be reduced. Once nonrenewable resources, such as oil and coal, are used up, it is unlikely more will become available because these resources take millions of years to form. Other resources, such as water and wind, are renewable resources. People can conserve renewable resources such as trees or biomass by careful management and use.

The Shrinking Aral Sea

Before 1960, the Aral Sea in Central Asia was the world's fourth largest lake. It supported villages and a small fishing industry. Then, people began using the water to irrigate crops. The sea shrank. The water became polluted with fertilizer. In 2000, the Aral Sea was less than half its historic size. By 2016, it had almost dried up.

2000   2008   2016

9. What do you think the Aral Sea will look like in 2024? Support your claim with evidence and reasoning.

Human Impact on Soil Distribution

Human actions affect the distribution of soil. Human actions can negatively change soil quality and can promote erosion. Soil polluted with pesticides and fertilizers is not a valuable resource. Repeatedly growing nutrient-depleting crops in the same fields can also lead to unhealthy soil. Unhealthy soil is less able to support plant growth, and its value as a resource is reduced. Strip mining, overgrazing cattle, and clearing forestland for building encourage soil erosion and can cause the loss of healthy soil. These processes may contribute to the expansion of deserts, a process called *desertification*. To protect soil resources, human activities can be designed to prevent soil loss or degradation. Planting diverse crops, rotating crops, planting trees and cover crops, and contour farming help prevent erosion and degradation of soil.

Human Activities and Soil Erosion

For years, Great Plains farmers over-plowed and overgrazed the land. In 1931, drought and poor farming practices caused extensive soil erosion. These practices caused the Dust Bowl.	Loss of tree cover increases soil erosion. Humans did not form the Sahara desert. But human activity, such as removing trees, allows the Sahara to grow. This is an example of desertification.	Crop rotation and contour plowing enrich soil and prevent erosion. Adding mulch retains water. Planting ground cover and trees holds soil in place. These practices protect soil resources.

10. Can human activities change the distribution of nonrenewable resources, such as oil or minerals? Could we change the distribution of renewable resources, such as sunlight and wind? Support your claim with evidence and reasoning.

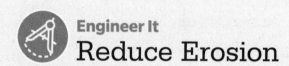

Engineer It
Reduce Erosion

Soil erosion caused by heavy rains is threatening to reduce the harvests of farms in your hilly community. Work with a small group to develop a solution to reduce erosion.

11. Identify the criteria and constraints for your problem. What needs must your solution address? What resources do you need to implement your solution? Describe any issues that limit your solutions.

12. Discuss Brainstorm and list ideas to prevent soil erosion. Be sure to consider the criteria and constraints. Choose the most promising solution based on your criteria and constraints.

Human Impact on Energy and Mineral Resources

Before humans can use minerals and fossil fuels, these resources must first be extracted from the ground. Extracting resources changes their distribution because the resources are removed and carried to a new location. For example, when oil is pumped out of the ground for human use, the amount of oil in that reservoir is reduced or completely depleted. Once nonrenewable energy and mineral resources are used, they are not replaced for millions of years. As humans extract and use nonrenewable mineral and energy resources, the total amount of these resources available for future use declines.

As deposits and reservoirs get smaller and disappear, we must find new deposits of the resources to use. These new deposits may be of lower quality or may be more challenging to acquire than the original deposits. We may also develop new technologies for extracting valuable resources. Some nonrenewable resources can be recycled. For example, gold can be extracted from some existing products, such as jewelry, and used again in other products, such as electronics. Recycling mineral resources reduces the need for mining and processing new ore deposits. Managing and reducing the use of nonrenewable minerals and fossil fuels is important to ensure that resources will remain available for future generations.

Gold Mining and Distribution

In 1848, gold was discovered at Sutter's Mill in California. Thousands of people moved to California to look for gold in the streams and hills of California in the years that followed.

Gold deposits are located in these mountains in Peru and on every continent. Some gold deposits are deep inside Earth, and others are at or near the surface.

Valuable gold deposits are rare. As gold is taken from a mine, less and less gold remains in that location. As the supply of gold at the mine gets smaller, miners must ask: Is there enough gold to continue mining this location?

Although some deposits have been depleted, the demand for gold continues. Used gold can be reclaimed and recycled. Recycling gold becomes more important as accessible and minable gold deposits become harder to find.

EVIDENCE NOTEBOOK

13. How does human activity change the distribution of gold? Record your evidence.

Human Impact on Freshwater Distribution

Humans cannot control Earth's water cycle, but they do change the distribution of fresh water on Earth. Humans cannot live without fresh water. We use water in most activities, including drinking and bathing, raising livestock and crops for food, manufacturing goods, and generating electrical energy.

Human activities can change the distribution of surface water. Dams block off flowing water to form reservoirs. As a result, water that would have flowed farther down the river stays in the area above the dam. Dams make more fresh water available upstream from the dam, but they make fresh water less available downstream. Humans also build canals to force water to flow in different directions. Canals are used to transport fresh water into and through regions where natural streams and rivers do not exist. Canals are also used to transport other materials by boat. Reservoirs and dams in dry areas also increase the rate of evaporation of freshwater supplies.

Humans extract groundwater from aquifers by using wells to pump the water up from below the surface. This process, called withdrawal, reduces the amount of water in the aquifer. In some places, water is used up faster than it is replenished by precipitation. The process by which water seeps through the ground and enters an aquifer is called *recharge*. When the rate of withdrawal exceeds the recharge rate, the water level in the aquifer may drop, and deeper wells have to be drilled. Over time, an aquifer can be completely drained if the rates of use and recharge remain unbalanced. Removal of too much groundwater may also destabilize the ground and cause sinkholes to form.

This canal diverts fresh water through the Arizona desert. These canals provide water for irrigation, industry, and personal use in an area that has few natural freshwater resources.

Hands-On Lab
Model Recharge and Withdrawal in an Aquifer

You will model an aquifer to explore how groundwater levels change.

Procedure

STEP 1 Build a landscape made up of permeable rock. In your landscape, make a depression to represent a low-lying area of land. What material models the permeable rock?

STEP 2 Add a few drops of blue food coloring to the pitcher of water to make the water a medium blue color. Carefully pour the blue water over your landscape until it partially fills the depression you made. What do the blue water and the depression represent?

MATERIALS
- fish tank hand siphon, pump, or syringe
- food coloring, blue
- graduated cylinders, 50 mL (2)
- gravel or aquarium pebbles, light colored, (3 cups)
- pitcher, with water
- plastic container, clear, large, rectangular
- ruler

STEP 3 Use a ruler to measure the height of the groundwater starting from the bottom of the container. Measure the height of the water in the depression starting from the bottom of the depression. Record your observations in the table.

STEP 4 Using a pump, model how a well can be used to withdraw groundwater from an aquifer. Pump out 50 mL of groundwater. Measure and record the depth of the groundwater and the surface water in the depression. Record your observations in the table.

STEP 5 An aquifer is refilled when precipitation occurs. Add 50 mL of water to the aquifer. Measure and record the depth of the groundwater and the surface water in the depression. Record your observations in the table.

	Groundwater depth (mm)	Surface water depth (mm)	Observations
STEP 3			
STEP 4			
STEP 5			

STEP 6 How do precipitation and pumping each affect the water in an aquifer? How do changes in the groundwater level affect the level of surface water?

STEP 7 How could you model the effects of humans using water from the aquifer more quickly than precipitation could recharge the aquifer?

STEP 8 In your model, you withdrew and added water in seconds. Explain how this differs from the rate at which groundwater levels change in the real world.

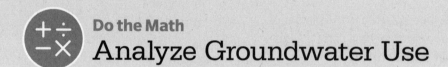

Do the Math

Analyze Groundwater Use

Caleb's farm uses groundwater from an aquifer that holds 100,000 gallons of water. The farm withdraws about 5,000 gallons per month. Precipitation adds about 2,000 gallons of water per month back into the aquifer.

---

14. Use the variables to write an equation to represent the overall change in volume per month, taking into account both withdrawal and recharge. Next use your equation to find the overall change in volume each month. Hint: For the rate of withdrawal, use a negative value.

> v = overall change in volume in one month
>
> s = starting volume
>
> w = withdrawal rate
>
> r = recharge rate

15. What will the total volume of water in the aquifer be after 6 months? Recall the initial volume is 100,000 gallons.

16. The well only reaches a certain depth into the aquifer. Once the aquifer's volume is less than 50,000 gallons, the well will no longer be able to pump water. At the current rate of usage, how long will this take?

Continue Your Exploration

Name: _____   **Date:** _____

Check out the path below or go online to choose one of the other paths shown.

Rare Earth Elements and Technology	• Hands-On Labs ✋ • Resources in Space • Propose Your Own Path	*Go online to choose one of these other paths.*

Suppose you send a text message. For you, it means tapping keys. For Earth, it means more rare earth elements (REEs) in shorter supply. Seventeen elements are considered REEs, and most are elements few people recognize, such as neodymium or terbium. Without them, cell phones, televisions, and all forms of state-of-the-art electronics would not work.

There are many uses for REEs. They are used to make rechargeable batteries and the world's strongest magnets. They are used to make light bulbs that give off more light for longer periods of time and to make images on television screens clear and bright. REEs are also used to reduce the amount of toxic emissions in automobile exhaust.

Extracting and Processing REEs

REEs are nonrenewable resources, and less than 1% are recycled. The demand for REEs increases daily as demand increases for technology. Scientists and engineers are trying to answer several questions about REEs. How many more REE deposits exist on Earth? Can other elements be substituted for REEs? Because REEs are nonrenewable, what will happen to technologies that depend on REEs if they are used up?

REEs accumulated on Earth as the planet was forming, so they are found deep below the surface. As a result, mining REE deposits with currently available tools and technology is difficult and costly.

When people get new cell phones, they can give their old ones to someone who can recycle REEs from them.

Continue Your Exploration

In the geosphere, REEs combine with other elements to form chemical compounds. Most REE compounds form as crystals. Processing REEs means separating the elements from the compounds in which they are found. The cost of processing REEs makes them expensive to use. The waste from these processes includes radioactive material and toxic chemicals. Disposal of the waste can endanger the environment, so safe disposal also adds to the cost of using REEs.

Because REEs have so many applications, we will eventually use up all of the REEs in the geosphere. Recycling REEs is critical to maintaining supplies. Most products contain very small amounts of REEs. The average television has trace amounts of yttrium, europium, and terbium. Cell phones may have lanthanum and neodymium. Even at trace amounts, recycling is worthwhile. However, recycling means collecting each REE individually from thousands of cell phones, laptops, and televisions.

1. What are some ways we could ensure that rare earth elements are used wisely? Circle all that apply.

   A. require recycling of used electronics

   B. eliminate their use in electronics

   C. develop ways to use less REEs per device

   D. replace REEs with common elements

   E. make electronics that last longer

2. As REEs are used up and the available supply goes down, do you think the cost of electronics, such as cell phones, will go up or down? Support your claim with evidence and reasoning.

3. What is a possible way to increase the supply of REEs other than recycling?

4. **Collaborate** With a partner, discuss ways to increase the number of people who recycle electronic products. Choose the idea that you think would work best and present it to the class.

Can You Explain It?

Name: _____ **Date:** _____

What determines where gold is found in nature?

EVIDENCE NOTEBOOK

Refer to the notes in your Evidence Notebook to help you construct an explanation about where gold is found in nature.

1. State your claim. Make sure your claim fully explains what determines where gold is located in nature. Explain whether natural processes, human activities, or both have an impact on these places.

2. Summarize the evidence you have gathered to support your claim and explain your reasoning.

Checkpoints

Answer the following questions to check your understanding of the lesson.

Use the diagram to answer Questions 3–4.

3. Number the statements to show the correct order of the processes displayed in the diagram.

_____ Weathered bits of the gold are eroded by water.

_____ Gold particles are deposited as they sink into depressions in the stream.

_____ Gold ore forms as magma cools beneath the surface.

_____ The gold ore is exposed to the surface and weathered.

4. Which of these processes is currently redistributing gold in the area in the diagram? Select all that apply.

A. evaporation of water

B. weathering

C. cooling magma

D. erosion

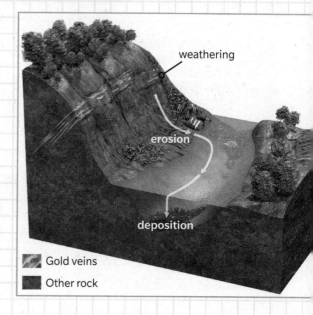

Gold veins

Other rock

5. Which of these activities or processes might affect the supply of groundwater in an aquifer? Select all that apply.

A. raising livestock on a farm

B. processing materials in a factory

C. drought

D. excessive rainfall

Use the table to answer Question 6.

6. Almost all of the diamonds on Earth formed billions of years ago in Earth's mantle. The diamonds were brought to the surface by volcanic eruptions. Over time, the volcanic rocks eroded and the diamonds were deposited in sediments. What can you infer about the geologic processes that shaped Russia and Africa from the table?

A. Russia has more active volcanoes than Africa does.

B. Both Russia and Africa only recently formed as continents.

C. Both Russia and Africa had volcanic eruptions in the past.

D. More weathering and erosion happens in Russia than in Africa.

Top Gem Diamond Producers in 2015	
Country and continent	**Amount of diamond produced (millions of carats)**
Russia (Asia)	21.5
Botswana, Angola, South Africa, DR Congo, Namibia (Africa)	35.5
Canada (North America)	12.0
All other countries	2.4

Source: Donald W. Olson, USGS, *Mineral Commodity Summaries*, 2015

Interactive Review

Complete this section to review the main concepts of the lesson.

The distribution of resources, such as minerals, soil, fossil fuels, and water, depends on both past and current geologic processes.

A. Explain why the distribution of mineral and freshwater resources is uneven in the Earth system.

As humans use nonrenewable resources, the distribution of those resources changes, and their availability becomes limited. Human activities can also affect the quality of some resources, such as water and soil.

B. Describe the cause-and-effect relationship between human use of a nonrenewable resource and the distribution of that resource on Earth.

Choose one of the activities to explore how this unit connects to other topics.

☐ Technology Connection

Asteroid Mining Some scientists, engineers, and aerospace businesses believe asteroid mining could yield important resources for use on Earth or in space colonies. They are starting to create long-term plans to mine asteroids or other planets for valuable resources during space missions.

Research possible destinations for the first asteroid mining missions and the technology that could be used to mine these asteroids. Collect information about what types of asteroids exist, and describe the natural resources that are found in these asteroids. Present your findings to the class.

☐ Physical Science Connection

Seabed Mining Nuggets of metal called "polymetallic nodules" are found on the sea floor around the world. In the 1970s, scientists and engineers began to investigate how to mine these nodules because they are a good source of four metals: nickel, copper, cobalt, and manganese.

Research the physical processes involved in the formation of polymetallic nodules. Create a short presentation that includes images of these nodules. Include information about challenges to recovering these nodules from the ocean floor. Share your presentation with the class.

☐ Social Studies Connection

Economic Geologists An economic geologist studies mineral resources such as minerals, ores, oil, and natural gas and the processes that cause their formation. Economic geologists are concerned with Earth materials that have some economic value or are considered valuable to society.

Research what economic geologists do on a daily basis. How do they locate deposits? Why is this role important to society? Write an essay that describes the types of natural resources an economic geologist researches and why this career is important.

Name: _____ Date: _____

Complete this review to check your understanding of the unit.

Use the map to answer Questions 1–2.

1. A promising place to look for coal today would be *West Virginia* / *Wisconsin.*
   Millions of years ago, the southern part of *Arizona* / *Illinois* was mostly swampland.

2. For which of these statements does the map provide evidence?

   A. In the past, there were large mountain ranges in Mississippi.

   B. In the past, the climate in Alaska was warmer than it is now.

   C. In the past, shallow seas covered parts of Wyoming.

   D. Mostly igneous rock is found today in Northern Louisiana.

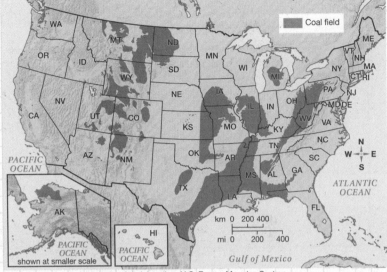

Source: U.S. Energy Information Administration, U.S. Energy Mapping System

Use the map to answer Questions 3–4.

3. Which of the following terms describe geothermal resources? Select all that apply.

   A. energy resource

   B. material resource

   C. renewable

   D. nonrenewable

4. The most favorable geothermal sites are in the *Central Plains* / *Rocky Mountains* / *Appalachian Mountains.* They are located there because of the *angle of the sun* / *movement of tectonic plates* / *proximity to the ocean.*

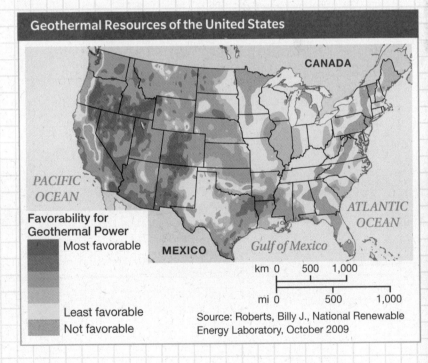

Geothermal Resources of the United States

Favorability for Geothermal Power
Most favorable
Least favorable
Not favorable

Source: Roberts, Billy J., National Renewable Energy Laboratory, October 2009

5. Complete the table by providing one example of how the following types of natural resources relate to each big concept.

Type of resource	Examples	Natural resource formation	How human use affects the resource
energy resources	fossil fuels		
material resources			
nonrenewable			
renewable			

Name: _____   Date: _____

Use the diagram to answer Questions 6–9.

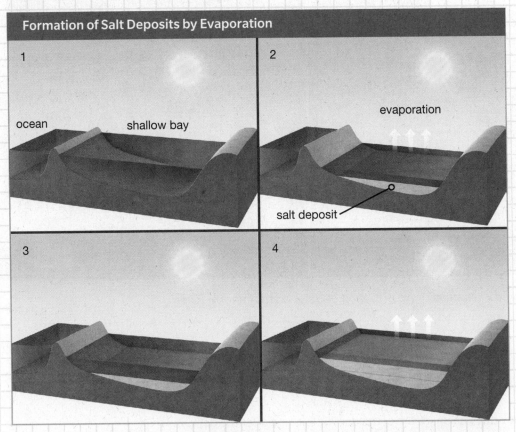

Formation of Salt Deposits by Evaporation

1   ocean   shallow bay

2   evaporation

    salt deposit

3

4

6. Write a statement that describes the geologic process by which the salt forms.

7. Do you think salt is a renewable or nonrenewable resource? Explain your reasoning.

8. In what types of areas would you expect to find salt deposits forming today? Use evidence and scientific reasoning to support your claim.

9. Large salt deposits are located in Poland, the Himalayas, and Michigan. These deposits may be several kilometers thick. How could these deposits have formed?

Use the satellite images to answer Questions 10–13.

Before and After Construction of China's Three Gorges Dam

before

after

dam

Source: NASA/USGS, *Landsat* Mission, 1987 and 2000

10. What natural processes affect the distribution of water on the Yangtze River in China?

11. The images show the area upstream of the dam before and after the dam was built. How did the construction of the Three Gorges Dam affect the distribution of water in the area?

12. How did the construction of the dam affect the distribution and availability of freshwater and soil resources upstream and downstream of the dam?

13. Has the dam changed the geologic processes that currently occur in the area? Use evidence and scientific reasoning to support your claim.

Name: _____   Date: _____

Which iron ore mine location is a better investment?

You have been asked to create a presentation for investors in an iron ore mining company. These investors were told that the company they will be investing in would be mining a banded iron formation (BIF) in Canada. The company has identified two locations to mine, and investors want to know which location would be a better investment. Create a presentation for the investors, explaining the geologic processes that formed the iron ore and which mine would be a better investment.

The steps below will help guide you in constructing a scientific explanation.

1. **Conduct Research** Research two different banded iron formations (BIFs) in Canada: Mine 1, an Algoma-type BIF located in Ontario, Canada, and Mine 2, a Superior-type BIF located in Labrador, Canada. Compare and contrast when they formed in Earth's past, the type of environment they formed in, the relative size of the formation, and the quality of iron ore.

2. **Construct an Explanation** Explain the geologic processes that formed the iron ore, and explain if BIFs are still forming today. Provide evidence for your explanation.

3. **Analyze Data** Based on the data you collected through your research, what criteria will you use to determine which mine site would be more profitable? Create a decision matrix to help make your decision.

4. **Identify and Recommend a Solution** Make a recommendation for whether the investors should support this mining effort. Which mine would you recommend for investment? Evaluate your decision matrix, and support your claim with evidence.

5. **Communicate** Create a multimedia presentation that explains how BIFs form and whether BIFs are a renewable or nonrenewable resource. Include your recommendation for whether the investors should support this mining effort and which mine is likely to yield more iron ore.

✓ **Self-Check**

	I researched two different types of BIFs.
	I created a decision matrix and analyzed my collected data on the mines.
	I constructed an explanation based on evidence for which mine is likely to produce more iron ore.
	I made a recommendation for whether the investors should support this mining effort and indicated which area to mine.
	I communicated my findings and recommendations in a multimedia presentation.

Using Resources

Lesson 1 Human Population and Resource Use 126

Lesson 2 Resource Use and Earth's Systems 148

Unit Review 171

Unit Performance Task 175

This bamboo water wheel is used to supply water for irrigation of crops in Vietnam. The amount of water used by humans changes as Earth's population grows.

Over time, humans have learned to use many natural resources found on Earth, such as minerals, water, food, and energy resources. Our consumption of these resources affects Earth's systems. In this unit, you will investigate how the use of resources by humans affects Earth's systems. You will analyze how increases in population and changes in an individual person's use of resources can cause changes in natural systems and the rates of change within those systems.

Why It Matters

Here are some questions to consider as you work through the unit. Can you answer any of the questions now? Revisit these questions at the end of the unit to apply what you discovered.

Questions	Notes
How do people use natural resources?	
What natural resources do you use regularly?	
How has human population changed over time?	
How has the growing human population changed the rate at which resources are used?	
How does the use of resources affect Earth's air, water, land, and living things?	
How does the use of resources affect the availability of resources for future generations?	

Unit Starter: Olive Oil Production and Consumption

Use this map to compare rates of production and consumption of olives and olive oil. The map also shows the average amount of olive oil used per person in each country.

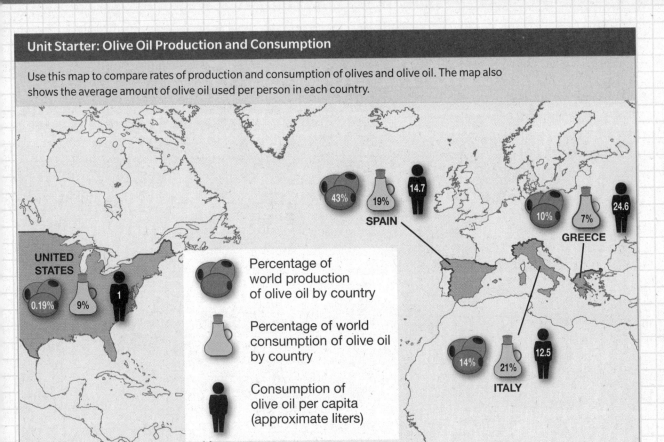

UNITED STATES

0.19% 9% 1

SPAIN

43% 19% 14.7

GREECE

10% 7% 24.6

ITALY

14% 21% 12.5

Percentage of world production of olive oil by country

Percentage of world consumption of olive oil by country

Consumption of olive oil per capita (approximate liters)

Source: The International Olive Council (IOC), 2011/2012 Forecast Reports

1. Each person in Spain uses more / less olive oil than each person in Italy uses.
   Each person in Spain uses more / less olive oil than each person in Greece uses.
   Spain most likely exports / imports olive oil.

2. Greece uses 24.6 L / 14.7 L of olive oil per person. Each person in the United States uses 1 L / 9 L of olive oil. However, Greece still uses less / more olive oil overall than the United States does because the United States has a much larger / smaller population than Greece.

 Go online to download the Unit Project Worksheet to help you plan your project.

Unit Project

Natural Resources and Earth Systems

Choose a natural resource, and identify patterns in its use relative to human population. Explain how that resource's acquisition, use, consumption, and disposal affects Earth systems on a local and global scale.

Human Population and Resource Use

Many farmers in Bali, Indonesia, use gradual steps, called *terraces*, to grow rice in steep, hilly areas. As human population grows, demand for rice gets higher.

By the end of this lesson . . .

you will be able to analyze population growth and per capita consumption of natural resources over time.

Go online to view the digital version of the Hands-On Lab for this lesson and to download additional lab resources.

CAN YOU EXPLAIN IT?

What might explain the patterns of population density in northern Africa?

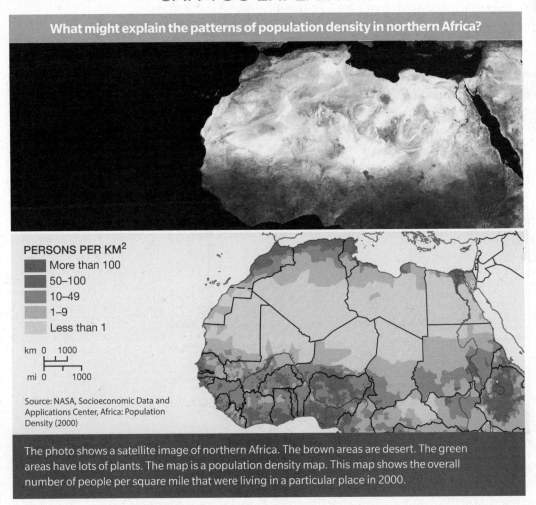

PERSONS PER KM²

- More than 100
- 50–100
- 10–49
- 1–9
- Less than 1

km 0   1000

mi 0   1000

Source: NASA, Socioeconomic Data and Applications Center, Africa: Population Density (2000)

The photo shows a satellite image of northern Africa. The brown areas are desert. The green areas have lots of plants. The map is a population density map. This map shows the overall number of people per square mile that were living in a particular place in 2000.

1. Compare the satellite image with the map. What do you notice on the satellite image about the places in northern Africa with the greatest population density?

EVIDENCE NOTEBOOK As you explore this lesson, gather evidence to help explain what might determine population density in northern Africa.

Analyzing Human Population Data

How many people do you think live on Earth? You might not be sure. Start by considering whether there are millions or billions of people. If you guessed billions, you are correct. In fact, more than 7 billion people live on Earth today.

World Population over Time

This graph shows the number of people on Earth over the last 12,000 years.

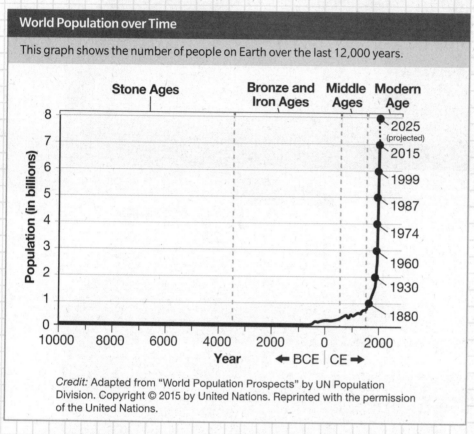

Credit: Adapted from "World Population Prospects" by UN Population Division. Copyright © 2015 by United Nations. Reprinted with the permission of the United Nations.

2. Look at the data in the graph. During what time period do you see the biggest change in the number of people on Earth? What factors do you think caused this change to happen?

Population

A **population** is a group of individuals of the same species living in the same place at the same time. Populations of every type of organism, including humans, are found on Earth. The human population can be analyzed on several levels. For example, you might think about the population of your school, your state, or the whole Earth.

For most of human history, the human population size was many times smaller than it is today. It did not change much. However, around 500 BCE the population began to increase. Then, less than 200 years ago, around the beginning of the Modern Age, the human population began to increase rapidly.

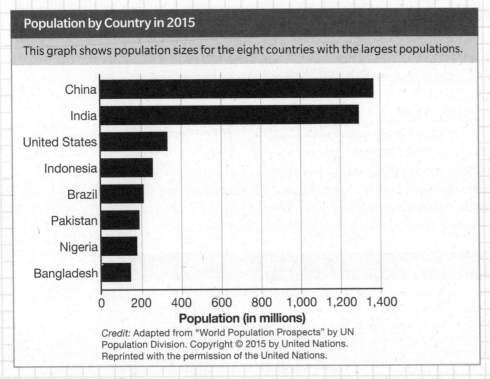

Population by Country in 2015

This graph shows population sizes for the eight countries with the largest populations.

Population (in millions)

Credit: Adapted from "World Population Prospects" by UN Population Division. Copyright © 2015 by United Nations. Reprinted with the permission of the United Nations.

3. According to the graph, how does the population of China compare to the population of the United States?

Data about Populations

Government agencies measure the populations of different areas. They find out more than the total number of people. For example, population data can include the distribution of ages and the ratio of males to females within the population. The data gathered are organized in databases that can be searched and sorted. They are analyzed to make inferences about a population.

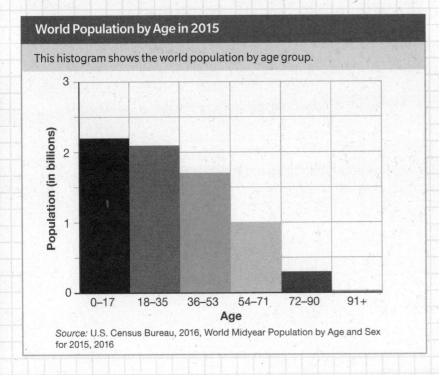

World Population by Age in 2015

This histogram shows the world population by age group.

Source: U.S. Census Bureau, 2016, World Midyear Population by Age and Sex for 2015, 2016

4. What can you conclude from the data shown in the graph?

A. The population is mostly made up of adults over the age of 17.

B. Most of the population that has lived to age 90 will continue to live for many more years.

C. Humans ages 54–71 make up about half the population.

D. People are not expected to live much past age 53.

Population Growth Rates

Population data can be used to calculate a growth rate. The growth rate indicates whether a population has grown and how fast it has grown. The growth rate of a population depends on the birth rate and death rate. It also depends on the migration of people into or out of a region. Birth rates, death rates, and growth rates are ratios. A ratio compares one amount to another amount. For example, birth rate compares the number of babies born to the total population size. If the birth rate is greater than the death rate, then a population will grow. For example, the birth rate in India in 2016 was 19 births per 1,000 people. The death rate for the same year was 7 deaths per 1,000 people. There were more births than deaths per 1,000 people. There was also not a large movement of people out of the country. As a result, the population grew. Taken all together, the trends in population data can tell a story about a particular region's population.

Birth Rate, Death Rate, and Population Size

Examine this graph to see how birth rate and death rate can affect population size.

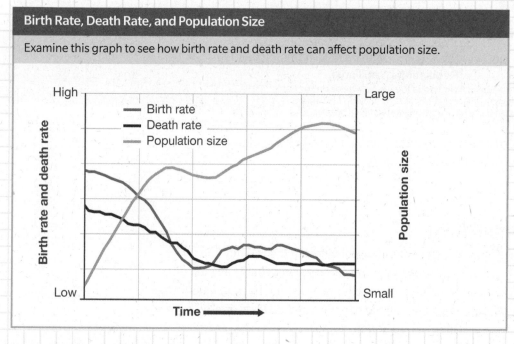

5. Examine the trends shown in this graph. How do trends in birth rate and death rate affect population size?

6. Do you think that all countries will follow the population size trend shown in this graph? Explain your reasoning.

Factors Affecting Population Growth

Rates of population change can be used to analyze causes of population change and to predict future changes. In other words, data tell a story. Significant changes in population are often related to environmental changes in a region or to events in history.

In the data shown earlier, several key factors influenced the huge increase in the world's population over a short period of time. Improvements in agriculture led to a larger and more reliable food supply. Technology and innovations led to increases in planting and harvesting crops. Thus, more food was available than when people relied on hunting and gathering. People invented and improved machines that used fossil fuels. These industrial developments increased the efficiency of agriculture, industry, and transportation. Improvements in sanitation, diet, and medical care led to population growth by increasing survival rates and the average human lifespan.

Factors That Affect Population Growth

Improvements in transportation and agriculture meant more food could be distributed to more places.

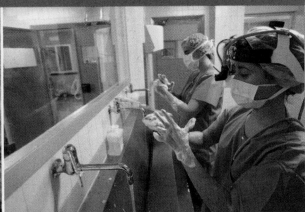

Improvements in sanitation and medicine helped to decrease death rates.

Population by World Region, 1750–2050

Population growth rates differ by region. The last bar shows projected population sizes. These sizes are estimated based on current data.

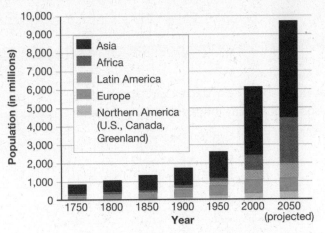

Credit: Adapted from "World Population Prospects" by UN Population Division. Copyright © 2015 by United Nations. Reprinted with the permission of the United Nations. Adapted from "The World at Six Billion" by UN Population Division. Copyright © 1999 by United Nations. Reprinted with the permission of the United Nations.

7. Which of the following likely contributed to increased global population growth between 1950 and 2000? Circle all that apply.

A. increases in birth rates

B. improvements in agriculture

C. increases in death rates in Europe

D. immigration from Latin America to Africa

Project Population Growth

Population data from a span of time can be used to project future population growth. To project population growth means to predict a future change in population based on current data. The table below shows the world's population size from 1900 to 2000.

Population Data						
Year	1900	1920	1940	1960	1980	2000
Population	1.7 billion	1.9 billion	2.3 billion	3 billion	4.4 billion	6 billion

8. **Draw** In the space provided, graph the data in the table to show global population change from 1900 to 2000. Label the x-axis "Years" and the y-axis "Population."

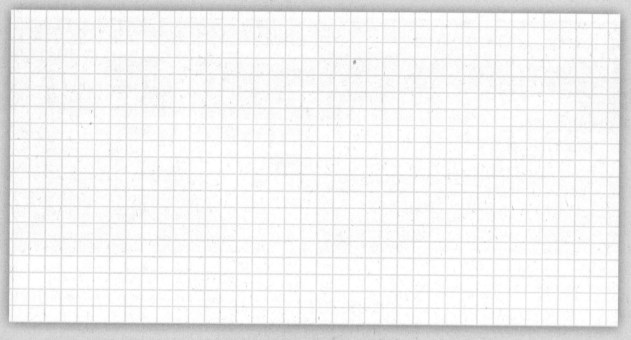

9. Use your graph to predict the world's population in 2040. Include a reason for your prediction.

_____

_____

_____

10. **Write** Describe an event or scenario that would increase or decrease the projected size of the world's population. Make an argument for why the event would affect the population. Support your argument with evidence.

_____

_____

_____

_____

_____

_____

Investigating Rates of Resource Use

Some materials provide your body with energy. Every day, they fuel your body's processes. All living things need energy sources, but they obtain energy in different ways. You get energy when your body breaks down the food you eat. Plants use energy from the sun to make food. They break down this food and use its stored energy. The sunlight that plants use is an endless source of energy. But other energy sources can run out.

This oil rig extracts oil from beneath the ocean floor.

11. Identify the natural resources that are shown or represented in the photo.

12. **Discuss** Together with a partner, discuss whether each resource identified in the photo can run out or whether its supply is unlimited.

Natural Resources

All human activity depends on natural resources. Some natural resources are renewable. They either cannot be used up or can be replaced at about the same rate at which they are used. Sunlight is renewable. Some resources are nonrenewable. They cannot be replaced as quickly as they are used. Coal and petroleum are nonrenewable.

Other resources can be either renewable or nonrenewable, depending on how the resource is used and managed. For example, bamboo and wood can be renewable or nonrenewable, depending on how fast the plants are cut down compared with how fast they are replaced. Water is renewable. However, pollution or overuse of water can use up clean drinking water faster than it can be replaced.

13. Think about the natural resources you need or use every day. What are some natural resources you need to live? How do you use them in your daily life? Explain your answer.

14. Complete the table to categorize the resources as renewable or nonrenewable.

Resource	Renewable	Nonrenewable
water	✓	
wind		
copper		

Renewable Resources

Wind and moving water are renewable resources that are used to generate electrical energy. Renewable resources are also used for materials, including plant fibers such as cotton and animal fibers such as wool. They are used to make clothing, insulation, and many other products.

Solar panels absorb the energy of sunlight. They convert this renewable resource into electrical energy. The electrical energy then moves through a utility grid to a community. Solar panels can be found on rooftops, in fields, offshore, and even on spacecraft.

The fleece of these alpacas is similar to wool, which is sheep hair. Like wool, alpaca fleece is used to make clothing such as sweaters, hats, and mittens.

 15. Engineer It The owner of two apartment buildings wants to install solar panels on the roof of each building. One building has twice as many people living in it than the other. How might the designs for the solar panels differ for each building? What other information would you want to know about each building before planning a design?

Nonrenewable Resources

Fossil fuels—coal, natural gas, and oil—formed from the remains of organisms that lived hundreds of millions of years ago. There were large swampy landscapes and seas at different times in Earth's history. In those conditions, massive amounts of organic material accumulated. Those materials were buried and slowly changed to form fossil fuels. They are nonrenewable because we use them much faster than they form. Other resources, such as metals and minerals, are also nonrenewable.

Coal is mainly used as a fuel that is burned to generate electrical energy.

How Natural Resources Are Used

Use of natural resources varies greatly from region to region. Resource use depends on several factors. For example, resource availability, cultural traditions, and the building of roads and facilities affect use. In general, populations of richer, industrialized nations use more natural resources than populations of less industrialized nations do. As societies become more industrialized, they tend to consume more resources. New technologies and more efficient practices can allow consumption to level off or decline.

 EVIDENCE NOTEBOOK

16. What natural resources do you think are available in northern Africa? How are these resources used? Record your evidence.

Hands-On Lab
Model Resource Use

You will model the relationship between population size and resource use.

MATERIALS
- beans
- cups, small

Procedure

STEP 1 Choose the number of people you want to have in your first model population. Set out one cup for each person. Place two beans in each cup to model resource use. Record the population and the total number of beans that were used by this population. Empty the cups.

STEP 2 Increase your population by one or more people (cups). Distribute the resources so that each person is again using two beans. Record the population and the total number of beans that were used by this population.

Analysis

STEP 3 Which of your model populations used more resources?

STEP 4 Use your models to support a general statement about the relationship between population growth and resource use.

STEP 5 Suppose the beans represented a nonrenewable resource. What impact could an increasing population have on a nonrenewable resource? How could you model this using the cups and beans?

Resource Use and Population Growth

Government agencies and other organizations track resource use in populations over time. The data collected can be used to show how rates of resource use change.

Resource Use Over Time

Resource use changes over time due to a variety of factors. For example, the use of oil increased greatly as the number of gasoline-powered vehicles increased. To compare resource use at different times, data can be measured as units used per time period. For example, the use of oil is generally measured in barrels of oil consumed per day or year. The data can be shown using models, such as graphs, which make comparisons easier.

Population Growth and Resource Use Over Time

The use of natural resources commonly increases as a population increases because more people are using these resources. However, more efficient use of a resource can also have an effect on overall use of that resource. For example, the graph shows that water use in the United States increased at a rate greater than the rate of population growth for many years. However, engineering and water use practices improved, and overall water use has decreased since 1980.

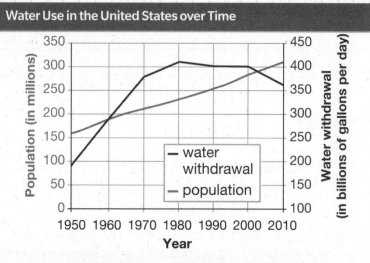

Water Use in the United States over Time

Source: USGS, "Estimated Use of Water in the United States in 2010," 2014;
Credit: Adapted from "World Population Prospects" by UN Population Division. Copyright ©2015 by United Nations. Reprinted with the permission of the United Nations.

The availability of resources also affects where people live. Throughout human history, higher population densities have occurred in areas with resources that humans use. These resources include food, water, and shelter. Improved transportation and engineering have allowed resources to be available in places where they were not available before. However, human populations still tend to be higher in and near areas that have more available resources.

Analyze Trends in Timber Consumption

17. Compare the data in the graph for population and lumber use. What trend or trends do you see in the population size and lumber use in the United States from 2003 to 2010?

_____
_____
_____
_____
_____
_____

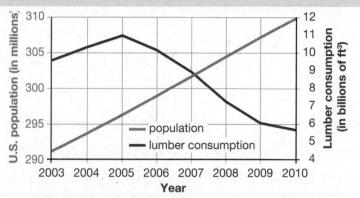

Lumber Use in the United States over Time

Wood that is used for building structures is called *lumber*. This graph shows population size and lumber use over time.

Source: U.S. Census Bureau, Statistical Abstract of the United States: 2012;
Credit: Adapted from "World Population Prospects" by UN Population Division. Copyright ©2015 by United Nations. Reprinted with the permission of the United Nations.

18. What might these trends indicate about changes in the use of lumber during this time period?

_____
_____
_____

Analyzing Per Capita Consumption

Analyzing how populations use resources can show large-scale changes and overall trends. These overall trends can be used to predict future resource use. This information can help people predict future needs. Understanding the trends can also help people develop ways to reduce resource use.

Individual resource use is also important. Each individual makes an impact on the availability of natural resources. The use of a resource by individuals, when added together, results in the overall resource use of a population. Consider the group of people eating peaches in the photos. The group will use more peaches if each person eats two peaches than if each person eats only one peach.

Both individual and group use of resources impact resource availability.

19. **Discuss** How does the way each individual person in your class uses resources impact the resource use of your class population?

Model Factors in Resource Use

You will model the use of a resource by individuals to determine how changes in individual use can affect the overall use of a resource by a population. The cups represent individuals, and the beans represent the resource.

MATERIALS
- beans (72)
- cups, small (18)

Procedure

STEP 1 Choose a certain number of people for your model A population. Decide how many beans each person will use. Distribute the beans. Record the results of your model in the table below.

STEP 2 Model two or three different scenarios with different populations using different amounts of the resource. Try to design your models so that you can draw conclusions about the factors that affect the overall use of a resource.

Model	Total Population	Beans used by each person	Total beans used	Total beans left over
A				
B				
C				
D				

Analysis

STEP 3 How can an increase in the amount of a resource each person uses affect the overall resource use if the population stays the same? What would happen if the population also increased? Use your models to support your answer.

STEP 4 Consider two equal-sized population models. Individuals in one model use fewer resources per person than individuals in the other model. How will total resource use of the models differ? What might account for the difference in two real populations represented by the models?

Per Capita Consumption

Resource use can be reported as the overall amount of a resource used by a population during a certain period. It may also be reported as the average amount of a resource used by each individual in a population. **Per capita consumption** is the amount of a resource that one person consumes in a given amount of time. Per capita consumption is a ratio. It is calculated by dividing the total amount of a resource used in a certain time period by the number of people in the population.

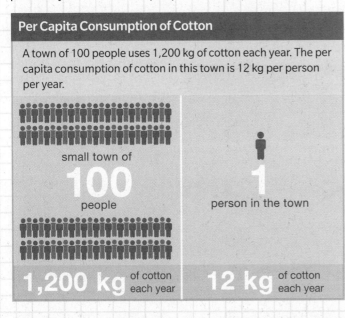

Per Capita Consumption of Cotton

A town of 100 people uses 1,200 kg of cotton each year. The per capita consumption of cotton in this town is 12 kg per person per year.

small town of
100
people

1,200 kg of cotton each year

1
person in the town

12 kg of cotton each year

20. How could you determine the per capita consumption of oranges in your town or city in kg per year?

   A. add up the kg of oranges that people in the population use in a year

   B. divide the total kg of oranges used in a year by the number of people in the population

   C. multiply the kg of oranges that one person uses in a year by the number of people in the population

21. Find the per capita consumption of oranges for each city in the diagram.

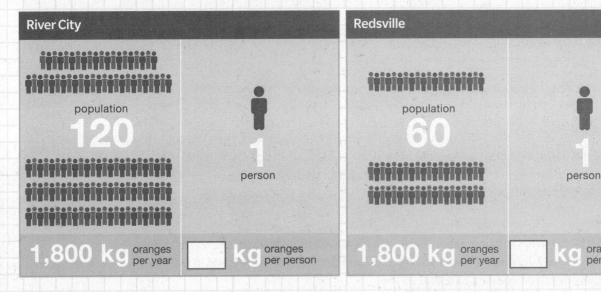

River City

population
120

1,800 kg oranges per year

1
person

☐ **kg** oranges per person

Redsville

population
60

1,800 kg oranges per year

1
person

☐ **kg** oranges per person

22. What factors might account for the different per capita consumptions of each of these two cities?

Trends in Per Capita Consumption

You can track per capita consumption over time by using tables and graphs. Look for trends in the per capita consumption of fish and shellfish in the table and graph.

Per Capita Consumption of Fish and Shellfish in the U.S.								
Year	2006	2007	2008	2009	2010	2011	2012	2013	2014
lbs	16.5	16.3	15.9	15.8	15.8	14.9	14.2	14.3	14.6
kgs	7.48	7.39	7.21	7.17	7.17	6.76	6.44	6.49	6.62

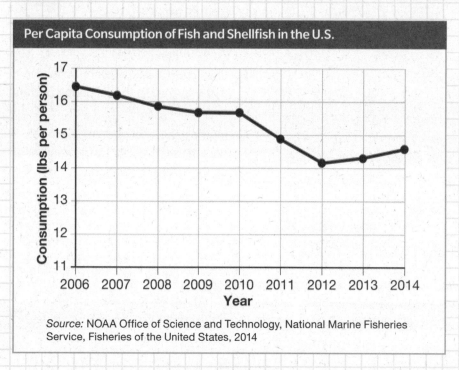

Per Capita Consumption of Fish and Shellfish in the U.S.

Source: NOAA Office of Science and Technology, National Marine Fisheries Service, Fisheries of the United States, 2014

23. Describe the trends you see in per capita consumption of fish and shellfish.

24. If the population stayed the same from 2006 to 2014, what could you conclude about the trend in overall consumption of fish and shellfish?

25. Data show that the population of the U.S. increased from 2006 to 2014. What additional information would you need in order to determine the trend in overall consumption between 2006 and 2014?

 EVIDENCE NOTEBOOK

26. How might the availability of a necessary resource in a region affect the number of people who can live in that region? Record your evidence.

Do the Math
Calculate Rate of Consumption

Suppose the population of a community is 10,000 people and the per capita consumption of fish is 6.6 kg per person each year. How much fish would be consumed per year if the population grows by 2,500 people?

A variety of fish is an important part of many human diets.

STEP 1 Use proportional reasoning to calculate the total fish consumption for the original population of 10,000.

$$\frac{6.6 \text{ kg}}{1 \text{ person}} \xrightarrow[\times 10,000]{\times 10,000} \frac{\boxed{} \text{ kg}}{10,000 \text{ people}}$$

STEP 2 Then use proportional reasoning to calculate the additional amount of fish that would be consumed by the additional 2,500 people.

$$\frac{6.6 \text{ kg}}{1 \text{ person}} \xrightarrow[\times 2,500]{\times 2,500} \frac{\boxed{} \text{ kg}}{2,500 \text{ people}}$$

STEP 3 Now add the two amounts together to find the total amount of fish resources expected to be consumed by the larger population. Record your answer in the table.

_____ kg of fish

---

27. The table below lists resources and their per capita consumption for the same community. How much will the total consumption of each resource be after the additional 2,500 people join the population?

Resource consumed	Per capita consumption	Overall resource consumption (after population increase)
fish and shellfish	6.6 kg/year	_____ kg per year
carrots	5.4 kg/year	
gasoline	1,514 L/year	

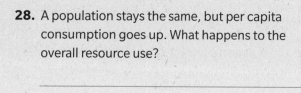

Relate Per Capita Consumption and Population Size

You may have heard news stories about increases in demand for certain resources or how long a particular nonrenewable resource will last. These predictions are based on per capita consumption and trends in population growth.

   Predict what will happen for each of the scenarios below. Provide an argument to support your reasoning.

Renewable resources such as vegetables are consumed daily.

28. A population stays the same, but per capita consumption goes up. What happens to the overall resource use?

_____

_____

_____

_____

_____

_____

29. The population stays the same, but per capita consumption goes down. What happens to the overall resource use?

_____

_____

_____

_____

_____

_____

30. The population increases, but per capita consumption stays the same. What happens to the overall resource use?

_____

_____

_____

_____

_____

_____

Continue Your Exploration

Name: _____   Date: _____

Check out the path below or go online to choose one of the other paths shown.

| Careers in Science | • Hands-On Labs  • Find Your Resource Use • Propose Your Own Path | Go online to choose one of these other paths. |

Conservation Scientist

Thousands of scientists work all across the world as conservation scientists. They provide input and expertise on questions about how to manage natural resources. A conservation scientist could work for or with any group or individual who owns or manages land. For example, they might work with a government group, an organization, a business, or a private landowner. These scientists may conduct research about the overall health or condition of an area of land or of a particular resource. They record, report, and interpret the data they gather. They often use computer modeling and mapping to make predictions and to identify trends.

Conservation scientists use a variety of equipment to help accurately gather, record, and map information about resources in an area.

Continue Your Exploration

The emerald ash borer (EAB) is an insect that can destroy ash trees. It is spreading across much of the United States. Ash trees are an important material resource. They are used for building furniture and other wooden items. Without treatment, ash trees infested with the EAB are expected to die. Treatment is possible but costly. Living, uninfested ash trees may be cut down to help prevent the spread of the EAB.

1. How does EAB affect the availability of resources? If human use remains the same, is ash wood a renewable or nonrenewable resource?

2. In what ways will treatment or removal of ash trees to prevent the spread of EAB affect overall and/or per capita use of ash trees as a resource?

3. How can human actions affect the rate at which infestations of the beetle spread? How would humans affect the rate at which ash resources could be renewed?

4. **Collaborate** The U.S. Forest Service outlined objectives for a nationwide management plan to address EAB threats. These objectives include:
   - prevent the spread of EAB and prepare for EAB infestations
   - detect, monitor, and respond to new EAB infestations
   - manage EAB infestations in forests
   - harvest ash trees—both infested and uninfested—for economic use and to prevent the spread of EAB
   - work to restore forest ecosystems that were affected by EAB

Source: U.S. Forest Service Department of Agriculture

Work with classmates to prioritize these objectives. Discuss which objectives you think are most important and should be given priority. Provide a rationale for all arguments. Order the objectives according to your decisions. Then compare your prioritized list and the list of another group. Discuss similarities and differences.

Can You Explain It?

Name: **Date:**

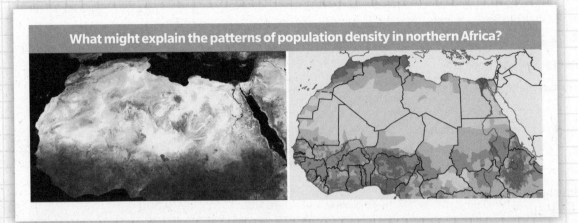

What might explain the patterns of population density in northern Africa?

EVIDENCE NOTEBOOK

Refer to the notes in your Evidence Notebook to help you construct an explanation for what might determine population density in northern Africa.

1. State your claim. Make sure your claim fully explains what might determine population density in northern Africa.

2. Summarize the evidence you have gathered to support your claim and explain your reasoning.

Checkpoints

Answer the following questions to check your understanding of the lesson.

3. Which factors contribute to population growth? Circle all that apply.

A. increase in births

B. increase in death rate

C. new farming technology

D. improvements in health care

Use the table to answer Question 4.

4. Which statement is supported by the data in the table?

A. The population of Toptown is increasing.

	Population	Consumption of rice (in kg)	Per capita consumption
Middleville	60,000	720,000	12.0 kg
Toptown	40,000	720,000	?

B. The per capita consumption of rice is higher in Toptown than in Middleville.

C. Per capita consumption of rice is decreasing in both Toptown and in Middleville.

D. Individuals in Middleville and Toptown consume the same amount of rice.

Use the graph to answer Question 5.

5. Which statement about the per capita consumption of yogurt is supported by the data in the graph?

A. In 2012, each person consumed more than twice the amount of yogurt they consumed in 2010.

B. More people ate yogurt in 2014 than in 2013.

C. Each person ate about 14.9 pounds of yogurt in 2014.

D. The U.S. consumed a total of 14 pounds of yogurt in 2012.

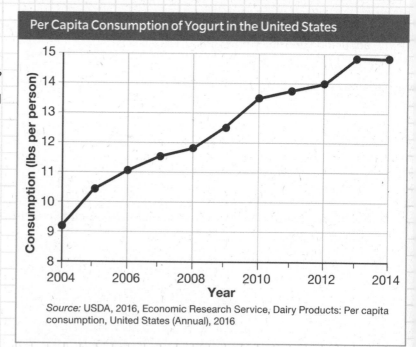

Per Capita Consumption of Yogurt in the United States

Source: USDA, 2016, Economic Research Service, Dairy Products: Per capita consumption, United States (Annual), 2016

---

6. In general, how is resource use related to population size?

A. Resource use is usually not affected by population size.

B. Resource use usually increases as population increases.

C. Resource use usually decreases as population stays the same.

D. Resource use usually increases as population decreases.

Interactive Review

Complete this section to review the main concepts of the lesson.

The rate of human population growth has increased significantly in the recent past.

A. What are some factors that contributed to the dramatic change in the rate of growth of the human population?

People rely on both renewable and nonrenewable resources to provide food, materials, and energy.

B. Summarize how population growth can impact resource use.

Per capita resource use is an average that describes the amount of a resource that one person consumes in a given amount of time.

C. If a population's size does not change, how would a change in per capita consumption affect the overall use of a particular resource?

Resource Use and Earth's Systems

This coastal community in Seward, Alaska, is home to a port used by cruise ships sailing through Alaska's waterways. This community is located near important natural resources.

By the end of this lesson . . .

you will provide evidence to show how resource use impacts Earth's systems.

Go online to view the digital version of the Hands-On Lab for this lesson and to download additional lab resources.

CAN YOU EXPLAIN IT?

Why does most of the water from the Colorado River no longer reach the ocean?

Upper basin
Lower basin
\ Dam location
★ Basin divide
• City

km 0   200
mi 0   100 200

Source: Colorado River Commission of Nevada, "Colorado River Basin Climate Variability and Change: Background, Tools, and Activities," 2008

The Colorado River is a valuable water resource in the western United States. It winds its way over about 2,300 km from the Rocky Mountains in Colorado to the ocean. In some places, the water creates raging whitewater rapids. Yet, little water from the river reaches the ocean.

1. How do people use water resources such as the Colorado River?

2. What are some reasons that a river's water level might drop?

 EVIDENCE NOTEBOOK As you explore the lesson, gather evidence to help explain why most of the water in the Colorado River does not reach the ocean.

Relating Rates of Resource Use to Impacts on Earth's Systems

Coaches are planning a soccer tournament. They need enough water for all of the players. They will need to supply more water if more teams play. More water will also be needed during hot weather when the players drink more water. The coaches need to consider the total number of players—the size of the population. They also need to think about the average amount of water each player will drink—the per capita consumption.

The water used at a soccer tournament and the land in a rain forest have something in common. They are both natural resources that are used by humans. The impact that total population and per capita consumption have on the use of natural resources is similar to the situation in the soccer tournament. Both the size of the population and the per capita consumption affect the amount of Earth's resources that humans use.

This area of rain forest near Altamira, Brazil, was clear-cut to provide resources, including land on which grow crops.

3. Which statements are likely reasons that forests in Brazil, like the one shown in the photo, were cut down? Select all that apply.

   A. The local population increased, and more land was needed for soybean farming.

   B. The local population decreased, and less land was needed for soybean farming.

   C. People around the world were using more products from soybean farming.

   D. People around the world were consuming fewer products from soybean farming.

Earth's Systems

The Earth system is made up of four subsystems—the atmosphere, biosphere, geosphere, and hydrosphere. The atmosphere is the mixture of gases that surrounds the planet. The biosphere is all of the living things on Earth, including humans. The geosphere is the solid part of Earth. The hydrosphere is all of the water on Earth.

Earth's four subsystems are interconnected. For example, the trees in the forest are rooted into the soil in the forest. The soil is part of the geosphere. The trees are also connected to the hydrosphere and atmosphere. Trees take in water from the ground and carbon dioxide from the air. They also give off water vapor to the atmosphere. Because the four different subsystems are interconnected, changes in one subsystem affect all of the others.

The Rate at Which We Use Resources

You are one of more than 7 billion people in the world using Earth's resources. People use resources to meet their needs. Needs may include food, water, shelter, clothing, and transportation. People in different places around the world may meet these needs in different ways. But they all use Earth's resources. Everything people use, from computers to table salt, comes from Earth's natural resources.

As the world population grows, more people will use Earth's resources. The consumption of natural resources commonly increases as population increases. Per capita consumption is the average amount a person uses. If it increases, resource use also increases even if the population stays the same. The graphs below show how resource use changes as the population and per capita consumption change.

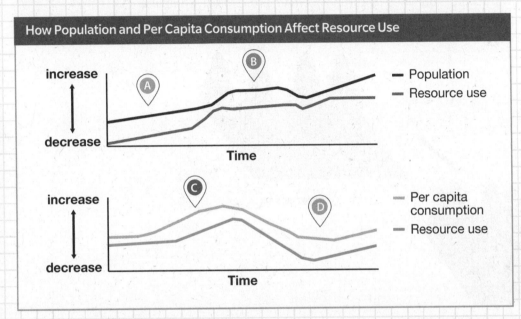

How Population and Per Capita Consumption Affect Resource Use

4. Look at the pointers on the graph. Circle the correct words to complete the statements that go with each pointer to explain why resource use is different at each point.

   (A) Resource use is *greater* / less at this point than at point B because the population is smaller and *more* / fewer people are using resources.

   (B) Resources use is *greater* / less at this point than at point A because the population is larger and *more* / fewer people are using resources.

   (C) Resource use is *greater* / less at this point than at point D because per capita consumption is higher. That is, the same number of people are using *more* / fewer resources.

   (D) Resource use is greater / *less* at this point than at point C because per capita consumption is lower, meaning the same number of people are using *more* / fewer resources.

5. **Discuss** In a small group, discuss how changes in your class population and per capita consumption affect the use of objects or materials used by the class, such as tablet computers or paper. Discuss how these changes impact the use of Earth's natural resources.

Impacts of Resource Use on Earth's Systems

Clear-cutting is the cutting down and removal of all of the trees in an area. Think about how clear-cutting in the rain forest causes changes to both the biosphere and the geosphere. The trees are cut to obtain timber or to clear land. People may put up buildings on the land. They may also use the land to grow crops or raise animals. At first, only a few trees may be removed, causing only small changes to the environment. Then, more trees may be cut down to provide for an increasing population or for an increasing demand by a stable population. As more trees are cut, the impact increases. An immediate effect of clear-cutting is that many living things lose their habitat. Over a longer time, water or wind may remove soil from the land.

6. The diagram shows resources obtained by cutting down trees in a forest. Complete the diagram by drawing in examples of how people might use the cleared land and timber from the trees.

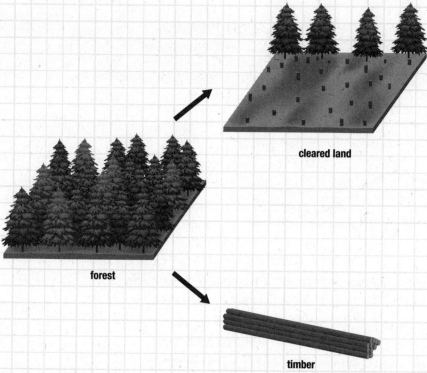

cleared land

forest

timber

7. Obtaining resources that people use may have positive / negative / both positive and negative effects on humans and positive / negative / both positive and negative effects on the environment. The impacts can be short term / long term / both short term and long term.

8. How will the environmental impact of obtaining and using resources change as the population increases and the demand for resources increases? Explain your reasoning.

The Impact of Resource Use

When humans use too much of a resource or use a resource too quickly, Earth's systems can be negatively affected. For example, deforestation leads to habitat loss for many species of animals. Trees cannot grow fast enough to replace the forest and provide new habitat for displaced animals. However, the negative impact can be reduced if resources are managed well. Effective management includes finding ways to reduce the per capita consumption of resources as populations grow. Negative impacts can also be reduced if the activities and technologies involved in getting resources are engineered in a way that gets rid of or reduces the environmental impact. Humans can also lessen the effects by finding ways to replenish renewable resources.

9. In order to reduce the negative impact of logging, what could be done to reduce the number of trees that are cut down?

Do the Math
Analyze Impacts to Earth's Systems

The *per capita consumption of land* is the average area of land used by one person. In one town, the per capita consumption of land is 12,000 m². The population is growing. More land is needed to build schools and housing. People in the town must decide to clear land in a nearby forest.

10. The town's current population is 4,790 people. It is expected to increase by 7.0% over the next 5 years. Based on the current per capita consumption, how much land must be cleared?

People in the town depend on the resources in the forest to build homes.

_____

_____

11. Urban planners want to reduce the impact of the town's growth on the environment. They want to reduce per capita land consumption by $\frac{1}{4}$. In this case, how much new land would need to be cleared in order to make space for the growing population? Use variables to write an expression that helps you solve this problem.

_____

_____

_____

EVIDENCE NOTEBOOK
12. How might the total consumption of water near the Colorado River have been changed by increases in population or changes in per capita consumption? Record your evidence.

Analyzing the Impact of Human Use of Water

When you use water to brush your teeth or to drink, you are using a resource. Think about how much water your family, your community, or your state might use each day. All this human use of water impacts Earth's systems. Sometimes the impact can be immediate, such as when people use more water than can be supplied. Other times, the impact can take many years to see, such as when lakes slowly dry up. Whether an impact is even noticeable depends on how much water is available, how much is used, and how it is used.

The hydrosphere is connected to the rest of Earth's systems. For example, the water lilies and other living things in and around this lake depend on its water.

13. How is the water in the lake important to the organisms in the photo?

The Impact of Obtaining and Using Resources from the Hydrosphere

Water makes up more than half of each human body. Without water, the processes that take place in your body to keep you alive and healthy cannot take place. People need water to live. So, people need a reliable supply of water. Humans also use water to generate electrical energy, to grow crops, to raise animals, to wash things, to mine and make materials, and for recreation.

About 71% of Earth's surface is water. However, fresh water is not always located where people need it. People collect water and direct it to where it is needed. They build dams and make reservoirs to store water. They build canals so that water can flow where it is needed. People also drill wells to get water that is stored underground. These activities can affect other parts of Earth's systems and may result in habitat destruction. A *habitat* is the natural environment of an organism. **Habitat destruction** happens when land inhabited by an organism is destroyed or changed.

As demand increases, impacts also increase. For example, habitat in several areas could be destroyed when canals are constructed to change the flow of river water.

14. What are the possible negative effects of increasing human use of a river's water?

Case Study: The Elwha River

To meet their needs for water, humans build structures that control where water goes and how fast it flows. Fresh water from rivers is stored in reservoirs behind dams so that it can be used when people need it. Dams also control water flow to prevent flooding. Many dams, including the Hoover Dam, have been built along the Colorado River.

The effects of a dam are not all positive. The Elwha River in Washington is an example. Water in the river flowed freely until the early 1900s. Then two dams were built to meet the needs of a growing population. One of the immediate impacts was that the land behind the dams flooded, forming lakes. Other impacts to the environment took years to observe.

The Impact of the Elwha River Dam

The first Elwha River Dam was finished in 1913 to provide hydroelectric power to paper mills.

 The dam kept sediments behind it. This kept sediments from moving downstream. Sediment is an essential part of the salmon habitat.

 The Elwha Dam was not engineered to allow fish to pass through it. So, fish such as salmon were unable to migrate up and down the river.

 Water flow below the dam decreased. This resulted in wetlands around the river drying up. A wetland is an important habitat that helps to purify water and control flooding. The slower water flow also caused temperature increases in the water. As a result, oxygen levels in the water decreased.

Each year, salmon swim up the Elwha River from the ocean to lay eggs. The dams on the river reduced salmon habitats by 90%. As a result, salmon populations declined rapidly. Before the dams changed the river, more than 400,000 salmon returned upstream each year. After the dams, only about 3,000 adult salmon returned each year.

Before the dams, sediment was carried to the mouth of the river. There, it expanded the delta and formed large beaches. The dams prevented sediment from flowing downstream.

Because of the dams' negative impacts, they were removed, starting in 2011. Efforts to restore the river and its habitats continue.

15. How might the impact of the Elwha River dams on the biosphere and geosphere have influenced the decision to remove the dams?

The Impact of Dam Removal on Sediment and Number of Salmon

The graph shows the amount of sediment flowing in the river and the number of salmon before and after dam removal.

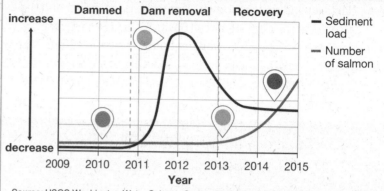

Source: USGS Washington Water Science Center, Elwha River Sediment Monitoring Maps, 2013

16. Write Use the graph to compare the sediment levels and the number of salmon when the dam was in place and when it was removed. On a separate sheet of paper, write an argument about how the dam negatively impacted the sediment flow, the number of salmon moving through the river, and salmon spawning.

The dam blocked most of the sediment from flowing down the river toward the ocean, which limited habitats for salmon to spawn. Few salmon swam in the river.

As the dam was removed, large amounts of sediment (500 mg of sediment per liter of water) flowed downstream.

As habitats were reconnected, the salmon population began increasing.

In the years after the dam was taken down, the amount of sediment flowing in the river leveled off to 100 mg/L. The salmon population continues to increase. It is expected to increase at a regular rate over the next 20 to 30 years.

 EVIDENCE NOTEBOOK

17. How could the use of dams affect the amount of water in the Colorado River that reaches the ocean? Record your evidence.

Analyze Water Use

18. Which statement about water consumption does the graph support?

A. Water use steadily increased as the population increased from 1990 to 2015.

B. Water use declined as population declined after 2008.

C. After 2007, per capita consumption decreased.

D. Per capita consumption was the same from 1990 to 2015.

Water Use and Population in Phoenix, AZ

The graph shows how water use changed as the population of Phoenix, Arizona, changed.

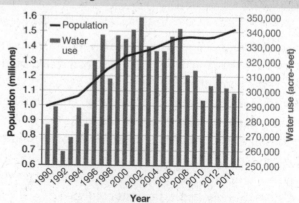

Credit: Adapted from "Historical Population and Water Use, 1990-2014" from the City of Phoenix. Reprinted by permission.

Analyzing the Impact of Human Use of Land Resources

Whether you live in a large city or a small town, you and everyone in your community depends on Earth's systems. Everyone depends on land for food and a place to live. Land is used for gardens and parks. Buildings and roads are built on land. Land also provides natural materials that are used to make products. For example, minerals, including most metals, are mined from the land. Many fuels that are used to produce electrical energy are mined from the land, including coal, petroleum, and natural gas.

Fertilizers contain chemicals that help plants grow. However, these chemicals can be harmful to the environment when they are used in large amounts, especially when they seep into streams and rivers.

19. How do the effects of one person using fertilizer differ from the effects of 100,000 people using the same fertilizer in the same town? Circle all that apply.

   A. The effects are the same when one person or 100,000 people use fertilizer.

   B. The effects of 100,000 people using fertilizer are greater than the effects of one person using fertilizer.

   C. The effects of 100,000 people using fertilizer spreads to a larger area than the effects of one person using fertilizer.

   D. The effects cannot be compared because different amounts of fertilizer are used.

The Impact of Obtaining and Using Resources from the Geosphere

When resources are removed from the land and used, all of Earth's systems can be affected. For example, the geosphere can be changed in a way that limits the space or nutrients available for plants. Such a change can negatively impact the whole Earth system. The atmosphere can be affected because plants add oxygen and remove carbon dioxide and other gases from air. Plants affect the geosphere by preventing erosion. Plants provide habitats for other organisms in the biosphere. And plants help the hydrosphere by filtering water in places such as marshes.

Many people depend on one kind of fuel resource—fossil fuels. These fuels must be mined from beneath Earth's surface. Many minerals that people use, such as copper and gold, are also mined. Mining causes immediate changes to the geosphere, as tunnels or holes are dug to access the resources. The removal process can add harmful materials to the air, water, and land and can harm living things.

Human Use of Coal

During the second half of the 1800s, the Industrial Revolution happened in the United States. The population grew rapidly. During this time, technology improved agricultural efficiency. Manufacturing increased and transportation systems expanded. One important invention—the steam engine—helped power the Industrial Revolution. Coal was burned to generate the steam. Coal was also burned to make steel, which was in great demand for many construction projects.

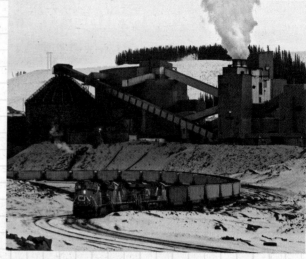

Most coal is burned to generate energy that is used for making other materials or is converted into electrical energy.

As people began to consume more products and more energy, the per capita consumption of coal increased. Because most coal is mined from underground deposits using large machinery, the increased need for coal had a significant impact on Earth's systems.

20. How do you think the increased use of coal during the Industrial Revolution might have affected Earth's systems?

Resource Use and Pollution

One negative effect of the Industrial Revolution was an increase in pollution. **Pollution** is an undesired change in air, water, or soil that negatively affects the health, survival, or activities of humans or other organisms. For example, burning coal and other fossil fuels causes air pollution because gases and other substances are released into the air. The gases that are given off can cause smog. The gases from burning fossil fuels can also combine with water in the atmosphere to form acids and cause acid rain. Burning fossil fuels also increases greenhouse gases in the atmosphere. Greenhouse gases absorb and reradiate energy in the atmosphere, which raises Earth's average global temperature.

Pollution can lead to other negative impacts on the Earth system because pollution changes the chemical and physical makeup of the atmosphere and hydrosphere. For example, acid rain can result in habitat destruction and the death of organisms. These changes alter the makeup of the biosphere.

Although we know that mining and using mineral and energy resources cause pollution, people will not necessarily stop using those resources. Society must balance the needs of people with the protection of the environment. Thus, scientific knowledge can inform people about the effects of human behaviors on Earth's systems. But this knowledge does not tell people how to act.

Case Study: Pollution in the Atmosphere

Some pollutants in the atmosphere are invisible. When fossil fuels are burned, carbon dioxide is one of the invisible gases produced. The concentration of carbon dioxide is about the same everywhere in the atmosphere. Humans add larger amounts of carbon dioxide to the atmosphere than any other greenhouse gas.

Increasing amounts of greenhouse gases warm the atmosphere, leading to changes in Earth's climate. A warmer atmosphere also affects the hydrosphere. For example, the ocean becomes warmer. Increasing amounts of carbon dioxide also change the chemical makeup of the ocean, making it more acidic. These changes can have negative effects on living things.

The concentration of greenhouse gases in the atmosphere has increased as populations around the world increase. As populations grow, more people drive cars that burn fossil fuels. They use more electrical energy and consume more products that are produced by using fossil fuels. These graphs show how the change in energy use correlates to increased carbon dioxide in the atmosphere.

21. What conclusions can you draw from the data shown in these two graphs? Circle all that apply.

A. The amount of energy used in the world is increasing as the population increases.

B. The amount of energy used in the world has leveled off as the population increases.

C. The amount of carbon dioxide in the atmosphere is increasing as the population increases.

D. The amount of carbon dioxide in the atmosphere has leveled off as the population increases.

As this case study shows, as human populations and per capita consumption of natural resources increase, so do the negative effects on Earth's systems. However, people can engineer processes, behaviors, or technologies to minimize the effects of human actions on the environment.

World Energy Consumption

Since the Industrial Revolution, the use of energy resources has increased. Most of this energy is generated by burning fossil fuels and biomass, which releases carbon dioxide and other greenhouse gases.

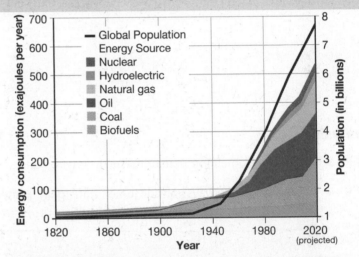

Credit: Adapted from "World Population Prospects" by UN Population Division. Copyright © 2015 by United Nations. Reprinted with the permission of the United Nations.
Credit: Adapted from Land and Irrigation dataset. Copyright © 2014 by Food and Agriculture Organization of the United Nations. Reproduced with permission.

Atmospheric Carbon Dioxide at Mauna Loa Observatory

Scientists have taken careful daily measurements of the amount of carbon dioxide in the air.

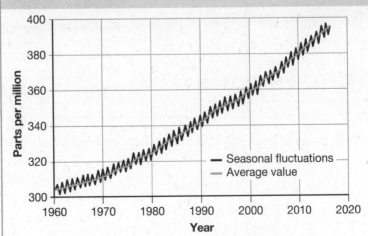

Source: Scripps Institution of Oceanography, NOAA Earth System Research Laboratory, "Atmospheric CO₂ at Mauna Loa Observatory," 2017

Hands-On Lab
Analyze Your Impact

You will track and analyze your daily use of water. Remember that all liquids that you consume are made up mostly of water.

Procedure

STEP 1 On a separate sheet of paper, track and record how many liters of water you use in a day.

STEP 2 Discuss with a partner how the water you used was obtained. For example, does your water come from a well or a reservoir? Record your ideas.

Analysis

STEP 3 Discuss how obtaining water impacts the environment.

STEP 4 Choose one of the ways you consumed water daily. In the table, record how using that water every day impacts each of Earth's systems.

System	Impact(s)
Geosphere	
Atmosphere	
Hydrosphere	
Biosphere	

STEP 5 How can you reduce your individual consumption of water to reduce your impact?

22. Engineer It Your individual use of fossil fuels depends largely on how much electrical energy you use in a day. What solutions could you design to reduce the amount of fossil fuels you use in a 24-hour period? On which solutions are you more likely to act, and why?

Analyze Arable Land Resources

Modern farmers use technologies that were designed to make farming more efficient. Some farmers use plants that have been engineered so that each plant produces more of the parts that humans use.

The graph shows the amount of available arable land and the world population from 1960 to 2020. The number for the 2020 world population is a prediction. Arable land is land that can be used to grow crops.

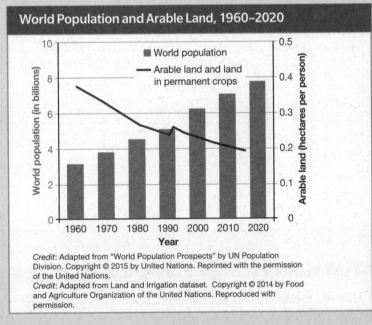

World Population and Arable Land, 1960–2020

Credit: Adapted from "World Population Prospects" by UN Population Division. Copyright © 2015 by United Nations. Reprinted with the permission of the United Nations.
Credit: Adapted from Land and Irrigation dataset. Copyright © 2014 by Food and Agriculture Organization of the United Nations. Reproduced with permission.

23. Which of Earth's systems are affected by farming? Circle all that apply.

A. atmosphere

B. biosphere

C. geosphere

D. hydrosphere

24. Describe the relationship shown by the graph.

_____

_____

25. What is a possible explanation for this relationship?

_____

_____

_____

_____

_____

Analyzing the Impact of Human Use of Plants and Animals

Changes humans make to the atmosphere, geosphere, and hydrosphere as they use resources also affect the biosphere. For example, when habitats on land or in water are damaged, many organisms can no longer live there. Pollution in the air and water can also have negative effects on organisms.

Humans also affect the biosphere by harvesting plants and animals as a resource. Harvesting is the gathering of living things for human consumption.

26. What are potential impacts of harvesting fish as human population increases and humans eat more fish? Fill in the table below.

A commercial fishing boat brings in a net full of salmon. Some groups of commercial vessels catch tons of fish daily.

Influence on resource use	Number of fish harvested	Impact of change on fish harvest
Human population increases	increases	Not enough fish left to meet demand
Per capita consumption of fish increases		
Human population and per capita consumption of fish increase		

The Harvesting of Living Resources

Humans harvest plants, animals, and other organisms from the biosphere. Examples of things humans harvest include corn, birds, and mushrooms. When humans harvest living things, the land, water, and air can also be affected.

Overharvesting results when a species is used so much that the population becomes very small. Overharvesting sometimes puts the survival of a species at risk. For example, overfishing is one type of overharvesting. The beluga sturgeon is a type of fish. Its eggs are used as food that many people want. The sturgeon has been overharvested. Now the species survives mostly because sturgeon are grown in fish hatcheries. When the sturgeon population decreases, many other living things are affected. For example, the populations of the small fish sturgeon eat may change. Some living things depend on sturgeon directly, and others depend on it indirectly. Any change in a species's population will affect all of Earth's systems that the organism interacts with.

Animal Resources

One type of horseshoe crab lays billions of tiny eggs in the Delaware Bay each spring. These eggs are food for many other organisms, including a bird called the red knot. Each spring, red knots migrate to the Delaware Bay just as the horseshoe crabs spawn. The red knots feed on the crab eggs. However, overfishing of the horseshoe crab for use as bait has caused the horseshoe crab population to decrease. As a result, the red knot population in the Delaware Bay area has also decreased.

passenger pigeon

Many plants and animals that were once common for people to eat are now endangered or extinct, such as the passenger pigeon.

27. Analyze the diagram about passenger pigeons. Why did the passenger pigeon go extinct? What might have been done to prevent its extinction?

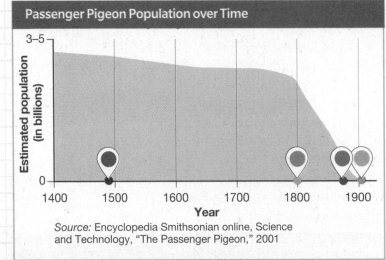

Passenger Pigeon Population over Time

Estimated population (in billions) vs Year

Source: Encyclopedia Smithsonian online, Science and Technology, "The Passenger Pigeon," 2001

- There were an estimated 3 to 5 billion passenger pigeons.
- Professional hunters began hunting and trapping passenger pigeons. They sold the birds at markets for people to eat.
- In 1878, one of the last known large nesting groups of passenger pigeons was hunted in Michigan at a rate of 50,000 birds per day for nearly 5 months.
- The last passenger pigeon died. The passenger pigeon was officially declared extinct.

Plant Resources

Trees are plant resources that have many uses. Sometimes, trees are harvested by cutting down or burning large forest areas. These actions destroy forest habitats. As a result, soil may erode and water in nearby lakes or streams may become polluted. The atmosphere is also affected because trees take in carbon dioxide from the air and give off oxygen.

28. How might an increasing human population cause the changes shown in the satellite images of the rain forest?

1985

2000

The satellite images show changes in a rain forest in Matto Grosso, Brazil, between 1985 and 2000.

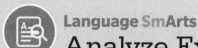
Analyze Extinctions and Land Use

The loss of habitat can have a negative effect on a species. As habitat destruction occurs, there is less space for individuals or populations to occupy. There is also less room for the plants and animals that the species depends on for food.

You learned how the loss of horseshoe crab eggs as a food source impacted the red knot. When human use of resources affects an animal's food source, other species that interact with the animal are also affected. If those species cannot find another source of food or another place to live, their populations will decrease. Some species may become extinct.

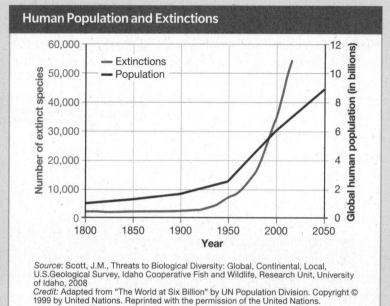

Human Population and Extinctions

Source: Scott, J.M., Threats to Biological Diversity: Global, Continental, Local, U.S.Geological Survey, Idaho Cooperative Fish and Wildlife, Research Unit, University of Idaho, 2008
Credit: Adapted from "The World at Six Billion" by UN Population Division. Copyright © 1999 by United Nations. Reprinted with the permission of the United Nations.

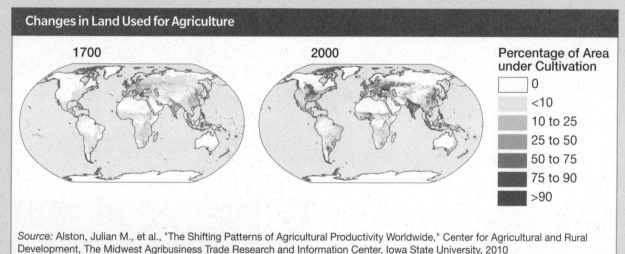

Changes in Land Used for Agriculture

Source: Alston, Julian M., et al., "The Shifting Patterns of Agricultural Productivity Worldwide," Center for Agricultural and Rural Development, The Midwest Agribusiness Trade Research and Information Center, Iowa State University, 2010

29. Construct an argument about how changes in global population relate to agricultural land use and species extinctions. Use evidence from the graph, map, and lesson to support your argument.

_____

_____

_____

_____

_____

_____

_____

_____

_____

Continue Your Exploration

Name: _____   Date: _____

Check out the path below or go online to choose one of the other paths shown.

The Atmosphere as a Resource

- **Hands-On Labs** 👋
- **The Need for More Resources**
- **Propose Your Own Path**

Go online to choose one of these other paths.

Suppose someone talks about Earth's energy resources. Which of Earth's systems do you think of? Often, people do not think of the atmosphere as an energy source.

A wind turbine is a device that captures the energy of moving air. Wind turbines use the movement of air to generate electrical energy. The kinetic energy of wind is transferred to the turbine when wind turns the turbine's large blades. This kinetic energy transforms into mechanical energy as it causes a shaft, or long cylinder, to turn. The spinning shaft turns a generator that transforms the mechanical energy of the spinning shaft into electrical energy.

Today, wind turbines are often grouped together in wind farms. These farms can generate a larger amount of electrical energy than a single turbine can. Wind farms are built in places that tend to be windy, such as the plains of West Texas or mountain passes in California. Wind energy is a renewable source of energy that is clean. It also uses almost no water. However, wind farms take up space on land.

Wind farms can consist of hundreds of wind turbines. The turbines in these farms are often placed relatively far apart. The land between them is used for other purposes, such as farming.

Continue Your Exploration

1. What are two positive impacts of using wind turbines to generate electrical energy?

2. How might the increasing use of renewable energy technologies, such as wind turbines and solar panels, have an impact on Earth's systems as the world population increases?

3. One of the negative impacts of wind turbines is the noise of the spinning turbine. Near the blades of the turbine, the noise level is similar to that of a lawn mower. Farther away, at around 400 meters from the turbine, the noise level is similar to that of a refrigerator. As a result, wind turbines cannot be put closer than 300 meters to the nearest house in some areas. How does this requirement affect the use of wind farms in areas where people live close together?

4. **Collaborate** Wind turbines and hydroelectric dams use the energy of motion to generate electrical energy. Brainstorm other motions in Earth's systems that could be used to generate electrical energy. Draw a simple model of how electrical energy would be generated by one of these motions.

Can You Explain It?

Name: _____ Date: _____

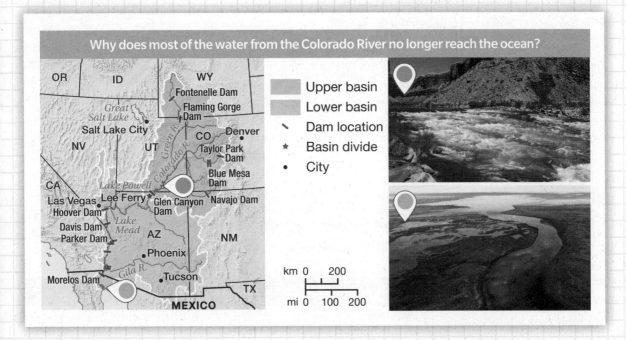

Why does most of the water from the Colorado River no longer reach the ocean?

Legend:
- Upper basin
- Lower basin
- Dam location
- Basin divide
- City

km 0   200
mi 0 100 200

 EVIDENCE NOTEBOOK

Refer to the notes in your Evidence Notebook to help you construct an explanation for the decreased flow of the Colorado River.

1. State your claim. Make sure your claim fully explains why most of the water in the Colorado River no longer reaches the ocean.

2. Summarize the evidence you have gathered to support your claim and explain your reasoning.

Checkpoints

Answer the following questions to check your understanding of the lesson.

Use the data in the table to answer Questions 3–4.

3. Circle the correct words to complete the sentences.

The number of cars decreases / increases / changes randomly as the population increases. This change in resource use will likely increase / decrease / not affect the negative impact of obtaining and using resources.

Population Growth and Car Ownership	
City Population	Number of Cars
3,500,000	2,082,500
3,530,000	2,100,350
3,700,000	2,201,500
3,800,000	2,261,000
3,890,000	2,314,550

4. How can the impacts of car use be reduced if the number of cars per person stays the same? Select all that apply.

   A. improving the bus and train system

   B. using carpools

   C. increasing the use of hybrid and electric cars, which produce less carbon dioxide

   D. finding new places to mine for the metals needed to make cars

Use the information in the graph to answer Questions 5–6.

5. The graph shows deforestation decreased / increased as the population decreased / increased. This trend has a positive / a negative / no effect on the geosphere and atmosphere.

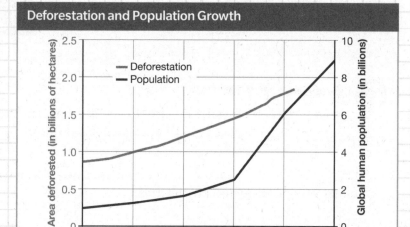

Deforestation and Population Growth

Credit: Adapted from "World Population Prospects" by UN Population Division. Copyright © 2015 by United Nations. Reprinted with the permission of the United Nations.
Credit: Adapted from "State of the World's Forests". Copyright © 2012 by Food and Agriculture Organization of the United Nations. Reproduced with permission.

6. How does deforestation directly affect the biosphere?

   A. It causes erosion.

   B. It causes poor water quality.

   C. It emits greenhouse gases.

   D. It reduces the population of trees.

7. A town wants to build a dam across a river. Which statements are evidence that the dam would negatively affect the environment? Select all that apply.

   A. It would reduce the flow of sediments.

   B. It would provide more habitat for salmon.

   C. It would decrease the number of wetlands along the river.

   D. It would provide a lake for recreation.

8. An herb that is used as medicine is threatened with extinction. How might human activities be contributing to this threat? Select all that apply.

   A. People have planted it as a crop in places where it is not native.

   B. The herb has become more popular as medicine, leading to overharvesting.

   C. Human population has grown in regions where the herb is a popular medicine.

Interactive Review

Complete this page to review the main concepts of the lesson.

Human use of resources affects all of Earth's systems. The environmental impact increases as resource use and consumption increase.

A. What happens to resource use as a population increases and per capita use does not change?

Human use of water resources impacts all of Earth's systems.

B. How does the human use of water affect Earth's systems?

Human use of land for buildings, for agriculture, and for resources such as metals and fossil fuels impacts all of Earth's systems.

C. How can obtaining and using resources from land impact Earth's systems?

Human use of plants and animals for food, materials, and fuel impacts all of Earth's systems.

D. How can overharvesting a resource impact Earth's systems?

Choose one of the activities to explore how this unit connects to other topics.

☐ Life Science Connection

Frogs and Pollution Frogs and other amphibians respire through their skins, so they are some of the most sensitive animals to pollution in the environment. Frog and toad species across the world are in danger of extinction because of pollution.

Research the effects of pollution on different species of frogs, toads, or salamanders. Explain the effects the pollution has on the amphibian and its environment. Create a poster or visual display that explains how frogs or other amphibians can be used to monitor the effects of resource use on Earth's systems.

☐ Social Studies Connection

Technological Ages The discovery and widespread use of crucial stone and metal resources have marked major periods of advancement in Africa, Asia, Europe, and the Middle East. Along with the discovery of these resources came a better ability to hunt, farm, and create buildings and artwork.

Choose one of the major technological ages, such as the Stone Age, Bronze Age, Iron Age, or Copper Age. Write a report that identifies when the technological age occurred, describes how resources were used in a new way, and summarizes the effects of the age on human culture.

☐ Health Connection

Vaccines and Population Growth The world's population has increased, in part, because of medical advancements made over the last century. Greater access to medications and immunizations has led to longer life expectancies and increases in population growth rates.

Research one disease that has been directly affected by vaccines. Diseases could include polio, smallpox, or measles. Research how common or widespread the disease was before the vaccine was developed and after. Describe how vaccination protocols have changed human population and the mortality rate associated with the disease itself. Create a visual presentation of your findings.

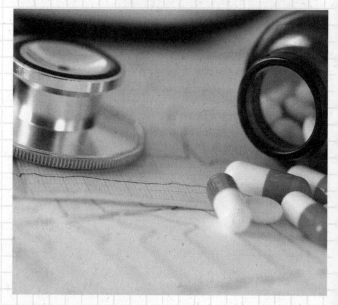

Name: _____   **Date:** _____

Complete this review to check your understanding of the unit.

Use the diagram to answer Questions 1–3.

1. The U.S. population is 330 million people. About how many trees does the United States consume as paper each year?

    A. 1.924 billion trees

    B. 597 million trees

    C. 1.234 billion trees

    D. 1.838 billion trees

Global Paper Consumption	
Number of 40-foot trees consumed per person each year	
Belgium	8.51
Japan	5.83
U.S.	5.57
Spain	3.74
China	1.81
India	0.28

Source: The Economist, How much paper does a person use on average in a year?,2012, based on data from RISI, Bureau of International Recycling, and the EPA

2. In 2010, China's population was 1.338 billion, India's population was 1.206 billion, and the United States' population was 309.3 million. China / India / The United States used the most trees as paper that year.

3. How does paper production from natural resources affect Earth's systems? Choose all that apply.

    A. Pollution from paper factories negatively affects the atmosphere.

    B. Paper production produces wastes that may contaminate water.

    C. When trees are harvested to make paper, exposed soil may erode.

    D. As trees are cut down for paper, habitat destruction occurs.

Use the graph to answer Questions 4–5.

4. Use the numbers 1–4 to order the countries from greatest to smallest producer of rice.

    _____ Bangladesh

    _____ China

    _____ India

    _____ Indonesia

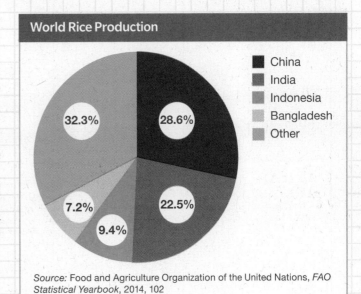

World Rice Production

- China
- India
- Indonesia
- Bangladesh
- Other

32.3% 28.6% 22.5% 9.4% 7.2%

Source: Food and Agriculture Organization of the United Nations, *FAO Statistical Yearbook*, 2014, 102

5. China consumes the most rice, followed by India, Indonesia, and Bangladesh. How could these countries ensure there is enough rice for their growing populations without negatively affecting Earth's systems?

    A. by using more land to produce rice

    B. by exporting more rice to other countries

    C. by decreasing the per capita use of rice

    D. by growing other crops instead of rice

6. Complete the table by providing an example of how these resources relate to each big concept.

Resource	Renewable or nonrenewable	How it is used	Effects of use on Earth's systems
Wind	Renewable		
Petroleum			
Fish			
Trees			

Name: _____   Date: _____

Use the graphs to answer Questions 7–10.

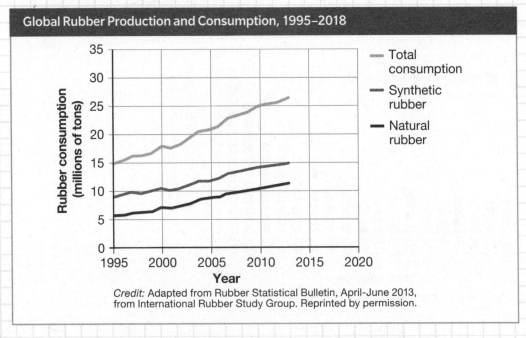

Global Rubber Production and Consumption, 1995–2018

Credit: Adapted from Rubber Statistical Bulletin, April-June 2013, from International Rubber Study Group. Reprinted by permission.

7. What trend can you see in the graph in the consumption of natural and synthetic rubber between 1995 and 2015?

8. What might account for the trend? Explain your reasoning.

9. How does an increase in rubber consumption affect Earth's systems?

10. Based on what you know about human population change, how would you expect the consumption of rubber, natural rubber, and synthetic rubber to change in the future? How might this change affect Earth's systems? Use evidence and scientific reasoning to justify your claims.

Use the graph to answer Questions 11–14.

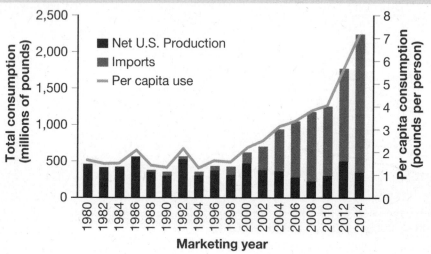

Avocado Production and Importation 1980–2014

This map shows the avocado production and importation in the United States over a thirty year time span.

Source: USDA, Economic Research Service, "Avocado imports grow to meet U.S. demand," 2016

11. How did the per capita use of avocados change between 1980 and 2015? What mathematical relationship(s) can you identify between the use in 1980 and 2015?

12. How does the per capita use of avocados relate to domestic production versus imports of avocados?

13. The population of the United States grew rapidly from 1998 to 2014. How do population growth and increase in per capita use explain a rise in the total amount of avocados consumed?

14. Avocados grow in tropical and subtropical climates, which most of the United States is not. If the per capita use of avocados in the United States continues to change at the same rate, how might the demand for avocados affect Earth's systems?

Name: Date:

How does population change affect energy consumption in Japan?

Since 1990, Japan's population growth has slowed significantly, and the nation's population began to decline after 2010. However, Japan's electrical energy consumption remains high, especially in rural areas. You have been asked to explain these trends to Japanese energy officials. Research how energy is generated and used in Japan, in Japan's cities, and in rural Japan. You may need to evaluate population change and demographics, regional differences in energy use, and per capita use. Present your findings as a multimedia presentation, animation, flow chart, or series of if-then statements that explains the patterns of population change and energy use in Japan.

Population Change and Electricity Consumption in Japan and in Rural Japan

The first figure shows the changes in population and electrical energy use for all of Japan. The second figure shows the same information for rural areas of Japan.

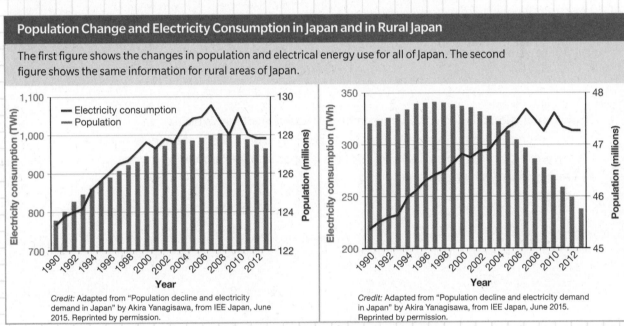

Credit: Adapted from "Population decline and electricity demand in Japan" by Akira Yanagisawa, from IEE Japan, June 2015. Reprinted by permission.

Credit: Adapted from "Population decline and electricity demand in Japan" by Akira Yanagisawa, from IEE Japan, June 2015. Reprinted by permission.

The steps below will help guide your research and help you draw conclusions.

1. **Ask a Question** Write a question that defines the problem you have been asked to solve. You may also want to list questions you have about population change and energy consumption in Japan. These questions may help guide your research.

2. **Conduct Research** How do people in Japan use energy? What type of resources do they use to generate electricity? What social or technological trends might affect how electrical energy is used in rural areas and in urban areas?

3. **Analyze the Data** Use the information you gathered to identify proportional relationships between population change, per capita use, and resource use in Japan. Describe the proportional relationships between the three variables, and identify how those patterns can be used to predict changes in electrical energy use in Japan.

4. **Draw Conclusions** Based on your research, draft a statement that explains electrical energy consumption patterns in Japan and makes predictions about how electrical energy consumption is likely to change in Japan's future. Support your claim by using evidence and scientific reasoning.

5. **Communicate** Present your findings to the board of energy officials in Japan. Use words and images to explain to them what has caused the energy consumption in Japan to remain high despite the drop in population.

✓ **Self-Check**

	I asked a question about how energy consumption relates to population change and trends in energy use.
	I researched how energy is used in Japan and the per capita use rates.
	I identified relationships between population change, per capita use, and energy use in Japan and used this information to make a claim.
	My conclusion was clearly stated and communicated to others.

Human Impacts on Earth Systems

Lesson 1 Human Impacts on the Environment 180

Lesson 2 Engineer It: Reducing Human Impacts
on the Environment 200

Lesson 3 Climate Change 224

Unit Review 247

Unit Performance Task 251

Human use of fossil fuels is a primary cause of rising temperatures on Earth. One of the effects of this temperature change is melting glaciers, such as the Perito Moreno Glacier in Argentina.

Humans impact Earth in many ways. One example is human use of fossil fuels as a source of energy, which causes many changes in the environment, including climate change. Human activity can cause global temperature rise. Rising global temperatures have effects such as habitat loss and melting sea ice. However, humans can take actions to reduce negative impacts on the environment. In this unit, you will explore the many ways we impact Earth. You will also investigate ways humans can reduce their impacts on Earth systems.

Why It Matters

Here are some questions to consider as you work through the unit. Can you answer
any of the questions now? Revisit these questions at the end of the unit to apply what
you discover.

Questions	Notes
How do you think humans are altering land and soil on Earth?	
What is causing global temperature change?	
What are some ways humans pollute, and how do these actions affect the environment?	
How could climate change affect your life?	
How are you contributing to climate change?	
What actions can you take to minimize your impact on Earth systems?	

Unit Starter: Interpreting Ozone Layer Data

Use your skills to analyze and interpret data about the "hole" in the ozone layer.

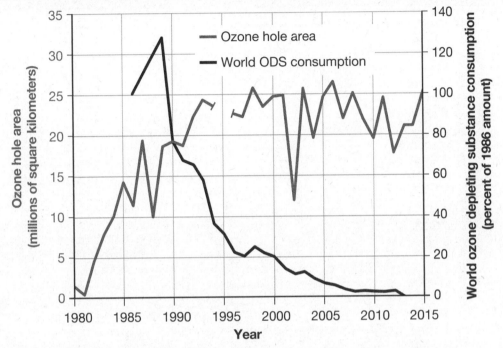

Source: NASA Ozone Watch, 2015; European Environment Agency, Production and consumption of ozone-depleting substances, 2016

1. What happened to the ozone hole area between 1984 and 2000?

   A. It became larger.

   B. It became smaller.

   C. It stayed the same.

2. In 1986, we started measuring the amount of ozone depleting substances (ODS) consumed worldwide each year. The amount consumed in 1986 was used as a baseline value, with later values being compared to the amount of ODS consumption in 1993, the ODS consumption was about 15% / 30% / 60% of the amount used in 1986. This means the ODS consumption was reduced by 40% / 60% / 85% from the amount used in 1986.

Go online to download the Unit Project Worksheet to help you plan your project.

Unit Project

Community Climate Change

You will research and design a community-based solution to reduce the effects of one human activity on greenhouse gas emissions that impact climate change.

Human Impacts on the Environment

The grass for this golf course in Arizona does not naturally grow in this area. It was brought here by humans.

By the end of this lesson . . .

you will be able to analyze the impacts of human activity on the environment.

Go online to view the digital version of the Hands-On Lab for this lesson and to download additional lab resources.

CAN YOU EXPLAIN IT?

How can farming on land contribute to the growth of algal blooms in the ocean?

Algae vary in color. When large amounts of algae are in a body of water, the color of the water may appear to change.

Algae are plant-like organisms that use the energy of sunlight to make sugars. They live in fresh water and salt water, which is where they get the nutrients they need. An algal bloom forms when the population of algae in a body of water increases rapidly. As an algae population grows, the algae use more oxygen, which depletes the amount of dissolved oxygen in the water.

1. Describe how land and oceans are connected.

2. What do you think might cause algae to start growing very rapidly?

EVIDENCE NOTEBOOK As you explore this lesson, gather evidence to help explain how farming on land relates to the growth of algal blooms in the ocean.

Exploring the Environment

All living things need certain materials to stay healthy. Organisms depend on their environment to provide those materials. A **habitat** is the place where an organism lives. It includes the living and nonliving factors that affect the organism, or the *environment* around the organism. The living and nonliving parts of the environment interact. Humans and other organisms rely on the environment for natural resources, such as water and soil, and for natural services, such as the filtering of pollutants from water.

3. Identify each factor in the beaver's habitat as living or nonliving.

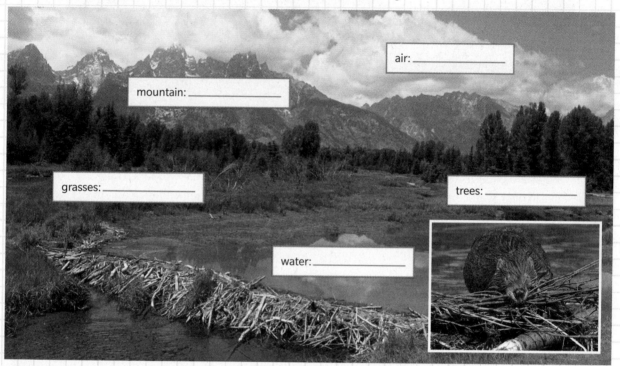

mountain: _____

air: _____

grasses: _____

trees: _____

water: _____

A beaver uses sticks and branches from nearby trees to build a dam in a river.

4. How might the beaver use or depend on at least three of the environmental factors labeled in the photo?

 EVIDENCE NOTEBOOK

5. Describe the environment of the algae shown at the beginning of the lesson. How are algae connected to their environment? Record your evidence.

Changes in the Environment

Changes in Earth systems happen all the time. Natural events cause some changes. For example, a flood caused by a severe rainstorm might destroy trees or remove topsoil. Humans also can cause change by actions such as damming a river or removing trees. Natural events and human activities can both disturb the environment. These disturbances can alter resources that living things need.

The path of a tornado can easily be seen in this forest.

Deforestation is the removal of trees and other plants from an area such as the forest shown in this photo.

6. **Discuss** With a partner, look at the images and compare the changes to a forest from a tornado and from deforestation.

Changes Caused by Natural Events

Some natural changes in the environment involve patterns. For example, in some places ocean tides change from high to low twice a day. Weather changes seasonally in many parts of Earth. It can become cooler and then warmer throughout a year. Because these events happen in a repeating pattern, many species have ways to deal with these changes. For example, fur color in Arctic hares changes from brown to white in the winter, an advantage when hiding from predators in the snow. Other natural changes happen suddenly or without a pattern. A forest fire caused by a lightning strike is a sudden natural event that can cause substantial changes to the environment.

Changes Caused by Human Activity

Human activities can have many different effects on Earth systems. For example, humans can change the shape of the land to meet their needs. Humans may use resources at a faster rate than they can be replaced. This use causes resources to become scarce in the environment and is called *resource depletion*. Humans also affect the environment when they pollute resources. *Pollution* is an undesirable change in a natural environment that is caused by adding substances that are harmful to living organisms.

7. Decide whether each example is caused by human actions or by natural events. Write H for human actions and N for natural events.

   A. asteroid impact flattens a forest _____

   B. flooding from a concrete dam _____

   C. flooding from a severe storm _____

   D. oil spill in the ocean _____

   E. deforestation to clear land for crops _____

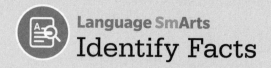

A *fact* is a statement that can be proven. An *opinion* is what someone believes about something. The following is an excerpt from a newspaper article about a dam and its impact on the environment. While you read the article, watch for statements that present facts and statements that present opinions.

The Three Gorges Dam

In 2003, the Three Gorges Dam opened across China's Yangtze River. The dam provides China with a sustainable source of electrical energy for a fast-growing population. It also helps decrease the risk of flooding in the river basin. In 2014, the dam produced 98.8 billion kilowatt-hours of electricity. By using flowing water rather than burning fossil fuels to produce electrical energy, about 120 million tons less carbon dioxide than what would have been produced without the dam entered the atmosphere during 2014.

   Although these results help the Chinese people, the construction of the dam is not as fantastic as it first appears. Building the dam required large amounts of concrete and released harmful chemicals and carbon dioxide into the air. Scientists think that earthquakes may result from water pressure in ground fissures near the dam's reservoir. Worse than these results is that people were moved from their villages. Sadly, many natural ecosystems were destroyed, and more than 500 species of rare plants and 300 species of fish were negatively affected. Many living things died because their ecosystems were lost. Building the dam helped the people. However, its effects on certain ecosystems were devastating.

8. Identify each statement as a *fact* or an *opinion*.

   A. The dam provides China with a sustainable energy source for producing electrical energy. _____

   B. The dam is not as fantastic as it first appears. _____

   C. It also helps decrease the risk of flooding in the river basin. _____

   D. Building the dam required large amounts of concrete. _____

9. Using factual evidence provided in the article, identify two different cause-effect relationships involving the construction of the Three Gorges Dam and the environment.

   _____

   _____

   _____

   _____

   _____

   _____

   _____

   _____

Relating Human Activity to the Environment

Human Activity in Earth Systems

Did you ever see someone throw a plastic cup on the ground and walk away? Some people might say, "Well, it is just one cup." People may not think about how pollution adds up when many people do the same thing.

Earth systems may be considered in four major parts: the hydrosphere, atmosphere, geosphere, and biosphere. Because these parts of Earth systems are interconnected, a human activity that directly affects one part may indirectly affect the other parts.

10. What are three human actions that impact the environment?

Recycling cell phones, which contain metals and plastics, reduces environmental pollution.

Human Impact on the Hydrosphere

All water on Earth is part of the *hydrosphere,* including polar ice caps, snow, groundwater, and surface water. Humans rely on surface water to drink, swim, fish, and transport goods. Farmers might divert water from rivers to give to crops or livestock. Humans also dig wells to pump groundwater to areas where surface water is unavailable. Human use of these water resources can lead to a scarcity of fresh and clean water in the environment.

Water pollution may result from human activities on or near water sources. Water pollution affects organisms that depend on the water supply. **Point-source pollution** occurs when harmful materials enter Earth's hydrosphere from a single, identifiable source such as a factory. **Nonpoint-source pollution** comes from many sources, including rainwater that picks up pollutants as it moves across land.

When wastes are dumped into Earth's hydrosphere, pollutants can travel to different parts of the environment.

Hands-On Lab
Model Ocean Pollution from Land

You will make a model to explore how land and ocean pollution are connected.

Procedure and Analysis

STEP 1 Make a prediction about how point-source pollution and nonpoint-source pollution on land may affect water pollution.

STEP 2 Use the materials provided to create a model of either point-source or nonpoint-source pollution on land near an ocean shore.

STEP 3 Explain how your model represents either point-source or nonpoint-source pollution.

STEP 4 Design a method to simulate precipitation with your model. Explore how precipitation affects the land pollution and ocean pollution. Record your observations.

STEP 5 Compare your observations with other groups. Is there a difference in how point-source pollution and nonpoint-source pollution on land impact ocean pollution? Explain.

STEP 6 **Draw** On a separate sheet of paper, draw a cartoon with three to four frames. Illustrate a human activity that could contribute to the process of pollution that you modeled in this activity. In your cartoon, show at least two effects on the environment of the human activity shown.

MATERIALS
- camera (optional)
- food coloring, blue
- food coloring, red
- metric ruler
- sand, coarse, wet (1/3 volume of washtub)
- spray bottle
- washtub, plastic
- water

 EVIDENCE NOTEBOOK

11. Identify the different materials that may enter a body of water by the same process explored in this lab. Record your evidence.

Human Impact on the Atmosphere

The *atmosphere* is the layer of gases that surrounds Earth. If you stand outside and look up, you might see blue sky and some clouds. You may not see air pollution because many air pollutants are colorless gases. Other pollutants may be in liquid or solid form, such as tiny particles suspended in the atmosphere. Air pollution may cause problems for humans and other species alike. Respiratory problems such as asthma can be made worse by air pollution. Many pollutants enter the atmosphere as the result of burning fossil fuels. Other pollutants such as dust may come from construction sites or agriculture as dry soil is carried by the wind.

Burning fossil fuels releases potentially harmful particles and gases into the atmosphere.

Human Impact on the Geosphere

The mostly solid, rocky part of Earth is called the *geosphere*. Humans change the geosphere when they reshape the land to meet their needs. Humans level land to build homes and offices. Humans may also change the land to mine for resources or to farm. Some farming and mining practices can degrade the soil. Degraded soil cannot support plants or crops, leaving the soil exposed. The exposed soil may then be swept away by wind or water, further changing the shape of the land. Humans may change the land to reduce the chance of erosion by planting different types of crops or by terracing sloped lands.

Mining provides people with materials they need, but it also changes the geosphere.

Human Impact on the Biosphere

The *biosphere* is all living things on Earth, including you. Humans affect the biosphere when they hunt, fish, or harvest plants. A species may become extinct if humans remove more organisms than can be replenished. A species is **extinct** when no more individuals remain on Earth. Human activity may also positively impact the biosphere. In many areas, deer populations no longer have natural predators. These deer populations may grow so large that their grazing negatively affects their ecosystem. Hunting deer in these areas can reduce the deer population to protect the forest ecosystem.

Commercial fishing can deplete the food for other species living in the area and add pollution to the water.

Changes to other Earth systems may indirectly affect the biosphere. For example, changes to land or water might degrade or destroy habitats. When an organism's habitat is degraded, the habitat may no longer be able to support the organism. Imagine that a lake is polluted or its water is removed for human use. In this example, organisms that depend on the water in the lake to survive either move to other sources, or, if they cannot move, they may not survive.

Connected Effects of Human Activity

Human activity may affect multiple parts of the Earth system. Burning fossil fuels releases particles and several different gases into the air. Some of these gases pollute the air. For example, gases such as nitrogen oxides and sulfur dioxide, react with water in the air to form acid rain. Acid rain may kill trees or crops and cause surface water to become more acidic. These effects can harm living organisms in the biosphere.

A mine in West Virginia, where the top of a mountain was removed to reach the coal in the ground.

12. Complete the paragraph with the words geosphere, hydrosphere, atmosphere, and biosphere.

    Surface mining changes the shape of the land, which impacts the _____. These land changes may fragment or destroy habitats in the area, which impacts the _____.
    Mining exposes new materials to the surface. Rain may carry these materials into rivers and streams, which impacts the _____. The process of mining can also cause small particles to enter the _____.

Human Impact on the Florida Panther

In the 1500s, the Florida panther roamed most of the southeastern United States. The Florida panther lives in forested areas, wetlands, and swamps.

13. How might a growing human population in the southeastern United States have affected the panther population?

Florida panther

As European settlers arrived in the 1600s, they clear-cut the land so they could grow crops. Today much of the area has been urbanized. The cutting of trees and building of roads and cities fragmented the panther's habitat. It reduced large, connected habitats to smaller, less connected areas. The panther was also hunted to protect livestock.

In 1967, the Florida panther was listed as an endangered species by the United States government and conservation efforts began. Conservation efforts included protecting and connecting panther habitats and making it illegal to hunt these large cats. In the early 1970s, there were approximately 20 adult wild panthers in southern Florida. Conservation efforts resulted in there being almost 200 in the same area in 2014. Despite the increase in numbers, Florida panthers still face many dangers. For example, 24 panthers were killed by cars while trying to cross roadways in 2014.

Human Impacts on the Florida Panther's Habitat

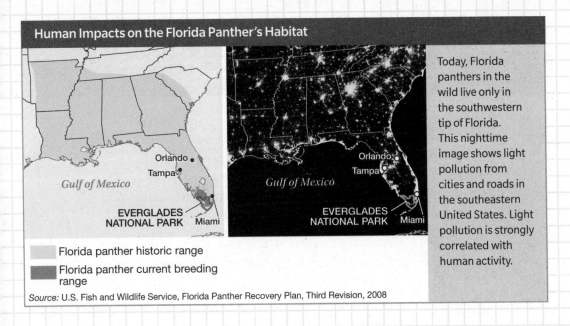

Florida panther historic range

Florida panther current breeding range

Today, Florida panthers in the wild live only in the southwestern tip of Florida. This nighttime image shows light pollution from cities and roads in the southeastern United States. Light pollution is strongly correlated with human activity.

Source: U.S. Fish and Wildlife Service, Florida Panther Recovery Plan, Third Revision, 2008

14. Look at the maps. How do the data in the maps support the claim that human activity has negatively affected the population of Florida panthers?

Engineer It
Evaluate Tradeoffs

Suppose you are an engineer who is designing a new drive system for an automobile. Two criteria for the product are that the design must keep the emission of carbon dioxide (CO_2) low, and that the cost of owning the product must be low. Use the graph to compare ownership costs with yearly CO_2 emissions for three drive system designs.

15. Which design has the greatest release of CO_2 per year in comparison to the others?

_____

16. Based on the design criteria, describe the tradeoff that must be made when choosing one of the three designs. Use the graph to support your argument.

_____
_____
_____

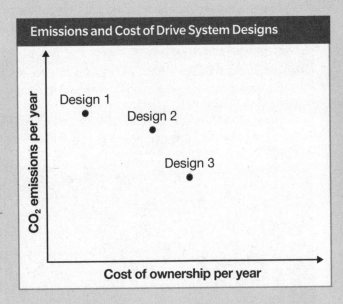

Emissions and Cost of Drive System Designs

Analyzing the Scale of Human Impacts on the Environment

Human impacts on the environment can vary in scale over time and space. Some effects are more noticeable in the long term, such as the increase in the acidity of oceans. Some effects can happen more quickly. For example, developers may fill in a wetland to build a neighborhood, which can impact the environment in the area in a short amount of time. A person cutting down a single tree affects a small area, but when large areas of trees are cut down, a larger area of the environment will be affected. The scale of a human impact on the environment affects the ability of the environment to recover or stabilize.

17. Discuss How might a human activity that impacts a small area affect a larger area over time?

Case Study: The Mississippi River

The Mississippi River is one of the largest rivers in the world. The river is an important shipping route and freshwater source for the midwestern United States. Human activity that affects the Mississippi River can have widespread effects due to the size of the river.

    Rivers naturally change course over time and occasionally flood due to natural events. The *mouth* of a river is where it empties into a larger body of water. Rivers naturally slow down near their mouths and deposit sediment in a fan-shaped area. This fan-shaped land mass is called the *delta* of the river. To protect cities near the river from floodwaters and to help maintain the course of the river, humans built levees along the river. A *levee* is a raised part of land either naturally occurring or human built to contain rising river waters. Levees prevent the river waters from spreading out, slowing down, and depositing sediment. Instead, sediment is carried beyond the river's mouth. The shape of the Mississippi River Delta has changed greatly during the twentieth century. A change this great over a short period of time, geologically speaking, indicates that human activity has had a role in changing the shape of the delta.

The Changing Mississippi River Delta

The images show the landmass and coastline of the Mississippi River Delta in 1932 and 2011. The main path of the river is shown in orange. Rising sea level and other factors have contributed to a large loss of land in the Mississippi River Delta over 79 years.

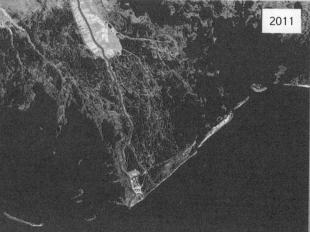

1932

2011

Human-Built Structures to Control the Mississippi River

Humans built several lock-and-dam systems so that larger boats could travel farther upstream on the Mississippi River. The lock portion allows boats passage, and the dam increases the depth of the water. The building of a dam can affect the environment in several ways.

Flow of a River Upstream of a Dam

River water carries sediment downstream. The sediment is suspended in the flowing water and makes the water cloudy or *turbid*. The flow of water slows down as it approaches a dam, and much of the sediment is deposited upstream of the dam.

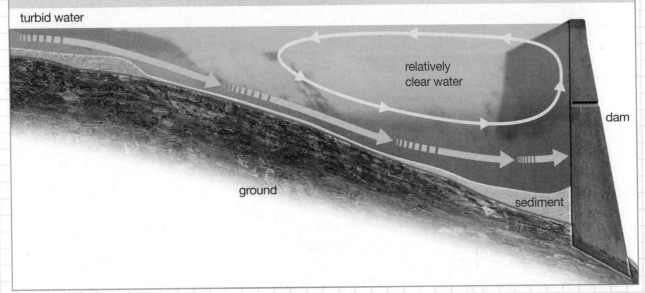

turbid water

relatively clear water

dam

ground

sediment

18. The following are effects of lock-and-dam systems in a river. Which effect will most likely impact the formation of land in the delta?

   A. They prevent the flow of sediments downstream.

   B. They can interfere with fish migration.

   C. They make navigation possible in places.

   D. They can affect water temperature.

For the cities in the Mississippi River Delta, it is important that the path of the Mississippi River does not change, as it would without human intervention. Many levees and other structures have been built to keep most of the flow of the Mississippi River along the same path it followed when cities in the area were established.

19. How might the building of levees have affected the shape of the Mississippi River Delta?

Levees limit rising river waters to an area near the banks of a river in the event of rising water level.

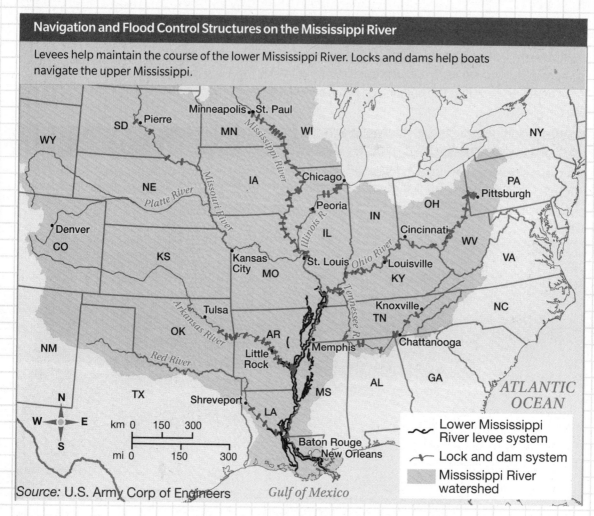

Navigation and Flood Control Structures on the Mississippi River

Levees help maintain the course of the lower Mississippi River. Locks and dams help boats navigate the upper Mississippi.

Lower Mississippi River levee system

Lock and dam system

Mississippi River watershed

Source: U.S. Army Corp of Engineers

20. How does the number of levees and dams on the Mississippi River affect the scale of human impact on the river and the organisms that depend on it?

Dead Zone at the Mouth of the Mississippi River

In 1972, humans first noticed that a large area in the ocean near the mouth of the Mississippi River, normally teaming with life, appeared dead. At first, this happened every few years, but later happened every year. This dead zone appears in the summer when the algae population in the Gulf of Mexico's warm water suddenly increases. The increase in algae reduces the amount of oxygen dissolved in the water. Organisms sensitive to oxygen levels in the water either die or leave the area. More oxygen is removed from the water as dead organisms decay. The result is a *dead zone*, an area where organisms cannot live. Fish leave the area to find waters with more oxygen. Fish-dependent species such as some kinds of birds must look elsewhere for food. The size of the dead zone varies each year. For the last several years, the average size of the dead zone has been almost 6,000 square miles. It is one of the largest dead zones in the world.

Mississippi River Watershed

A *watershed* is an area of land drained by a river system. Forty-one percent of the continental United States is part of the Mississippi River watershed, which drains into the Gulf of Mexico.

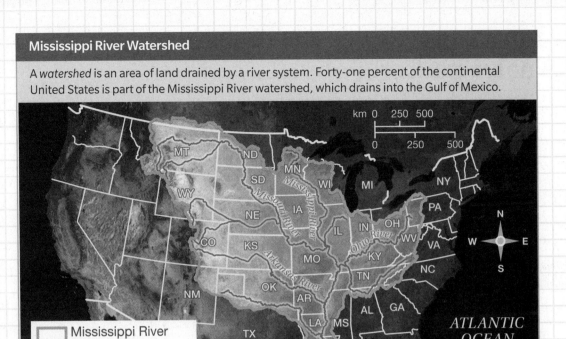

Source: NOAA National Centers for Coastal Ocean Science, Hypoxia and Eutrophication

The Mississippi River watershed includes many cities and farms. Human activities in the watershed contribute to pollution in the water. Some pollutants are directly added to the waterways. Other pollutants are picked up from cities and farms by the rain that runs into streams and rivers. The pollutants include contaminants from roadways and fertilizers that farmers apply to crops to help them grow.

21. Explain how wastewater from a manufacturing plant in southern Ohio could impact fish in the Mississippi River. Use the watershed map to support your answer.

22. Farmers often apply extra nutrients to their crops in the form of fertilizer. Describe how these extra nutrients might impact the Mississippi River.

EVIDENCE NOTEBOOK

23. What materials might runoff in the Mississippi watershed contain that could contribute to algae growth in waterways? Record your evidence.

Analyze a Cod Population

Renewable resources must be used carefully to maintain the availability of the resource. For centuries, humans fished for cod off the coast of Newfoundland, Canada. Then, in the mid-twentieth century, new technologies allowed cod to be harvested in much greater numbers than in previous years. Soon after, the cod population declined rapidly. In 1992, Canada introduced a ban on cod fishing in the area. Even after the ban started, the cod population failed to recover as quickly as expected. One possible reason that the cod population remains low is the decrease in phytoplankton, the main food source for cod in the area. Also, the few cod that remain are more susceptible to environmental changes.

Northern Cod Landings

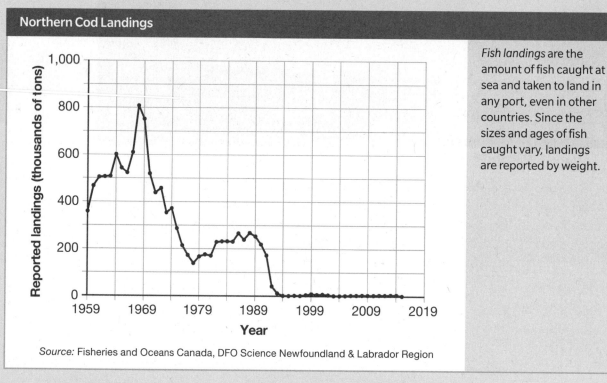

Fish landings are the amount of fish caught at sea and taken to land in any port, even in other countries. Since the sizes and ages of fish caught vary, landings are reported by weight.

Source: Fisheries and Oceans Canada, DFO Science Newfoundland & Labrador Region

24. Use the graph to answer the following questions.

   A. What is the average weight of fish caught per year from 1959–1969, to the nearest 20,000 tons? _____

   B. What is the average weight of fish caught per year from 1979–1989, to the nearest 20,000 tons? _____

   C. About what percentage of the average in part A is the average in part B, to the nearest 5%? _____

25. Why do you think the fishing industry was unable to continue catching the same amount of fish in the decades after the 1960s as had been caught in the 1960s?

_____

_____

_____

_____

_____

Continue Your Exploration

Name: _____   Date: _____

Check out the path below or go online to choose one of the other paths shown.

Chernobyl Nuclear Disaster

- **Hands-On Labs** ✋
- **Impact of** *Deepwater Horizon* **Oil Well Accident**
- **Propose Your Own Path**

Go online to choose one of these other paths.

Under normal operating conditions, nuclear power generation is safe and releases minimal pollutants into the atmosphere. But in 1986, an accident at the Chernobyl Nuclear Power Plant in Ukraine released huge amounts of radioactive material into the environment. Soon after the incident, the government closed the area within 30 kilometers of the plant and evacuated about 115,000 people. In the following years, 220,000 more people were evacuated to reduce their risk of radiation exposure.

The effects of radiation sickness on people and other organisms vary with the type of radiation, and the level and duration of exposure. Minor exposure may lead to nausea, hair loss, vomiting, headaches, and fevers. More severe exposure may significantly reduce an organism's life expectancy. Within four months after the incident, 28 people had died from severe radiation exposure and thermal burns. About 6,000 cases of thyroid cancer in children have been linked to the accident. Radioactive material is hard to clean up, and it continues to be dangerous as it breaks down slowly over time—sometimes over centuries. As of 2017, the Chernobyl area is still closed to the general population.

Human Exposure to Radiation

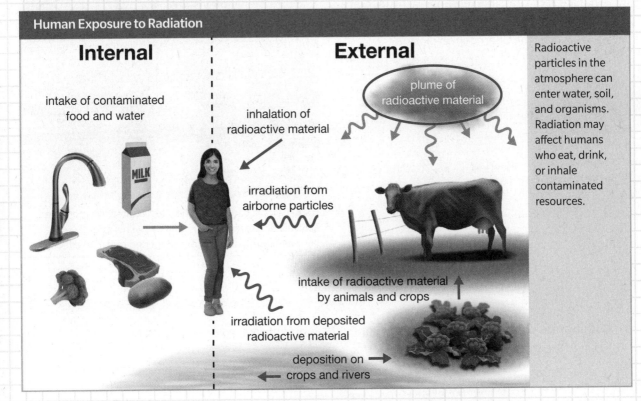

Internal

intake of contaminated food and water

MILK

External

plume of radioactive material

inhalation of radioactive material

irradiation from airborne particles

intake of radioactive material by animals and crops

irradiation from deposited radioactive material

deposition on crops and rivers

Radioactive particles in the atmosphere can enter water, soil, and organisms. Radiation may affect humans who eat, drink, or inhale contaminated resources.

Continue Your Exploration

1. Which are some of the effects of radiation poisoning? Select all that apply.

   A. headaches

   B. vomiting

   C. hair loss

   D. death/reduced life span

2. By what process did the radiation spread across such a large area?

3. Why is the impact of the Chernobyl disaster so long lasting?

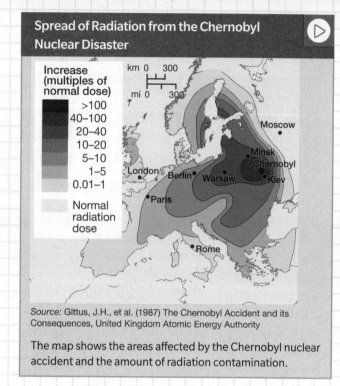

Spread of Radiation from the Chernobyl Nuclear Disaster

Increase (multiples of normal dose)
- >100
- 40–100
- 20–40
- 10–20
- 5–10
- 1–5
- 0.01–1

Normal radiation dose

Source: Gittus, J.H., et al. (1987) The Chernobyl Accident and its Consequences, United Kingdom Atomic Energy Authority

The map shows the areas affected by the Chernobyl nuclear accident and the amount of radiation contamination.

4. What are some possible reasons for the increase in the number of wildlife in the affected areas 25 years after the Chernobyl explosion?

Humans have been out of the affected areas for more than 25 years. In the absence of humans, wildlife numbers have increased, despite some lingering radiation effects.

5. **Collaborate** Research changes made to improve safety of nuclear power plants as a result of the accident at the Chernobyl Nuclear Power Plant.

Can You Explain It?

Name: _____   **Date:** _____

How can farming on land contribute to the growth of algal blooms in the ocean?

EVIDENCE NOTEBOOK

Refer to the notes in your Evidence Notebook to help you construct an explanation for how farming on land can contribute to the growth of algal blooms in the ocean.

1. State your claim. Make sure your claim fully explains how farming on land can contribute to algal blooms in the ocean.

2. Summarize the evidence you have gathered to support your claim and explain your reasoning.

Checkpoints

Answer the following questions to check your understanding of the lesson.

Use the photo to answer Question 3.

3. How might these wind turbines impact the environment?

   A. impact the biosphere by endangering birds in flight

   B. impact the geosphere when installed

   C. impact the atmosphere by polluting the air

   D. impact the hydrosphere by changing ocean currents

Use the photo to answer Questions 4–5.

4. The area in the photo was originally a forested mountain. Building the structures and ski slopes probably affected the environment in a positive / negative way, by fragmenting / preserving natural habitats.

5. The snowmakers shown on the left of the image use a freshwater source to create snow for the resort. Which of the following questions should scientists investigate to determine if these snowmakers impact the environment? Select all that apply.

   A. What is the water source for the snowmakers?

   B. Where do the snowmakers get their power?

   C. Are the snowmakers ugly?

   D. Are the snowmakers a danger to birds in the area?

6. Because a change in one part of the Earth system can / cannot affect other parts, it may be easy / difficult to fully analyze the effects of a human activity. Scientists must collect and analyze data to determine whether a change in the environment is caused by human activity.

7. Creating new roads can alter the biosphere by destroying rocks / habitats. Human actions, such as overfishing, can negatively affect the biosphere by causing some species to become better adapted / extinct.

Interactive Review

Complete this section to review the main concepts of the lesson.

All living things depend on their environment to provide the things they need. A change in the environment may be caused by natural events or human actions, or both.

A. How could natural events and human actions change a coastline?

Human actions can affect all parts of the Earth system, which include the hydrosphere, atmosphere, geosphere, and biosphere.

B. How might a change to the hydrosphere affect the biosphere?

Human impacts on the environment can be positive or negative and vary in scale over time and space.

C. Give an example of a human activity that has a greater impact over a longer period of time than it does in the short term.

(b) ©Climate.gov/National Oceanic And Atmospheric Administration (NOAA)

Reducing Human Impacts on the Environment

A wildlife overpass allows wildlife to safely move between the parts of their habitat, which has been split by a highway.

By the end of this lesson . . .

you will be able to develop methods to monitor and reduce human impacts on the environment.

Go online to view the digital version of the Hands-On Lab for this lesson and to download additional lab resources.

CAN YOU EXPLAIN IT?

What are two environmental problems that contour farming solves?

Farmers can plow the ground and plant crops in straight lines. They can also use contour farming. Contour farming follows the shape of the land when farmers plow and plant.

1. When rain falls on the farm in the photo, what will happen to the water? What factors determine what happens to water that falls on the farm?

2. How can water flowing over land change the shape of the land?

 EVIDENCE NOTEBOOK As you explore this lesson, gather evidence to explain the effects of contour farming on the environment.

Describing Methods for Monitoring Human Impacts on the Environment

Humans affect the environment in many ways. Sometimes, our actions have unwanted or even catastrophic effects. In order to prevent or correct effects that harm the environment or human health, people gather data. For example, water quality data can be used to find out if water is safe to drink. Some pollutants may not be visible. So, special tools or methods may be needed to determine water safety.

The quality of water varies depending on where it is from.

3. Think about some of the things that might make water unsafe to drink. How can you decide if the water in each beaker in the photo is safe to drink?

Resource Use

The environment provides many resources for humans, such as land, water, and air. Human use of a resource may make that resource unavailable or unsuitable for other purposes. For example, some land uses can destroy or fragment a habitat. This negatively affects the organisms that live there.

There are organizations around the world that record data about the use of land and water. In the United States, much of this data is collected by the United States Geological Survey (USGS). Water or land use may also be regulated and measured by local governments or organizations.

Collection of Resource Use Data

People may take photos or use specialized sensors to measure and record data. Data may be collected locally or remotely. Meters measure the amount of water that is pumped from an aquifer or the amount used at a specific place. Satellite cameras and instruments remotely collect data about larger areas, such as an area the size of a city or larger.

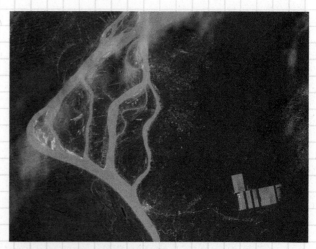

The satellite photo shows how an area of forest near a river has been cleared by humans.

Analysis of Resource Use Data

Once data are collected, the data must be analyzed. Resource use data may be shown in many ways, such as a photo, map, table, or chart. Scientists look at trends when they analyze data. They also use the data to determine correlations. Data are correlated when two data sets have related trends. For example, if one variable increases, another variable increases or decreases at the same time. When data are strongly correlated, scientists look at the data or collect more data to find out if there is a cause-and-effect relationship between the two variables. For a relationship to be cause-and-effect, there must be a mechanism by which one variable causes change in the other.

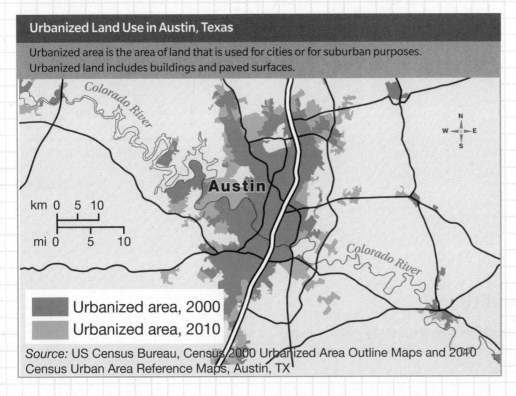

Urbanized Land Use in Austin, Texas

Urbanized area is the area of land that is used for cities or for suburban purposes. Urbanized land includes buildings and paved surfaces.

Urbanized area, 2000
Urbanized area, 2010

Source: US Census Bureau, Census 2000 Urbanized Area Outline Maps and 2010 Census Urban Area Reference Maps, Austin, TX

4. Analyze the map. What does the change in urbanized area indicate about the change in land use of the city? How might that change affect the environment?

Data about water use are collected so that people can keep track of the amount of water that remains available. Most places on Earth have water beneath the ground in aquifers. People pump this groundwater to the surface for drinking, irrigation, and industrial uses. Groundwater in an aquifer is replaced slowly as water from the surface flows through permeable soil or rock. However, water is not likely to be absorbed if it cannot seep through the land surface or if the land slopes steeply. Impermeable surfaces, such as concrete, do not allow water to enter soil. Instead, the water runs off the land as surface water, ending up in rivers, lakes, and oceans.

When an aquifer is depleted, it can cause the ground to sink. Another effect of a depleted aquifer is the contamination of the remaining water with salt from nearby oceans or other contaminants. Contaminated or salty groundwater is unusable for most of the purposes for which groundwater is used by humans.

5. Assume the trend of pumping water from the aquifer continues at its current rate. Predict the water level in the aquifer in the years after 2016. Support your claim with evidence and reasoning.

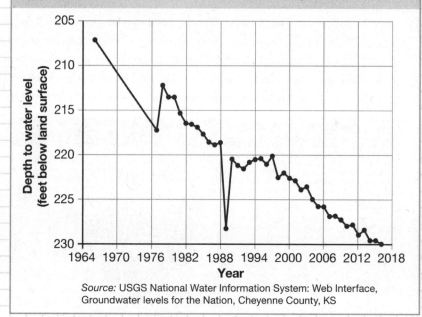

Water Level of a Well in the High Plains Aquifer

This graph shows the water level in a well getting farther from the surface of the ground. This means that the amount of water in the aquifer has decreased.

Source: USGS National Water Information System: Web Interface, Groundwater levels for the Nation, Cheyenne County, KS

Resource Quality

Air, soil, and water are essential resources for humans. When these resources become polluted by human activities, their usefulness decreases. This affects humans and other organisms in many ways.

Do the Math
Compare Concentrations

Pollution levels are usually described in terms of concentration. The concentration of a pollutant is the amount of the polluting substance compared to the total amount of the sample. For example, a concentration of 1% is one unit (gram or mL) of pollutant in 100 units total. However, amounts of pollutants much smaller than 1% can be harmful. Therefore, pollution may be measured in parts per million or parts per billion. One part per million (1 ppm) is one unit of pollutant in one million units total. One part per billion (1 ppb) is one unit per one billion units.

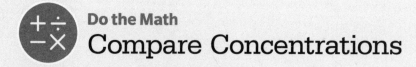

6. A concentration of 1% is 10,000 times greater / less than 1 ppm.
A concentration of 1 ppm is 1,000 times greater / less than 1 ppb.
A concentration of 1 ppb is 10,000,000 times greater / less than 1%.

Collection of Resource Quality Data

There are different ways to collect data about pollution in the environment. Some pollution can be observed directly, like when you smell smoke in the air or see color changes in water. Other pollution can be monitored by observing their effects on living things, such as by causing the leaves of plants to change color or fall off. Scientists also use tools that can measure substances in air, water, or soil. They can take a sample to a lab or use instruments to analyze data in the field. Some equipment can take measurements from far away, such as sensors on satellites, and send data to computers at remote locations.

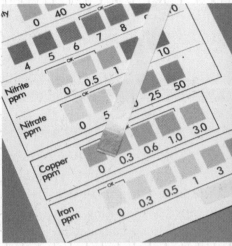

7. The Environmental Protection Agency (EPA) is a government organization that regulates pollutants. The EPA set the maximum safe amount of copper in drinking water at 1.3 ppm. The test result for a sample of water is shown in the photo. According to this test, the water is / is not safe to drink.

The test results show the amount of copper in a sample of drinking water.

Analysis of Resource Quality Data

The amount of pollutants in a resource affects the quality of the resource. Acceptable concentrations of different pollutants are generally set by state or federal agencies, such as the Environmental Protection Agency (EPA). The acceptable concentration of a pollutant depends on the pollutant, its effects on the health of humans or other organisms, and the way the resource is used. For example, drinking water has different acceptable limits for pollutants than water used for watering crops.

Scientists may also measure concentrations of nonpolluting substances to make sure the levels are acceptable. Soil quality measures may include testing for certain nutrients, to make sure the soil can support certain crops.

8. This photo shows water flooding a farm field. How can the effects of runoff from this field be monitored?

Water flows between rows of crops on a farm. As the water flows, it picks up dirt and other substances, including fertilizers or pesticides.

9. What substances might runoff from a farm contain? How might these substances affect the quality of nearby surface water or of the soil in the field? Record your evidence.

Propose How to Monitor Human Impacts

Surface and groundwater resources near cities receive pollutants from many different sources. To minimize impacts of urban areas on the environment, city officials must monitor the sources of pollution.

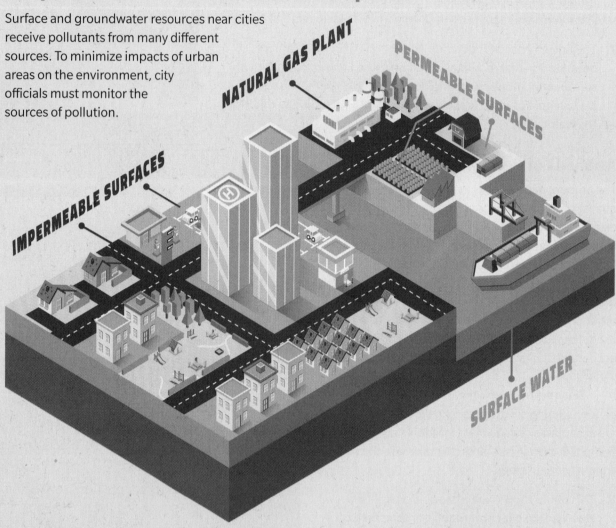

10. The town in the drawing formed a committee to work on ways to detect possible problems with the quality of groundwater and surface water. As a member of the committee, propose what sources of pollution should be monitored and how they should be checked.

_____

_____

_____

_____

_____

_____

Developing a Method to Monitor a Human Impact on the Environment

Once scientists know that a human activity impacts the environment, they can develop methods to monitor the activity and its impact. Monitoring is necessary to determine if changes in human activity affect the impact on the environment.

11. Think about some of the things you disposed of today or in the past week. How could you monitor the solid waste you generate in a week?

Solid Waste

Solid waste includes organic and inorganic materials. Organic materials, such as paper, are found in or made from living things. Some organic materials decay quickly. Sometimes humans change organic materials in ways that make them take longer to decay. For example, pressure-treated wood is chemically treated so that it is more durable. Inorganic materials, such as glass and metals, may take very long periods of time to break down by natural processes.

Every day, about 2 kilograms (kg) of solid waste per person is generated in the United States. Solid waste is typically taken to a landfill when it is discarded. Most landfills are designed to prevent pollution, but waste can dissolve and pollute groundwater or surface water. When some organic materials decay without oxygen, as they do in a landfill, they produce methane. Methane is a greenhouse gas. But it can also be burned to produce electrical energy. Particularly hazardous solid waste goes to specially designed landfills. About one-third of the solid waste in the United States is either recycled or composted.

Some landfills cover large areas of land. Natural processes break down the solid waste over time, which can cause pollution in the area.

Under certain conditions, some organic materials, such as plants, decay into compost.

Compost is a nutrient-rich material. It looks like soil and can be used as a natural fertilizer.

The Engineering Design Process

You can use the engineering design process (EDP) to develop a way to monitor a human activity to determine its environmental impact. The first step of the EDP is identifying the problem, for example "how do we monitor solid waste produced by a school?" Engineering design is an iterative process. That means you might not develop the best solution on the first try. Instead, you assess the results and then adjust your solution. The solution you choose depends on the criteria and constraints. To ensure a solution will solve the problem, you must make sure criteria and constraints are well defined.

The Engineering Design Process Flow Chart

12. Write each step of the engineering design process in the correct location in the flow chart.

- Define   • Research   • Model
- Evaluate   • Brainstorm   • Test
- ~~Identify~~

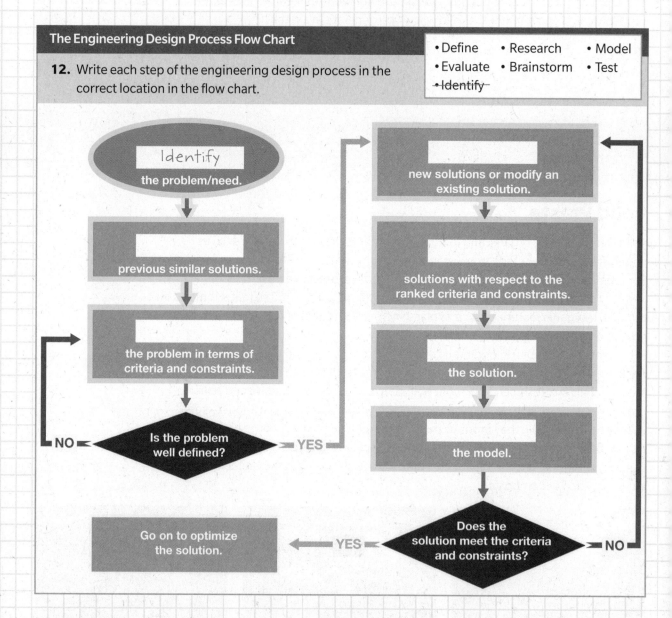

13. Each time the EDP is used, steps may be completed in a different sequence. You may return to any previous step in the process at any time, but you may not skip steps. For example, you must always model / optimize the solution before you can test / identify the model. The problem must be well defined / tested before you research / brainstorm possible solutions.

Hands-On Lab

Design a Method to Monitor Solid Waste from a School

You will use the engineering design process to develop a method to monitor the amount and types of solid waste generated by your school.

Scientists know that solid waste in a landfill has a negative impact on the environment. Reducing the amount of solid waste sent to landfills can reduce the negative impact on the environment.

MATERIALS

• computer, for research (optional)

Procedure and Analysis

STEP 1 **Research the Problem** With your group, research the problem of monitoring the amount and types of solid waste and identify existing solutions for similar problems.

STEP 2 **Define the Problem** State the problem related to monitoring your school's waste. Then add at least one constraint to more completely define the problem of monitoring solid waste from your school.

Problem:

Criterion	Constraint
1. Information is measurable.	1. Students must not handle hazardous waste.
2. Data can be collected by students.	2. All activities must occur during school hours.
3. Waste to be evaluated currently goes to a large trash container outside.	3.

STEP 3 **Brainstorm Solutions** Based on your research, brainstorm possible methods that could be used to monitor the solid waste generated by your school. Record all possible solutions on a separate paper.

STEP 4 **Language SmArts | Choose a Promising Solution** Evaluate all of the possible solutions from Step 3. Choose the solution that you think will best satisfy the criteria and constraints of the problem. On a separate sheet of paper, write a paragraph to describe the solution you chose. Explain why you think the solution will work.

STEP 5 **Choose a Solution to Be Tested** Draw a diagram of your chosen solution.

STEP 6 **Propose a Test** Before a solution can be implemented, it must be tested. The test results should show whether the solution fully meets the criteria and constraints. In the space below, describe how you would test your solution.

Monitor Solid Waste from a Neighborhood

14. In what ways might the waste from a neighborhood be different from or similar to the waste from a school?

_____

_____

_____

_____

_____

_____

Homes generate many different types of solid waste.

15. Could you use the same method to monitor the waste from your school and the waste from a neighborhood? Explain why or why not.

_____

_____

_____

_____

_____

Describing Methods to Reduce Human Impacts on the Environment

Scientists monitor the environment in many ways. When data show that a human activity impacts the environment in a negative way, scientists and engineers develop ways to reduce these negative impacts. A change in behavior may reduce human impacts on the environment. A new technology might also be needed.

16. You are going on a three-day camping trip with friends. You are able to bring only one gallon of water per person per day. How might you change the way you use water to make sure your supply lasts long enough?

When you are away from a clean water supply, you need to carry drinking water with you. You might also use a tool or process to purify water that you find so that it is safe to drink.

Resource Availability

Using a resource in a sustainable way means that the resource continues to be available. Renewable resources are resources that can, under certain circumstances, be replaced as fast as they are used. For example, new trees can replace a forest when old trees are cut down. In order for these resources to be sustainable, they cannot be used faster than they can be replaced. Other resources, such as metals that are mined or oil that is pumped from the ground, are nonrenewable. No new metal or oil replaces them once they are used. A nonrenewable resource will eventually be used up. Use of nonrenewable resources must be minimized to make sure the resource is available for as long as possible.

Careful Use of Resources

What are some ways that humans can reduce the rate at which we consume resources and make them more sustainable? It is possible to reduce use by changing the way we behave. For example, you can turn on the faucet only to rinse your mouth and toothbrush. You will use less water this way than if you leave the water running while you brush your teeth. Better technology can also reduce resource use. Modern air conditioning units are more efficient than older ones due to improved technology. They use less energy to cool buildings and so reduce the use of energy resources. If you monitor how you use resources and are careful to use only the amount you need, you can often reduce your resource use.

17. Do the Math A hotel installs dual-flush toilets to help conserve water. The new toilets use 1.6 gallons for one full flush and 0.9 gallons for one partial flush. Measurements show that in the first week there were 1,190 full flushes and 3,150 partial flushes. How many gallons of water were saved for the week compared to a week in which all the flushes were full flushes?

This toilet has two types of flushes. One uses much less water than the other.

Resource Reuse and Recycling

Another way to make resource use more sustainable is to make products last longer by reusing them. A plastic bag or a sturdy canvas bag can be used many times when shopping. Each time you reuse the bag, you reduce the number of new bags that are needed. That saves resources. Things that cannot be reused can often be recycled as materials for new products. Used paper can be recycled to make new paper to reduce the need for harvesting trees. Recycling metal, plastic, or glass containers provides materials for new products. It reduces the use of resources. The diagram shows how recycling aluminum reduces the amount of aluminum that is mined.

Mining bauxite to produce aluminum has a large impact on the environment. Aluminum is made into many products. These products can be recycled over and over, saving material and energy resources needed to mine bauxite.

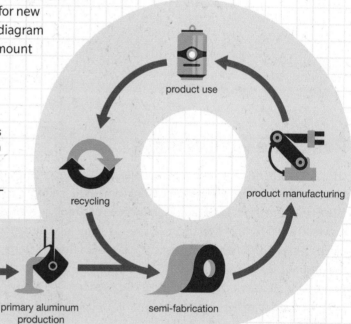

product use

recycling

product manufacturing

bauxite mining

alumina refining

primary aluminum production

semi-fabrication

18. How does recycling aluminum reduce the environmental impact of the human use of aluminum?

Resource Quality

The quality of a resource determines its value and usefulness to people and affects the health of people and the environment. Some human activities affect the quality of resources like water or soil. Quality of resources can be negatively affected by overuse, by improper use, and by pollution.

Behavior Change

Sometimes the quality of a resource can be maintained or improved if people change their behavior. A person may choose to buy food grown locally rather than food that is shipped from another state or country. This change in behavior may reduce air pollution, because foods are often shipped in vehicles or trains that use fossil fuels for energy. Some people leave trash and other items on beaches. These items may then be washed into the ocean, adding to water pollution. By changing their behavior to make sure that these items are disposed of responsibly, people can reduce water pollution.

19. What are some questions you could investigate to determine if a change in behavior would impact resource quality?

Technology Development and Use

New technologies take time and money to develop. Newer technology often costs more than existing technology. Often, without a catastrophic event, people may not see the need to switch to a newer technology. For years, people dumped raw sewage into the same bodies of water from which they drank. It was not until people started getting sick from the polluted water that communities invested in methods to filter and treat drinking water. Since the 1800s, humans have been burning coal to generate electrical energy. Burning coal adds greenhouse gases and other pollutants to the air. Mining coal may also cause air, water, and soil pollution if it is not done carefully. Due to societal needs and regulations, scientists have worked to develop technologies to reduce the pollution produced by mining and burning coal. Scientists have also developed technologies such as wind turbines. Wind turbines generate clean energy because they do not create air pollution when they are running. However, building wind turbines does require resources. Obtaining those resources may impact the environment negatively.

20. **Discuss** With a partner, discuss reasons that humans may continue to use technology that negatively affects the environment when technology with fewer negative effects exists.

Case Study: The Dust Bowl

The Great Plains in the central part of the United States was once a vast grassland. The grasses had deep roots and were adapted to the climate of the plains. Herds of animals lived on these plains and fed on the grasses. In the 1800s, few people used the land to farm crops. In the early 1900s, new technologies made it easier to farm large areas of land. As the price of grain increased, more farmers began plowing the soil and planting grain crops over large areas of land. The grain plants did not have deep roots like the native grasses. When a long drought happened in the 1930s, the fields became dry and crops died. Heavy winds picked up the dry soil and formed giant dust storms. These dust storms caused respiratory problems. Sometimes humans and animals in the area died. Swarms of grasshoppers ate many remaining crops, leading to even less protection for the soil. The loss of fertile topsoil made it more difficult to grow crops.

Native grasses have deep roots that hold soil in place and keep the soil healthy.

Without deep roots to hold the soil in place, the soil was carried away by the wind in massive dust storms.

21. Dust storms occurred after humans changed the environment. Which activities contributed to severe dust storms? Select all that apply.

    A. plowing soil for crop planting

    B. overgrazing herds of cattle

    C. removing native grasses

    D. building towns and dirt roads

22. **Write** In the 1950s, a drought similar to the one in the 1930s was predicted. The United States Congress offered farmers money to turn farmland back into grassland to avoid another dust bowl. Farmers had to decide whether to accept the offer or to continue farming their land as they had been doing. Think about the situation from the farmers' point of view. On a separate sheet of paper, write a letter responding to this offer as a farmer in the area at the time. Say whether you would or would not accept the government offer and explain your reasoning.

23. How does the slope of land or direction of plowing affect how water runs over the land? What method or technology could reduce the runoff? Record your evidence.

Analyze the Environmental Impact of a Power Plant

Conventional power plants burn fuel to heat water and make steam. This steam turns a turbine to generate electrical energy. The steam is then cooled so that the water can be heated again. This heating and cooling repeats in a cycle. The water used to cool the steam is often drawn from nearby surface water. The steam transfers thermal energy to the water, which makes the water hotter and the steam cooler. The hot water is released into a nearby body of water. It causes thermal pollution that may make the body of water too warm for plants and animals living in it. In a combined heat and power (CHP) plant, shown in the diagram, the hot water heats buildings instead of being discharged into the nearby body of water.

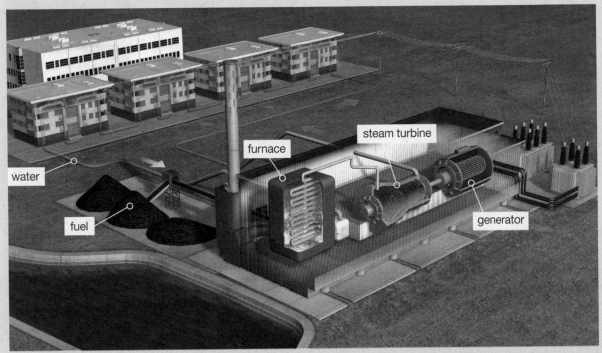

Follow the path of the water through the furnace and steam turbine. Then notice how the hot water passes through the buildings. The water cools down as the buildings are heated. The cool water then returns to the furnace in a continuous cycle.

24. Which of the following are ways in which the CHP plant has a lower impact on the environment than a traditional power plant? Select all that apply.

A. It uses thermal energy more efficiently than the traditional plant.

B. It causes less thermal pollution in the nearby body of water.

C. It uses fuel that causes less pollution than a traditional plant.

D. It does not produce greenhouse gases when fuels are burned.

Developing a Method to Reduce a Human Impact on the Environment

Define and Evaluate a Problem Related to Solid Waste

Recall that the engineering design process is a tool that you can use anytime you want to develop a solution for a specific problem. Solutions may be a process or a physical object. The first step of the engineering design process is to identify the problem. An engineering problem must be stated very clearly so that a solution can be developed to address the exact problem. The purpose of the criteria and constraints is to define the problem in a way that makes it possible to measure how well the solution works. Engineers begin with as many ideas as possible, then evaluate the solutions to choose a solution they think will be the most successful. A promising solution can then be tested and improved until all the criteria and constraints are satisfied.

The trash in this can is all going to a landfill. But some of this waste could be disposed of in a different way.

25. Which of the following changes might reduce the impact of your school's solid waste on the environment? Select all that apply.

   A. Start school later in the morning.

   B. Compost food waste to make garden fertilizer.

   C. Reuse the back of worksheets as scratch paper.

   D. Collect plastic bottles for recycling.

26. **Discuss** With a partner or group, discuss the sources and types of solid waste that are generated in your school.

Hands-On Lab

Evaluate a Method to Reduce the Impact of Solid Waste on the Environment

You will use the engineering design process to develop a method for reducing the environmental impact of solid waste generated by your school.

MATERIALS
- camera (optional)
- meterstick (optional)
- scale (optional)

Procedure and Analysis

STEP 1 **Research the Problem** Research the problem and possible solutions for reducing the impact of solid waste.

STEP 2 **Define the Problem** State the engineering problem related to reducing the environmental impact of your school's waste. Then determine criteria and constraints for your problem.

Problem:	
Criterion	Constraint
1. Can be directed by students	1. Does not require any money
2.	2.
3.	3.
4.	4.

STEP 3 **Brainstorm Solutions** Based on your research, brainstorm possible methods that you could use to reduce the amount of solid waste that is generated by your school and goes to a landfill. Record all possible solutions on a separate sheet of paper.

STEP 4 **Choose a Solution** Choose the most promising solution from your brainstorming step. Describe your solution and explain how it addresses the engineering problem.

STEP 5 **Design and Implement a Test** Decide the best method for testing your solution. Perform the test and record your test results on a separate sheet of paper.

STEP 6 **Analyze Results** Analyze the results to determine whether your solution would work for the whole school. Use evidence and reasoning to support your claim.

STEP 7 **Evaluate the Solution** Based on your test results, can your chosen solution be used to reduce the environmental impact of solid waste generated by your school? If yes, explain how the solution could be used to reduce the school's environmental impact. If no, how would you change your solution to make it more likely to solve the problem?

Reduce the Energy Use of a School

Schools require electrical energy for many different needs. The environmental impact of the electrical energy used by a school depends on the source of the power.

27. Examine the graph. Brainstorm ways that the school might reduce its energy use. A constraint of this problem is that the recommended change cannot require a lot of money.

_____

_____

_____

_____

_____

_____

_____

_____

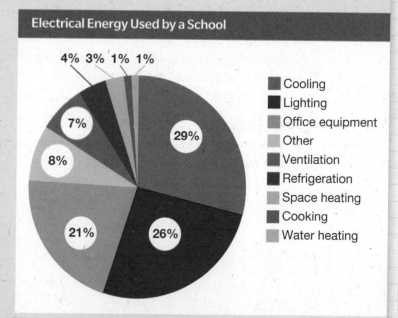

Electrical Energy Used by a School

4% 3% 1% 1%
7%
8%
29%
21%
26%

- Cooling
- Lighting
- Office equipment
- Other
- Ventilation
- Refrigeration
- Space heating
- Cooking
- Water heating

Continue Your Exploration

Name: _____   Date: _____

Check out the path below or go online to choose one of the other paths shown.

Urban Planning to Reduce Impact

- **Hands-On Labs** ✋
- **Air Pollution Past and Present**
- **Propose Your Own Path**

Go online to choose one of these other paths.

In 2016, about 54% of the world's population lived in cities. A city can have a large impact on the environment, due to the large human population of the city. Urban planners design transportation systems. They also design systems to provide water, electrical energy, and sewage services to all the people in a city. The design of these systems affects the environmental impact of a city. Planned public transportation, such as trains and buses, helps reduce the use of cars. Some cities, such as Copenhagen, Denmark, build infrastructure to make it easier for people to use bicycles instead of cars to get to and from work.

Compare the populations of New York City and Tokyo. How are the people in these cities distributed?

_____

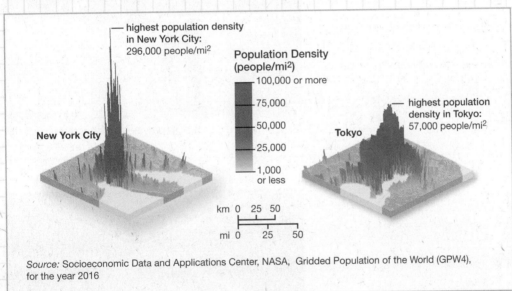

Source: Socioeconomic Data and Applications Center, NASA, Gridded Population of the World (GPW4), for the year 2016

1. The population of Tokyo is a little greater than the population of New York City. Each year, about 1.6 billion people ride the subway in New York City, but about 3.7 billion ride the subway in Tokyo. Can the population distribution for each city be used to explain the large difference in the number of subway riders each year? What other information might you need to explain this difference?

Continue Your Exploration

2. Some urban planners design transportation systems that reduce human impact. How might redesigning a roadway to add a protected bike lane impact the environment?

Riding a bicycle on a busy street is dangerous. Drivers often do not see cyclists or they drive closer to cyclists than is safe.

3. Urban planners redesign a roadway to encourage people to bike from place to place. How can they monitor or measure environmental impacts related to the new bike lanes?

An unprotected bike lane improves safety. But the cyclist still must deal with vehicles moving in and out of the bike lane.

This protected bike lane is located between parked cars and the sidewalk. The parked cars protect bicyclists from moving vehicles.

4. **Collaborate** With a small group, brainstorm non-transportation-related ways that cities can reduce their environmental impact. Make a brochure to present your ideas to city officials.

Can You Explain It?

Name: _____   Date: _____

What are two environmental problems that contour farming solves?

 EVIDENCE NOTEBOOK

Refer to the notes in your Evidence Notebook to help you construct an explanation for the effects of contour farming on the environment.

1. State your claim. Make sure your claim fully explains how contour farming can solve two environmental problems.

2. Summarize the evidence you have gathered to support your claim and explain your reasoning.

Checkpoints

Answer the following questions to check your understanding of the lesson.

Use the photo to answer Questions 3 and 4.

3. Which problem does the storm drain label solve?

   A. It keeps waterways from flooding.

   B. It stops people from overfishing.

   C. It protects groundwater from pollution.

   D. It discourages people from polluting waterways.

4. Which of these criteria appear to be satisfied by the label in the photo? Select all that apply.

   A. It is low cost.

   B. It does not require new technology.

   C. It stops all possible pollution.

   D. It records data on the effectiveness of the solution.

Use the chart to answer Questions 5 and 6.

5. About how many times more water is needed to produce a pound of beef than a pound of lentils?

   A. 0.5 times

   B. 1.9 times

   C. 13.5 times

   D. 1450 times

6. A family chooses to eat lentils instead of beef for dinner to reduce the family's impact on the environment. The chart does / does not support this reasoning, because raising beef for food requires less / more water than lentils. Using more water has a greater / lesser impact on the environment, because water is an important and often scarce resource.

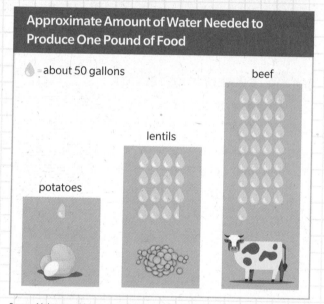

Approximate Amount of Water Needed to Produce One Pound of Food

= about 50 gallons

potatoes
lentils
beef

Source: Mekonnen, M.M. and Hoekstra, A.Y. (2010), Value of Water Research Report Series Nos. 47 and 48, UNESCO-IHE, Delft, the Netherlands

7. Which of the following data for monitoring human impacts on the environment can be collected by a satellite?

   A. land use in a rural area

   B. quality of a body of water

   C. air quality around a city

   D. water use per person in a city

8. A new city program encourages people to bike rather than drive a car to work. It is hoped that this program will monitor / reduce air pollution in the city. The program effectiveness could be monitored / reduced by surveying residents to see how they commute.

Interactive Review

Complete this section to review the main concepts of the lesson.

Scientists monitor resource use and quality to determine how humans impact the environment.

A. What types of resources do scientists monitor and how do they monitor them?

The engineering design process can be used to develop a method for monitoring human impacts on the environment.

B. How can the engineering design process be used to develop a method for monitoring the environmental impact of a human activity?

People can reduce their impact on the environment by changing their behavior or by using new or different technologies.

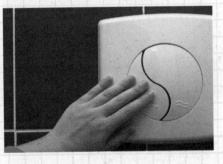

C. How might the effect on the environment of the human activity of traveling be reduced?

The engineering design process can be used to develop ways to reduce human impacts on the environment.

D. Why would a community decide to use the engineering design process as they look for a solution for an environmental problem?

Climate Change

Ice is an important habitat for many seals. When the pack ice breaks up earlier than usual, these seals may starve or drown.

By the end of this lesson . . .

you will be able to examine evidence of factors that have caused the rise in global temperatures over the past century.

Go online to view the digital version of the Hands-On Lab for this lesson and to download additional lab resources.

CAN YOU EXPLAIN IT?

What could be causing ice and permafrost to melt in Shishmaref?

The 400-year-old fishing village of Shishmaref, Alaska, used to be surrounded by thick sea ice every winter. Over the last century, less sea ice has been forming and ocean waves have eroded much of the shoreline.

The ground here used to be frozen throughout the year. This *permafrost* has started melting in recent years. The resulting loose soil erodes quickly, damaging buildings and houses in Shishmaref.

1. The amount of sea ice and permafrost have steadily decreased near Shishmaref, Alaska, over the last century. The loss of ice has allowed ocean waves to erode the land and destroy property. What might be causing this melting?

EVIDENCE NOTEBOOK As you explore this lesson, gather evidence to help explain why ice and permafrost are melting in Shishmaref.

GRILLO/AP Images

Exploring Earth's Climate

Climate

Weather can change from day to day or even several times in one day. *Weather* describes the conditions of the atmosphere over a short period. "A hot, sunny afternoon" or a "cold, snowy day" are descriptions of weather. By contrast, *climate* describes the weather conditions in an area over a long period, such as 30 years. For example, a tropical rain forest climate is warm and rainy throughout the year.

The average climate of Earth can also be described. *Global climate* is often expressed as Earth's average surface temperature, which is currently 16 °C (61°F). Earth's average surface temperature is a combination of the sea surface temperature and the near-surface air temperature.

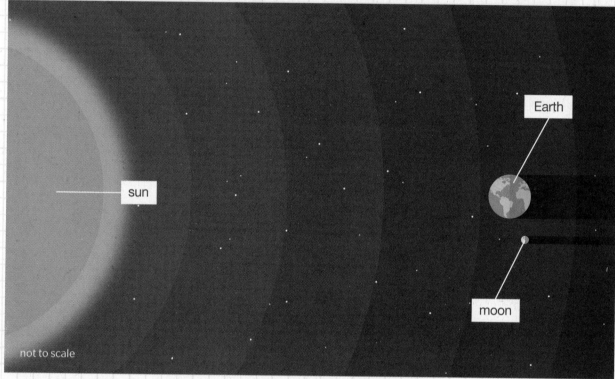

not to scale

Earth and the moon are about the same distance from the sun. Earth's temperatures range from about –88 °C to 58 °C (–126 °F to 136 °F). The moon's temperatures range from about –233 °C to 123 °C (–387 °F to 253 °F).

2. **Discuss** Why do you think the temperature range on Earth is so different from the temperature range on the moon? Make a list of ideas with a partner.

Earth's Climate System

Earth's climate is the result of complex interactions between the biosphere, geosphere, hydrosphere, and atmosphere. These interactions are driven by energy from the sun. Earth's atmosphere and surface absorb and reflect incoming sunlight. Darker surfaces absorb more sunlight than lighter surfaces do. For example, soil and ocean water absorb more sunlight than clouds, ice, and snow do.

The total amount of energy that enters the Earth system almost exactly equals the total amount of energy that leaves the Earth system. However, solar energy can remain in the Earth system for different periods of time. For example, oceans retain solar energy for a longer period of time than land does. This energy is transferred around the globe by ocean currents and is a major influence on weather and climate patterns.

The Greenhouse Effect

Just like a greenhouse regulates temperatures for plants, Earth's atmosphere regulates temperatures on Earth. The **greenhouse effect** is the warming of the surface and lower atmosphere of Earth that occurs when greenhouse gases absorb and reradiate energy. Greenhouse gases include carbon dioxide, methane, water vapor, and other gases. The processes that cause the greenhouse effect are shown in the diagram. Solar energy is absorbed and reflected by Earth's atmosphere and surface. The absorbed energy is eventually radiated back out as infrared radiation. Some infrared radiation goes back out to space while some is absorbed again by greenhouse gases. The infrared radiation absorbed by greenhouse gases is reradiated and some is reabsorbed. As a result, energy stays in the Earth system longer than it would stay if there were no greenhouse gases.

The greenhouse effect keeps the temperature range on Earth suitable for life as we know it. If the concentration of greenhouse gases increases, more radiation is absorbed and reradiated within the Earth system. As a result, Earth's average surface temperature increases. If the concentration of greenhouse gases decreases, Earth's average surface temperature decreases.

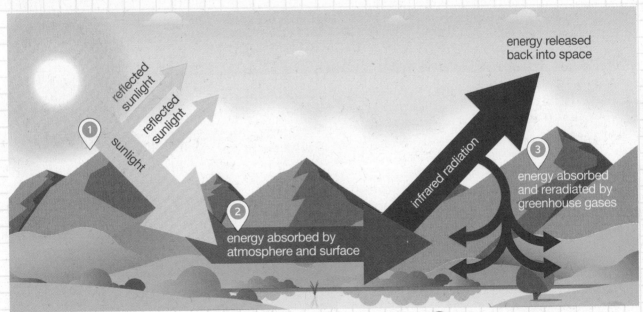

① Sunlight travels through space and reaches Earth. Some solar energy is reflected by the atmosphere and Earth's surface.

② Some solar energy is absorbed by the atmosphere and surface. It is transformed into infrared radiation and is reradiated.

③ Greenhouse gases absorb some of the outgoing infrared radiation and reradiate it back into the Earth system.

Hands-On Lab
Model the Greenhouse Effect

In this experiment, you will construct and use a physical model to explain how greenhouse gases affect Earth's temperature.

Procedure and Analysis

STEP 1   Pour dark soil into both bottles so the depth of soil is about 5 cm. Why do you think dark soil is used in this model?

STEP 2   Cover the top of one bottle with clear plastic wrap. Tape the plastic wrap to the bottle so that air cannot escape.

STEP 3   Set up a data table to record the temperature of the air in each bottle every minute for a total of 15 minutes.

STEP 4   Place the two bottles in direct sunlight. Use the temperature probes to measure and record the temperature of each bottle every minute for a total of 15 minutes. Record your data.

MATERIALS
- bottle, plastic, 2L, with the top cut off (2)
- masking tape
- plastic wrap, clear
- ruler
- soil, dark
- temperature probe (2)

Analysis

STEP 5 The bottle with / without the plastic wrap models the greenhouse effect. The air in the bottle with / without plastic wrap became warmer than the bottle with / without the plastic wrap did.

STEP 6 In this model, the bottle represents the Earth system. The atmosphere is represented by the air and the plastic wrap, and the surface is represented by the soil in the bottle. Models are used to represent the real-world, however, no model is perfect. What are some differences between your model and the real-world?

STEP 7 How could you improve your model to better represent the Earth system?

STEP 8 How might you modify your model to show that changes in the concentration of greenhouse gases in the atmosphere affect temperature over time?

Language SmArts

Explain Temperature Ranges on Earth and the Moon

3. Think about the temperature ranges on Earth and the moon. Unlike Earth, the moon has almost no atmosphere. Explain why the range of temperatures on Earth is so different from that on the moon. Cite evidence to support your explanation.

_____

_____

_____

_____

_____

_____

Identifying Global Climate Change Factors

Global Climate Change

Global climate has changed throughout Earth's history, due to both natural processes and human activities. Some climate scientists study how climate has changed in the past and compare that to how the climate is currently changing.

4. One-hundred-million-year-old fossils of tropical ferns have been found in Antarctica. Tropical ferns grow in tropical climates. Therefore, Antarctica's climate was warm and rainy / cold and dry 100 million years ago. Now, Antarctica's climate is warm and rainy / cold and dry.

Climate Data

Systematic measurement of temperatures across Earth's surface began around 1880. Today, satellites and other instruments collect detailed data. But how do we know what the climate was like thousands, or even millions, of years ago? This information comes from paleoclimate data. Look at the photos. *Paleoclimate data* contain clues about past climates and are found in rocks, fossils, tree rings, and ice cores. For example, coal commonly forms from plants that grow in swamps. Finding a 150-million-year-old layer of coal provides evidence that the area was likely a swamp 150 million years ago.

Tables, graphs, and maps are made from paleoclimate data to show trends in climate over time and in different areas on Earth. Both paleoclimate data and recent climate data are used in computer models to explore the causes and effects of climate change. Some climate models are used to predict future climate changes.

An ancient glacier passed over this rock and formed these scratches. This is evidence that the climate was very cold when the glacier existed.

Tree rings form each year as a tree grows. Wider rings form when the tree grows faster due to warmer, wetter conditions.

Fossils are the remains of living things from long ago that can give us clues about past climates. This fossil is of an animal that lived in a warm, shallow sea.

Scientists identify different gases trapped in ice that formed thousands of years ago. These data can tell scientists about the levels of greenhouse gases in Earth's past atmosphere.

Paleoclimate Temperature Reconstruction from Antarctic Ice Core Data

These data show how temperature in Antarctica changed over the last 800,000 years. Scientists use these data and others to reconstruct Earth's global climate history.

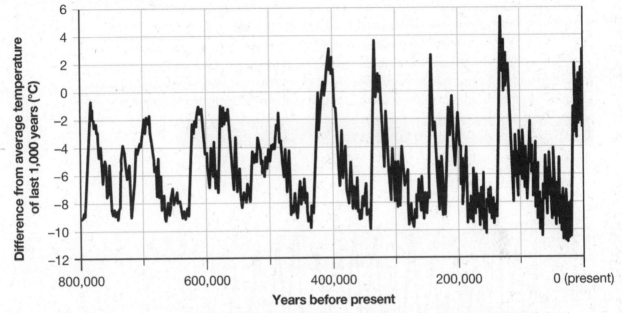

Source: National Oceanic and Atmospheric Administration, Paleoclimatology Program at NOAA's National Centers for Environmental Information.

5. The graph shows that the average surface temperature in Antarctica has changed / not changed over the last 800,000 years. Scientists think that Earth's average temperature has followed a similar pattern. If so, Earth's average temperature is currently experiencing a cooling / warming trend.

Causes of Global Climate Change

The stability of the global climate can be disturbed by short-term or sudden events. For example, explosive volcanic eruptions can temporarily lower Earth's average surface temperature for a period of weeks or for a few years. This temperature drop happens because explosive eruptions send ash particles into the atmosphere. The ash particles reflect a portion of incoming sunlight. Gradual changes also affect global climate. For example, changes in the shape of Earth's orbit occur over a period of about 100,000 years. These changes affect the amount of incoming solar radiation that reaches Earth and its distribution across Earth's surface, which affect global climate.

Human activities also cause global climate change. For example, daily activities such as driving vehicles and raising livestock emit greenhouse gases. The increased concentration of greenhouse gases in the atmosphere results in an increase in global surface temperatures. How long the temperature remains higher depends on how long the greenhouse gases remain in the atmosphere. If greenhouse gas concentrations continue to increase in the atmosphere, the temperature will continue to rise. If concentrations of greenhouse gases decrease, the temperature will stop rising and will begin to decrease.

Astronomical Changes

The shape of Earth's orbit affects global climate, and so do changes in Earth's tilt on its axis. Earth's tilt varies between about 22 to 25 degrees. These changes take place on cycles of about 41,000 years. When the tilt angle is higher, summers are warmer and winters are colder. Earth also wobbles on its axis as it orbits the sun. Over about 26,000 years, this wobble changes the timing of the seasons relative to Earth's distance from the sun. As a result, the intensity of the seasons changes.

Sunspot activity relates to the amount of solar energy that reaches Earth. However, scientific studies show that recent solar energy changes have had very little impact when compared to the changes in greenhouse gas concentrations in Earth's atmosphere.

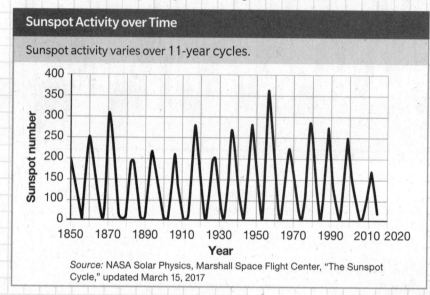

Sunspot Activity over Time

Sunspot activity varies over 11-year cycles.

Source: NASA Solar Physics, Marshall Space Flight Center, "The Sunspot Cycle," updated March 15, 2017

Changes on Earth's Surface

Earth's surface is made up of oceans, forests, deserts, ice sheets, rock, and soil. Changes in the materials exposed at Earth's surface affect global climate. Different Earth materials absorb and reflect different amounts of solar energy, and different materials retain solar energy for different amounts of time. For example, rock absorbs more solar energy than water does, but water retains energy longer than land does. In addition, some materials absorb greenhouse gases from the atmosphere. For example, forests, soils, and oceans absorb carbon dioxide from the atmosphere.

1940

2006

6. As Grinnell Glacier in Montana melts, dark soil and rock are exposed. The soil and rock absorb more / less solar energy than the ice absorbed. The result is an increase / decrease in temperature.

Both natural processes and human activities alter Earth's surface. Human activities generally change Earth's surface more quickly than natural processes do. For example, dark pavement and rooftops in a development could replace forested areas in a matter of months or years.

Changes in Earth's Atmosphere

Earth's atmosphere plays a large role in global climate. For example, the concentration of greenhouse gases is currently increasing in the atmosphere. The increase in concentration of these gases leads to an increase in the average global temperature.

Greenhouse gases enter the atmosphere from natural and human sources. For example, burning fossil fuels releases greenhouse gases into the atmosphere. Humans burn fossil fuels to power vehicles and to generate electrical energy. Mining, agriculture, and cement production also release greenhouse gases into the atmosphere.

Volcanic eruptions are natural processes that release greenhouse gases into the atmosphere. However, human activities release a larger quantity of greenhouse gases than volcanoes do. Furthermore, explosive eruptions release particles into the atmosphere that reflect sunlight and result in a slight decrease in the global temperature. This effect usually lasts for a period of months or years.

In 1991, Mount Pinatubo erupted in the Philippines. This explosive eruption sent ash into the atmosphere that was spread around the world by global winds. As a result, global temperatures had dropped by about 0.5 °C one year later.

 EVIDENCE NOTEBOOK

7. Which climate change factors might be contributing to phenomena occurring in Shishmaref? Think about how changes can be gradual, sudden, natural, or human caused. Record your evidence.

 Do the Math
Compare Quantities of Carbon Dioxide

8. Use the word bank to complete the statements to compare the amounts of carbon dioxide released by human activities and by volcanoes.

In 2015, human activities added about 40 trillion kilograms of carbon dioxide into the atmosphere. On average, volcanoes release about 600 billion kilograms of carbon dioxide into the atmosphere every year.

40,000,000,000,000 kg / 600,000,000,000 kg is about 67.

Therefore, _____ release about 67 times more carbon dioxide than _____ do.

WORD BANK
- human activities
- volcanoes

Analyzing Recent Climate Change

Is Earth's average global temperature changing? The maps below show how Earth's surface temperature has changed over time. The colors on each map show how the temperature in a given time period compares to the average temperature during the years 1951 to 1981.

9. The maps show global temperature changes over time. Different locations have warmed and cooled by different amounts, but the overall global temperature has increased / decreased / stayed the same.

Explore ONLINE!

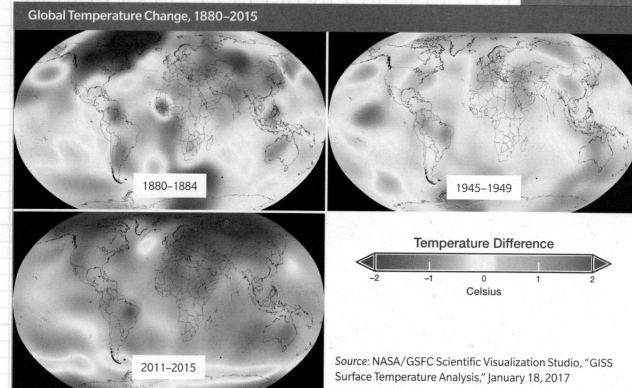

Global Temperature Change, 1880–2015

1880–1884

1945–1949

2011–2015

Temperature Difference

-2 -1 0 1 2

Celsius

Source: NASA/GSFC Scientific Visualization Studio, "GISS Surface Temperature Analysis," January 18, 2017

Recent Climate Change

Scientists use the term *climate change* to refer to the effects of Earth's increasing global temperature. This recent rise in temperature has been more rapid and has lasted longer than any period of warming that happened over the previous nine centuries. Earth's average global surface temperature has increased over the last century by about 0.6 °C.

This change might seem small, but a change in only a few degrees can completely alter an environment and the things that live there. For example, many organisms in polar regions rely on permafrost. *Permafrost* is a soil that is frozen throughout the year. But small increases in temperatures cause this soil to thaw. When the ice in permafrost melts, the soil becomes more vulnerable to erosion. It no longer supports the trees and other plants that live in the soil. It also releases a greenhouse gas called *methane* into the atmosphere. This gas absorbs solar energy and makes the atmosphere warmer, which thaws more permafrost. These processes form a feedback loop that contributes to the increasing warming of the planet.

Indicators of a Warming World

10. Look at the diagram. Write the words *increasing* or *decreasing* to tell whether the labeled features are increasing or decreasing as a result of climate warming.

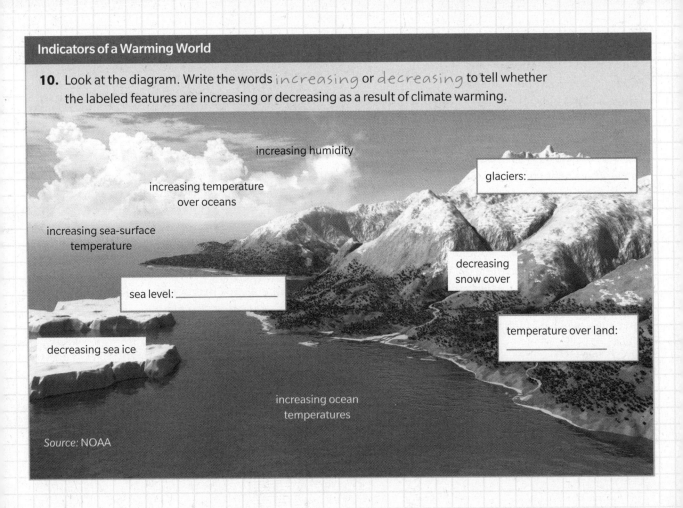

increasing humidity

increasing temperature over oceans

glaciers: _____

increasing sea-surface temperature

decreasing snow cover

sea level: _____

temperature over land: _____

decreasing sea ice

increasing ocean temperatures

Source: NOAA

Do the Math
Identify Correlation and Causation

Correlation with Causation Scientists compare trends in global temperature data to trends in other data to identify whether a correlation exists. A *correlation* means that as one variable increases, another variable increases or decreases in a similar pattern. In these graphs, there is a correlation: temperature and ice cream sales decrease in a similar pattern over the same time period. The goal of many climate scientists is to identify all of the factors that contribute to the recent rapid increase in global temperatures. To do this, more than a correlation between variables is needed.

Causation means that one variable causes the other variable to change. It is reasonable to think that more ice cream is sold when the temperatures are warmer because people want a cold treat. A scientist would gather data to test whether this relationship is true.

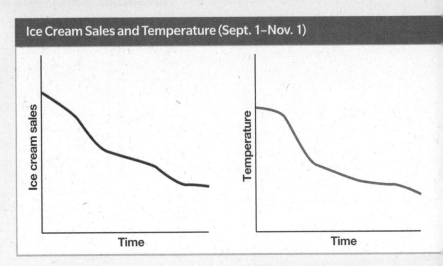

Ice Cream Sales and Temperature (Sept. 1–Nov. 1)

Ice cream sales — Time

Temperature — Time

Correlation Without Causation The graphs of pet adoptions and temperature also show a correlation. They both have in the same pattern in the same time period. However, causation is unlikely as there is no logical explanation of how one factor relates to another. A correlation does not always mean that variables are related.

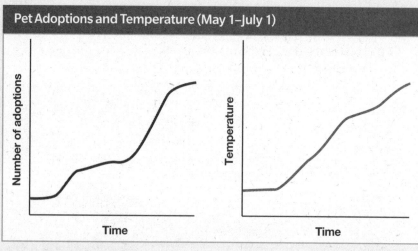

Pet Adoptions and Temperature (May 1–July 1)

You can investigate whether there is causation when there is a correlation and it seems likely that one factor could affect the other factor. In order to show causation, you must be able to explain why one factor affects the other. You may find evidence in existing scientific knowledge or by conducting your own investigation.

These graphs show the levels of carbon dioxide in the atmosphere and the average global temperature over time.

11. Analyze the data shown in each graph. Is there a correlation? Explain.

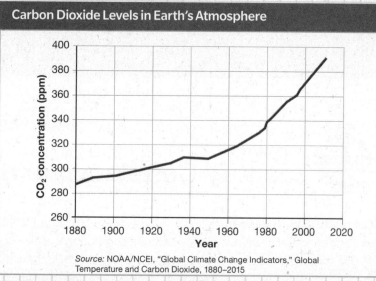

Carbon Dioxide Levels in Earth's Atmosphere

Source: NOAA/NCEI, "Global Climate Change Indicators," Global Temperature and Carbon Dioxide, 1880–2015

12. What questions would you want to investigate to confirm a causal relationship between CO_2 in the atmosphere and the average global temperature?

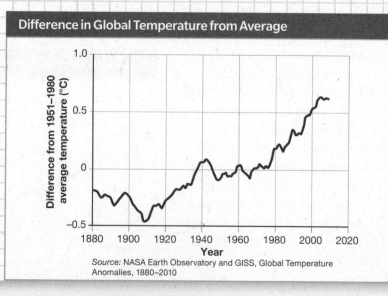

Difference in Global Temperature from Average

Source: NASA Earth Observatory and GISS, Global Temperature Anomalies, 1880–2010

13. **Discuss** With a partner, discuss your answers to questions on the previous page. Create a list of additional questions you could investigate about other possible factors that might impact climate change. Identify what evidence you would need to find to answer those questions.

Causes of Recent Climate Change

Most scientists agree that the primary cause of the recent increase in the average global temperature is a rapid increase in greenhouse gas concentrations. The current levels of carbon dioxide and methane in the atmosphere are higher than they have been in the past 420,000 years. Carbon dioxide levels may be higher than they have been in the past 2–3 million years. The rapid increase in greenhouse gas concentrations intensifies the greenhouse effect. This is often referred to as the *enhanced greenhouse effect*.

Most of the carbon dioxide that has entered the atmosphere in the last century is from the burning of fossil fuels for transportation and to generate electrical energy.

EVIDENCE NOTEBOOK

14. How might the erosion in Shishmaref, Alaska, be related to the recent rise in global temperature? Record your evidence.

Describe Cause and Effect

Positive feedback loops are one cause of rapid climate change. A *positive feedback loop* occurs when a change in one quantity changes a second quantity, and the second quantity then amplifies the changes in the first quantity.

15. As temperatures rapidly increase, sea ice is melting. Ocean water is darker / lighter than ice is. Darker surfaces absorb more / less solar energy than light surfaces do. Therefore, ocean water absorbs more / less solar energy than ice does. This warms / cools ocean water over time, which melts more sea ice.

Understanding the Effects of Climate Change

Climate change is more extreme in some places than in others. For example, the average temperatures near Earth's poles have increased at a more rapid rate than temperatures have increased elsewhere.

The environment in North America was quite different 12,000 years ago. Many animals that thrived in that cooler environment, such as woolly mammoths, no longer exist today.

16. **Draw** During the last "ice age," the average global temperature was about 11 °C (52 °F). Today, it is 16 °C (61 °F). Draw what the area shown might look like now. Describe what it might look like if temperatures were 5 °C (9 °F) warmer than they are today?

Effects of Recent Climate Change

The effects of rapidly changing climate in the past century include sea level rise and changes in habitats. Changes are more extreme in some places. For example, over the past 60 years, the average temperature in Alaska has increased by about 1.5 °C (2.7 °F). That rate of increase is almost twice as fast as that of the rest of the United States.

Changes in the Biosphere

A region's climate affects its organisms. For example, as the climate warms in Alaska, plants begin to grow earlier in the season than they did in the past. This affects any organisms that depend on those plants. As climate changes a habitat, populations of organisms must adapt, move, or die out. In some places, climate is changing so rapidly that some organisms can't adapt or move quickly enough to survive the changes.

Changes in Ice

Earth's ice contains a large volume of water and keeps that water out of the oceans. Recent climate change has caused frozen soil called *permafrost,* continental ice sheets, and glaciers to melt. The meltwater from the ice flows into the ocean, which causes sea levels to rise. As ice melts, animals such as polar bears and seals that rest, breed, and hunt for food on ice lose their habitats. Structures built on permafrost can shift and sink into the soil as it thaws.

Sea ice protects the coastline. When sea ice melts, the coastline can be exposed to erosion from ocean waves.

Changes in the Oceans

Recent climate change has increased ocean temperatures, which affects ocean currents, weather patterns, and sea level. Warmer surface waters generate more powerful tropical storms, hurricanes, and typhoons. Wave action and high winds erode beaches and damage ocean and coastal ecosystems. Rising sea levels flood low-lying coastal areas with ocean water, which kills organisms. Erosion increases as water reaches farther onto shore during storms, often reaching areas that were once protected.

Thawing permafrost is no longer supported by the solid ice crystals it once contained. As a result, the soil may sink, crack, or collapse. It is also more easily eroded by waves and rain.

Earth's oceans support a diversity of organisms, many of which are important human food sources. Increasing ocean temperatures affect the kinds of organisms that live in particular locations, the migration and breeding patterns of animals, and sensitive marine ecosystems, such as coral reefs and coastal wetlands. As the amount of carbon dioxide in the atmosphere increases, the amount that dissolves in ocean water also increases. This process makes ocean water more acidic, making it difficult for many marine organisms to form hard skeletons or shells.

Increased ocean temperatures harm coral that live in reefs. In a process called *coral bleaching*, algae that the coral needs for food leave, and the coral turns white.

EVIDENCE NOTEBOOK

17. Describe how the increase in global temperatures over the last century could be related to the events in Shishmaref. Record your evidence.

Human Activity and Climate Change

Human activities are adding greenhouse gases into the atmosphere at an increasingly rapid rate. To reduce the effects of greenhouse gases on global climate, humans must find ways to reduce the amount of greenhouse gases that are being added to the atmosphere. In order to reduce greenhouse gases, scientists and engineers are improving technologies that use wind and solar resources to generate electrical energy. They are also researching ways to absorb and contain greenhouse gases.

Humans and Greenhouse Gases

Understanding human sources of greenhouse gases in the atmosphere is a key part of finding solutions. Reducing human impacts on climate change takes a commitment from individuals, businesses, and governments. Individuals and businesses can make smarter choices about energy and resource use. Governments can work both domestically and internationally to develop laws and programs to reduce greenhouse gas emissions.

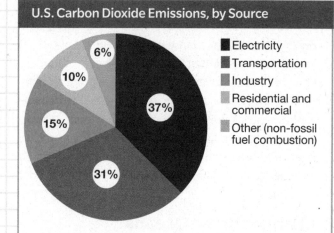

U.S. Carbon Dioxide Emissions, by Source

- Electricity
- Transportation
- Industry
- Residential and commercial
- Other (non-fossil fuel combustion)

37% · 31% · 15% · 10% · 6%

Source: EPA, Inventory of U.S. Greenhouse Gas Emissions and Sinks: 1990–2015

18. Fill in the table with your ideas for ways that each group of people could reduce carbon dioxide emissions.

Ideas for Reducing Carbon Dioxide Emissions		
Individuals	Businesses	Governments

Engineer It
Evaluate Solutions for Climate Change

Engineers solve problems by proposing and evaluating solutions.

Engineering Problem: Carbon dioxide in the atmosphere is causing global temperatures to rise. How can the concentration of carbon dioxide in the atmosphere be reduced?

Solution 1: Remove carbon dioxide from the atmosphere by planting trees in deforested areas.

Solution 2: Add fertilizer to ocean water to encourage the growth of green algae that will remove carbon dioxide from the atmosphere.

19. Evaluate the solutions to find strengths and weaknesses. Think about any unwanted effects. Recommend whether each solution should be considered further.

_____

_____

_____

_____

_____

Continue Your Exploration

Name: _____   Date: _____

Check out the path below or go online to choose one of the other paths shown.

Careers in Science

- **Hands-On Labs** ✋
- **Disappearing Coral Reefs**
- **Propose Your Own Path**

Go online to choose one of these other paths.

Geeta G. Persad, Postdoctoral Research Scientist

As a freshman in college, Dr. Geeta Persad attended a scientific conference about climate that motivated her to focus on climate science. She believes that one of climate scientists' duties is to inform the public and policymakers about climate research and why it is important.

Scientists like Dr. Persad use computer models to determine how different substances affect the atmosphere and climate. These models include factors such as the amounts of different gases, liquids, and solids in the atmosphere. Scientists change the factors in the climate model to help them understand how each factor may affect climate. Scientists use these models to make predictions about how climate may change in the future.

Dr. Persad's work with climate models has focused on the effects of tiny particles called *aerosols*. These particles affect how clouds form. Dr. Persad has applied what she has learned about aerosols and clouds to computer models, so that clouds can be modeled realistically. These data help the computer climate models more accurately recreate the conditions that cause clouds to form and dissipate. These models help scientists understand how clouds, weather, and climate behave and how climate may change in the future.

Dr. Geeta Persad visited the Franz Josef Glacier in New Zealand, which is shrinking as a result of recent climate change.

Continue Your Exploration

1. How does Dr. Persad's work on clouds contribute to our understanding of climate and climate change?

2. Scientists have developed a number of different global climate models. Why do climate scientists use computer models to study changes in climate?

3. A scientist is developing a computer model to study the effects of a certain substance in the atmosphere on climate. Which factors might the scientist need to adjust in the model? Select all that apply.

   A. changes in the sun's output

   B. amount of the substance in the atmosphere

   C. Earth's distance from the sun

   D. whether the substance causes a positive or negative feedback

   E. the source of the substance

4. **Collaborate** With a partner, write at least three questions that you would like to ask Dr. Persad about evidence related to factors that affect climate change.

Can You Explain It?

Name: _____   Date: _____

What could be causing ice and permafrost to melt in Shishmaref?

EVIDENCE NOTEBOOK

Refer to the notes in your Evidence Notebook to help you explain why ice and permafrost are melting in Shishmaref.

1. State your claim. Make sure your claim fully explains why sea ice and permafrost are melting and leading to destructive erosion in Shishmaref.

2. Summarize the evidence you have gathered to support your claim and explain your reasoning.

©AL GRILLO/AP Images

Checkpoints

Answer the following questions to check your understanding of the lesson.

Use the graph to answer Questions 3–5.

3. Which statement is supported by the data in the graph?

   A. The amount of carbon dioxide in the atmosphere does not change.

   B. Melting sea ice is caused by rising levels of carbon dioxide in the atmosphere.

   C. Adding more carbon dioxide to the atmosphere causes Earth's climate to warm.

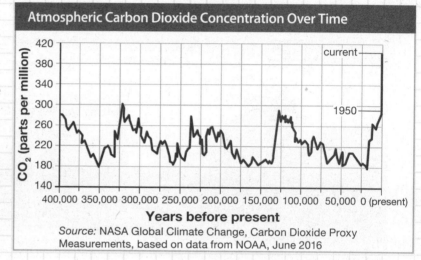

Atmospheric Carbon Dioxide Concentration Over Time

Source: NASA Global Climate Change, Carbon Dioxide Proxy Measurements, based on data from NOAA, June 2016

   D. Carbon dioxide concentration in the atmosphere is higher now than at any other time in the last 400,000 years.

4. Based on the concentration of carbon dioxide in the atmosphere, Earth's global temperature likely was higher / lower 125,000 years ago than it was 25,000 years ago.

5. The rate at which carbon dioxide is being added to the atmosphere now is higher / lower than ever before.

6. Complete the table by matching the factors provided in the word bank with the effect they have on global temperature.

WORD BANK
- volcanic eruption
- less incoming solar radiation
- more greenhouse gases
- shrinking polar ice caps

Makes Earth Warmer	Makes Earth Cooler

7. When greenhouse gas concentrations in the atmosphere are high, less / more energy is absorbed by the atmosphere. As a result, thermal energy stays in the Earth system for a longer / shorter time and Earth's average surface temperature rises / drops.

8. Select all of the factors in the list below that would lead to an increase in the temperature of Earth's atmosphere.

   A. exposing dark rock or soil to the sun

   B. reducing greenhouse gas emissions

   C. using wind and solar energy resources

   D. reducing the size of polar ice caps

Interactive Review

Complete this section to review the main concepts of the lesson.

Climate is driven by energy from the sun and interactions of the Earth system. Greenhouse gases in the atmosphere absorb energy from the sun.

A. How is the temperature range on Earth affected by Earth's atmosphere?

Both natural processes and human activities affect climate. Earth's climate can be changed by sudden events or by gradual changes over time.

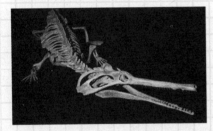

B. Describe how one natural process and one human activity affect climate change.

Earth's average global temperature has increased over the last century. The main cause of this increase is carbon dioxide that is released when humans burn fossil fuels as an energy source.

C. How do correlation and causation relate to understanding how natural processes and human activities affect climate change?

Minimizing the effects of climate change requires reducing greenhouse gas emissions from human activities and understanding effects of climate change on Earth systems.

D. Give an example of how humans burning fossil fuels affects each of Earth's major systems (atmosphere, biosphere, geosphere, hydrosphere).

(c) ©Alexandra Gl/Fotolia; (b) ©Accent Alaska.com/Alamy

Choose one of the activities to explore how this unit connects to other topics.

Music Connection

Songs about Saving Earth Many songwriters and singers have been inspired by human effects on the environment. These artists use music to share information and to encourage action and change regarding issues that are important to them.

Identify a song that was inspired by human impacts on the environment. Read the lyrics. Then write a brief essay explaining how the song is related to natural resources or environmental conservation. Identify Earth systems and natural resources that are mentioned in the song. Then present your findings by playing the song and leading a group discussion.

Social Studies Connection

Science and Activism Some individuals find an environmental cause they feel strongly about and do bold things to raise awareness. Often these people are called "activists." Some activists walk in marches or plan demonstrations to inform others about environmental causes. These activities can raise awareness about environmental issues and motivate people to help make changes.

What else would you like to know about science and activism? Research an environmental activist to find out about the activist's cause and efforts. Create a multimedia presentation to share with the class.

Computer Science Connection

Satellite Imaging Scientists and citizens use satellite images to monitor different features on Earth's surface. Because satellites are becoming less expensive to make, there are now hundreds of satellites gathering data about Earth every day. Many of these satellite images are used to study how our planet changes over time.

Research how satellites take images of Earth's surface to monitor environmental changes. Create a slide-show presentation of images and explanations describing how satellite images highlight Earth's changing surface and contribute to scientific studies.

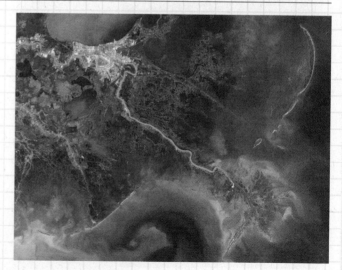

Name: _____

Date: _____

Complete this review to check your understanding of the unit.

Use the graph to answer Questions 1–2.

1. Which of the following statements describes how rising global temperature affects the caterpillars?

   A. More caterpillars survive and mate each year.

   B. The caterpillars hatch earlier in the season.

   C. The caterpillars move to a new habitat.

   D. The caterpillars change the food they eat.

2. What physical or behavioral adaptations will determine how well the birds survive the change in climate? Select all that apply.

   A. the number of eggs the birds lay

   B. the variety of foods the birds can eat

   C. the timing of the birds' mating and laying seasons

   D. the location and size of the birds' range

Effects of Climate Change on Birds and Caterpillars

Before Climate Change

After Climate Change

— Eggs laid by birds — Birds needing food — Caterpillars hatched

Use the decision matrix to answer Questions 3–5

3. Complete the decision matrix by calculating the totals for each product.

| Product | Criteria | | | | Totals |
	Can be used for at least 3 days (2)	Inexpensive (3)	Produces little waste (5)	Requires little energy to make (5)	
Liquid soap in plastic bottle	2	2	2	2	
Bar soap in paper wrapper	2	3	4	4	

4. Which product would you choose for the guest rooms of an ecologically friendly hotel?

   A. Liquid soap, because it is the least expensive.

   B. Solid bar soap, because it has the highest total score in my decision matrix.

   C. Liquid soap, because it has the lowest total score in my decision matrix.

   D. Bar soap, because it produces more waste than liquid soap.

5. If the liquid soap in a plastic bottle produced less waste, would it change your decision?

   A. No, it still scores lower in my decision matrix.

   B. No, it still scores higher in my decision matrix.

   C. Yes, less waste outweighs the other categories.

   D. Yes, bar soap is harder to clean up when the guests leave.

6. Complete the table by explaining how the following categories are related to each concept.

Topic Category	Cause and Effect	Patterns	Stability	Change
Climate	A variety of natural processes and human activities cause changes in Earth's climate.			
Human Activities				
Climate Monitoring Methods				
Greenhouse Gases				

Name: _____   **Date:** _____

Use the plastic usage diagram to answer Questions 7–10.

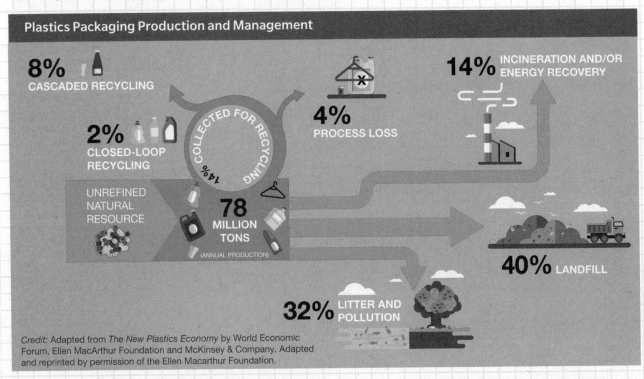

Plastics Packaging Production and Management

8% CASCADED RECYCLING

2% CLOSED-LOOP RECYCLING

UNREFINED NATURAL RESOURCE

COLLECTED FOR RECYCLING

14%

78 MILLION TONS (ANNUAL PRODUCTION)

4% PROCESS LOSS

14% INCINERATION AND/OR ENERGY RECOVERY

40% LANDFILL

32% LITTER AND POLLUTION

Credit: Adapted from *The New Plastics Economy* by World Economic Forum, Ellen MacArthur Foundation and McKinsey & Company. Adapted and reprinted by permission of the Ellen Macarthur Foundation.

This diagram represents an analysis of the life cycle of plastic packaging around the globe. Plastic packaging collection and recycling are not the same in every region and country.

7. Approximately how many tons of plastic are recycled each year?

8. After a plastic bottle has been used, what four outcomes could it experience? List these four outcomes in order from the most likely to the least.

9. Explain why not all of the plastic products that are produced are recycled.

10. Suggest at least three ways human behaviors could be changed to minimize the impacts of plastic packaging materials on Earth's systems.

Use the infographic to answer Questions 11–14.

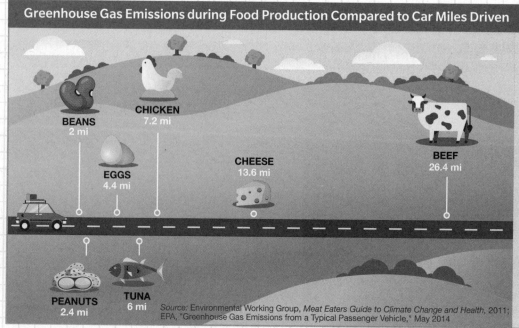

Greenhouse Gas Emissions during Food Production Compared to Car Miles Driven

CHICKEN
7.2 mi

BEANS
2 mi

EGGS
4.4 mi

CHEESE
13.6 mi

BEEF
26.4 mi

PEANUTS
2.4 mi

TUNA
6 mi

This image compares the amount of greenhouse gases emitted during the production of one pound of food to the amount of carbon dioxide produced per mile driven in a car.

Source: Environmental Working Group, *Meat Eaters Guide to Climate Change and Health*, 2011; EPA, "Greenhouse Gas Emissions from a Typical Passenger Vehicle," May 2014

11. Why is the comparison shown in the image useful?

12. Global Warming Potential (GWP) is a measure of how much heat a greenhouse gas absorbs. Higher GWP means the gas absorbs more heat. The GWP of CO_2 is 1 and the GWP of methane is 21. Producing beef and dairy products releases a lot of methane. Driving a car releases a lot of carbon dioxide. Which action has a greater potential impact on global temperature? Explain your reasoning.

13. If a round-trip distance to the grocery store is 20 miles, which would reduce your greenhouse gas emissions more: making one less trip to the store or eating one less pound of beef? Explain your reasoning.

14. If you wanted to reduce your greenhouse gas emissions, how might you change your diet to have the greatest impact? Use evidence and scientific reasoning to support your claim.

Name: _____   Date: _____

How can air travel be improved to reduce impacts on Earth systems?

Air travel is an important part of our global culture and economy. However, it causes significant greenhouse gas emissions and requires large amounts of natural resources. Greener Skies is an initiative that is being implemented to help decrease airport emissions. It improves upon existing area navigation (RNAV) procedures. These new procedures allow aircraft to fly a different course to reduce mileage and, therefore, the amount of fuel burned during the flight. Research Greener Skies procedures that have been put into place at Seattle-Tacoma Airport and other airports and determine whether any of these procedures would benefit an airport near you.

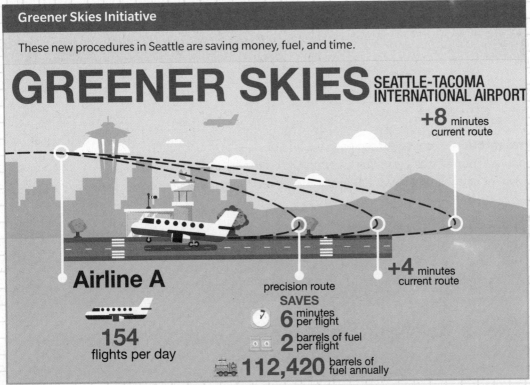

Greener Skies Initiative

These new procedures in Seattle are saving money, fuel, and time.

GREENER SKIES SEATTLE-TACOMA INTERNATIONAL AIRPORT

+8 minutes current route

+4 minutes current route

Airline A

154 flights per day

precision route **SAVES**
6 minutes per flight
2 barrels of fuel per flight
112,420 barrels of fuel annually

Source: Federal Aviation Administration, U.S. Department of Transportation, and Alaska Airlines, June 27, 2014

The steps below will help guide your research.

1. **Define the Problem** What questions do you have about the goal of the Greener Skies initiative? Write a statement defining a problem that Greener Skies is trying to solve.

2. **Analyze Data** In a test of the new procedures, a single airline was able to save 87 gallons of fuel per flight and shorten flight times by 9 minutes. As a result, they reduced greenhouse gas emissions by 1 metric ton every time a plane landed at the Seattle-Tacoma Airport. Across all airlines, about 206,085 flights landed at Seattle-Tacoma in 2016. Calculate the amount of fuel and the amount of greenhouse-gas emissions that would be saved using the Greener Skies initiative at Seattle-Tacoma Airport over the course of one year and ten years.

3. **Conduct Research** Research the Greener Skies procedures enacted at the airport in Seattle and other test airports around the country. Consider how the Greener Skies procedures could be implemented at another airport of your choice, taking into consideration the air-traffic patterns at that airport.

4. **Develop a Presentation** Propose strategies that could be used at your chosen airport to improve airport efficiency and reduce impacts on the environment. Use evidence from other airports that have implemented Greener Skies initiatives to support your recommendation.

5. **Communicate** Present your proposal to your class.

✓ **Self-Check**

	I defined the problem that the Greener Skies program is trying to solve.
	I analyzed data about carbon emissions caused by airplane flights and how Greener Skies procedures can reduce them.
	I researched air traffic patterns and procedures at another airport of my choice in order to evaluate which initiatives could be implemented there.
	I developed a presentation that proposed strategies to improve efficiency at my airport and reduce human impacts on the environment.
	My proposal was supported by evidence and clearly communicated.

Glossary

Pronunciation Key							
Sound	Symbol	Example	Respelling	Sound	Symbol	Example	Respelling
ă	a	pat	PAT	ŏ	ah	bottle	BAHT'l
ā	ay	pay	PAY	ō	oh	toe	TOH
âr	air	care	KAIR	ô	aw	caught	KAWT
ä	ah	father	FAH•ther	ôr	ohr	roar	ROHR
är	ar	argue	AR•gyoo	oi	oy	noisy	NOYZ•ee
ch	ch	chase	CHAYS	o͞o	u	book	BUK
ĕ	e	pet	PET	o͞o	oo	boot	BOOT
ĕ (at end of a syllable)	eh	settee lessee	seh•TEE leh•SEE	ou	ow	pound	POWND
ĕr	ehr	merry	MEHR•ee	s	s	center	SEN•ter
ē	ee	beach	BEECH	sh	sh	cache	CASH
g	g	gas	GAS	ŭ	uh	flood	FLUHD
ĭ	i	pit	PIT	ûr	er	bird	BERD
ĭ (at end of a syllable)	ih	guitar	gih•TAR	z	z	xylophone	ZY•luh•fohn
ī	y eye (only for a complete syllable)	pie island	PY EYE•luhnd	z	z	bags	BAGZ
îr	ir	hear	HIR	zh	zh	decision	dih•SIZH•uhn
j	j	germ	JERM	ə	uh	around broken focus	uh•ROWND BROH•kuhn FOH•kuhs
k	k	kick	KIK	ər	er	winner	WIN•er
ng	ng	thing	THING	th	th	thin they	THIN THAY
ngk	ngk	bank	BANGK	w	w	one	WUHN
				wh	hw	whether	HWETH•er

extinct (ek•STINGKT)

describes a species that has died out completely (187)

extinto término que describe a una especie que ha desaparecido por completo

greenhouse effect (GREEN•hows ih•FEKT)

the warming of the surface and lower atmosphere of Earth that occurs when water vapor, carbon dioxide, and other gases absorb and reradiate energy (227)

efecto invernadero calentamiento de la superficie y las capas inferiores de la atmósfera terrestre que se produce cuando el vapor de agua, el dióxido de carbono y demás gases absorben energía y la vuelven a irradiar

habitat (HAB•ih•tat)

the place where an organism usually lives (182)

hábitat el lugar donde usualmente vive un organismo

habitat destruction (HAB•ih•tat dih•STRUK•shuhn)

the ruin or alteration of a place inhabited by an ecological community (154)

destrucción de hábitat ruina o alteración de un lugar habitado por una comunidad ecológica

mitigate (MIT•ih•gayt)

to reduce the severity or impact of something (50)

mitigar reducir la gravedad o los efectos de algo

natural disaster (NACH•uhr•uhl dih•ZAS•ter)

widespread injury, death, and property damage caused by a natural hazard (7)

desastre natural gran cantidad de heridos, muertos y daños materiales causados por un riesgo natural

natural hazard (NACH•uhr•uhl HAZ•erd)

a natural process or phenomenon that may cause widespread injury, death, and property damage (6)

riesgo natural proceso o fenómeno natural que puede provocar gran cantidad de heridos, muertos y daños materiales

natural resource (NACH•uhr•uhl REE•sohrs)

any natural material or energy source that is used by humans, such as water, petroleum, minerals, forests, and animals (78)

recurso natural cualquier material o fuente de energía de la naturaleza que usan los seres humanos, como el agua, el petróleo, los minerales, los bosques y los animales

nonpoint-source pollution (nahn•POYNT SOHRS puh•LOO•shuhn)

pollution that comes from many sources rather than from a single, specific site (185)

contaminación no puntual contaminación que proviene de muchas fuentes, en lugar de provenir de un solo sitio específico

nonrenewable resource (nahn•rih•NOO•uh•buhl REE•sohrs)

a resource that forms at a rate that is much slower than the rate at which the resource is consumed (85)

recurso no renovable un recurso que se forma a una tasa que es mucho más lenta que la tasa a la que se consume

per capita consumption (PER CAP•it•uh kuhn•SUHMP•shuhn)

the average consumption per person within a population (139)

consumo per cápita consumo promedio por persona en una población determinada

point-source pollution (POYNT SOHRS puh•LOO•shuhn)

pollution that comes from a specific site (185)

contaminación puntual contaminación que proviene de un lugar específico

pollution (puh•LOO•shuhn)

an unwanted change in the environment caused by substances or forms of energy (158)

contaminación un cambio indeseable en el ambiente producido por sustancias o formas de energía

population (pahp•yuh•LAY•shuhn)

a group of organisms of the same species that live in a specific geographical area (128)

población un grupo de organismos de la misma especie que viven en un área geográfica específica

renewable resource (rih•NOO•uh•buhl REE•sohrs)

a natural resource that can be replaced at the same rate at which the resource is consumed (85)

recurso renovable un recurso natural que puede reemplazarse a la misma tasa a la que se consume

Index

Note: Italic page numbers represent illustrative material, such as figures, tables, margin elements, photographs, and illustrations. Boldface page numbers represent page numbers for definitions.

A

acid rain, 89, 158, 188
active volcano, 12, 15, 33, 34
agriculture
    contour farming, 201, *201*
    crop rotation, 105, *106*
    Dust Bowl, 208, *208*, 214, *214*
    land use, 164, *164*
    role in population growth, 127
    terraced farming, 106, *106*
air
    as natural resource, 78
    as renewable resource, 85
air travel emissions, 251
algae, 91, *91*, 181, *181*, 192, 193, *239*
amphibian, 170, *170*
Analysis
    of building sites near volcanoes, 15
    of data, 86
    of design solution, 59
    of environmental impact of a power
      plant, 209
    of greenhouse effect, 228–229
    of impact to Earth's systems, 153
    of landslides, 31
    of method of reducing solid waste,
      217
    of monitoring methods, 209
    of ocean pollution, 186
    of resource data, 203
    of resource quality data, 205
    of resource use, 135, 138
    of your impact, 160
animal
    impact of climate change, 238
    impact of human use of, 152–153,
      162, *162*
    as natural resource, 78, *78*
    needs of, 78
    as renewable resource, 85, 134,
      163, *163*
animal fats, 91, *92*

aquifer, 103, *104*, 108, 109-110, 203
Aral Sea, 105
arctic seal, *222*
ash fall, 14, *14*
ash trees, 144
Assessment
    Lesson Self-Check, 23–25, 45–47,
      63–65, 93–95, 113–115, 145–147,
      167–169, 197–199, 221–223,
      243–245
    Unit Performance Task, 71–72,
      121–122, 175–176, 251–252
    Unit Review, 67–70, 115–118,
      171–174, 243–246
asteroid impacts, 43–44, *43*, *44*
asteroid mining, 116, *116*
astronomical change, 232
atmosphere, 148
    changes in, 221
    gases in, 158
    greenhouse gases and, 89
    human impact on, 162, 187, *187*,
      188
    as natural resource, *79*
    pollution in, *159*
    as source of natural resources, 78

B

Bali, 126
bamboo, 59, *59*, 87, *87*, 133
bamboo water wheel, *123*
Barringer Crater, *43*
bauxite, *75*
behavior change, 213
biofuel, 83, 91–92, *92*
biomass
    as energy resource, 81, 91–92
    percentage of energy sources used,
      82
    as renewable resource, 85, 101

biomass engineer, 91–92
biosphere, 148
    effect on climate, 238
    effects of climate change, 227, *227*
    human impact on, 157, 160–161,
      179, 187, *187*, 188
    impact of human population
      growth, 162, *162*
    as source of natural resources, 78
birth rate, 130, *130*
blizzard, 9, *9*, 64, *64*
Brainstorm Solutions, 58, 209, 217

C

canal, 108, *108*, 154
Can You Explain It? 5, 23, 27, 45, 49,
    63, 77, 93, 97, 113, 127, 145, 149,
    167, 181, 197, 201, 221, 225, 243
carbon dioxide, 150, 157, 233, 237
    absorption of, 232
    acid rain and, 184
    emissions in U.S., *189*, *240*
    as greenhouse gas, 159, 227
    levels near Mauna Loa, *159*
    used by trees, 163
Careers in Engineering:
    Geotechnical Engineer, 61–62
Careers in Engineering: Biomass
    Engineer, 91–92
Careers in Science: Conservation
    Scientist, 143–144, *143*
Careers in Science: Postdoctoral
    Research Scientist, 241–242
Case Study: The Dust Bowl, 214, *214*
Case Study: The Elwha River,
    155–156, *155*, *156*
Case Study: The Mississippi River,
    190–193
Case Study: Pollution in the
    Atmosphere, 159, *159*
Cassiterite, *85*

causation, 235–236

change

astronomical change, 244

causes of climate change, 230–233, 237, 245

climate change, 179, 224–245

in Earth's surface, *220*

effects of climate change, 177, *177*, 224–227, *227*

in environment, 177

natural changes, 177

reducing effects of climate change, 238–240, 245

Checkpoint, 24, 46, 64, 94, 114, 146, 168, 198, 222, 244

Chernobyl nuclear disaster, 195–196

circle graph, *82, 218, 240*

classification of tornadoes, 19, *19*

clear-cutting, 152

climate

defined, 37, 230

global climate, 230–231

impact on water distribution, 103

climate change, 159, 224–228

analyzing recent change, 234–237

astronomical change, 232, *232*

causes of, 231, 232, 237

changes in atmosphere, 233

changes on Earth's surface, *232*

Earth's climate, 226–227

Earth's climate system, 227

effects of, 177, *177*, 226–227, *227*

greenhouse effect, 237

identifying global climate change factors, 230–233

reducing effects of, 238–240

climate data, 218

climate hazard, 8, 9, *9*, 37–41, *47*

coal, 90, *90*, 207

formation of, 99, *100*

human use of, 158

location of, *100*

mining of, *156, 167*

as natural resource, 77, 79, *79*, 81, 133

as nonrenewable resource, 85, *93, 100*, 134

percentage of energy sources used, 82, *82*

use of, *130*

world consumption of, *157*

coastal floods, 41

Collaborate, 22, 44, 62, 92, 112, 144, 166, 196, 220, 242

Colorado River, *149*

reduced flow of, *155*

Communicate, 72, 122, 176, 252

compost, 207, *207*

Computer Science Connection

Satellite Imaging, 246

Conduct Research, 72, 176, 252

Connections. *see* Unit Connections

consequences, 88–90

conservation of natural resources, 85, *88*

conservation scientist, 143–144, *143*

constraint, 56, 57, 58, 208, 216

contour farming, 201, *201, 221*

coral, 239, *239*

correlation, 203, 235–236

criterion, 51, 56, 57, 209

crop resource, *84*

crop rotation, 106, *106*

Crosscurricular Connections. *see* **Unit Connections**

currents, ocean, 227, 239

D

dam, 108, 154, 155, *155*,156, 183, 184, 191, *191*

data

analysis of, 28, 50, 72, 86, 120, 170, 197, 199, 239

application of, 50

on climate, 218

collection of, 28, 38, 50, 53, 196, 199, 234

of eruptions of Mauna Loa, *34*

evaluation of, 60

on human impact on environment, 196

on human population, 124–128

interpretation of, 72, 86, *173*

making predictions from, 29

on natural hazards, 10–11, *10–11*

of past eruptions, *34*

patterns in tornado data, 18–20, *18, 19, 20*

on resource use, 131–132

on tornadoes, 38, *39*

volcanic data, 12–14, *17, 33*

dead zone, 192

death rate, 130, *130*

decision-making tool, 57

decision matrix, 57, *247*

deforestation, 153, *168, 183, 247*

Delaware Bay, 163

delta, 190, *190*

desert, 75, *75*, 103, 105, 106, *106*, 232

desertification, 105, *106*

Design a Solution, 72

diagram, *13, 14, 104, 114, 117, 150, 165, 213, 214, 215, 223, 238*

diamonds, *114*

Discuss, 2 33, 44, 50, 78, 84, 88, 98, 106, 129, 133, 137, 151, 183, 190, 213, 216, 226, 237

disease, 66, 170

dissolution, 102

dome home, *48*

dormant volcano, 12

Do the Math, 57, 212

Analyze a Cod Population, 194

Analyze Eruption Data, 17

Analyze Groundwater Use, 110

Analyze Impacts to Earth's Systems, 153

Calculate Rate of Consumption, 141

Compare Concentrations, 204

Compare Quantities of Carbon Dioxide, 233

Compare Rates of Renewal, 87

Explain Earthquake Probability, 36

Identify Correlation and Causation, 235–236

Interpret Natural Disaster Data, 11

Draw, 8, 80, 132, 186, 238
drive system designs, 189
drought, 9, 9, 106, *106*
    number and cost, 22
    number of occurrences, *8*
    number of people affected by, *11*
    wildfires caused by, 8
Dust Bowl, 214, *214*

E

Earth
    average surface temperature, 226, *226*
    changes in atmosphere, 233
    changes in surface of, 232
    climate, 226–227
    distance from the sun, *226*
    surface of, *78*
    tilt of, 232
earthquake
    cause of, 9, 59
    effects of, *1, 12, 32, 35, 50*
    frequency on Mauna Loa, *35*
    location of, *29, 32*
    location of in U.S., *10*
    mitigation plan, 55
    mitigation solutions, 53
    monitoring of, 59
    number of occurrences, *8*
    predicting, 35
    probability of 7.0 near
      Yellowstone, *36*
    risk in U.S., *6, 10*
    tsunamis caused by, 8
earthquake risk map, *35*
Earth's climate system, 227
Earth's system, 76, *76, 78*
    average surface temperature, 226
    human impact on, 207
    impact of human use of land,
      157–158
    impact of human use of plants and
      animals, 162–164
    impact of human use of water,
      156–156,

    orbital changes, 230–232
    relating rates of resource use to
      impacts on, 150–153
    resources of, 73, 76–92
    resource use and, *150*
    role of soil in, 99
    solar energy in, 227
    as source of natural resources, 78
    your impact, 162
ecological succession, 66, *66*
economic geologist, 116, *116*
EDP (engineering design process),
    214, *214,* 216, 217
effects of natural hazards, 10, 28
electricity
    generation of, 156, 171, 233
    production of, 134, 207
emergency kit, 51
emergency management agency, 51
endangered species, 188
energy
    absorption of, 227
    change of form, 81
    conservation of, 81
    reduce use at school, 218, *218*
    from the sun, 78, 227, *227*
energy resource, 81–83, 95
    human impact on distribution, 107
    U.S. energy consumption by source,
      82
engineering design principles, 53
engineering design process (EDP),
    214, *214,* 216, 217
    analyze and interpret data, 72
    analyze data, 120, 239
    ask a question, 71
    brainstorm solutions, 56, 58
    choose and test solutions, 59
    communicate, 72, 120, 239
    conduct research, 72, 119, 239
    construct an explanation, 120
    criteria and constraints, 56, 58
    define the problem, 55, 58, 239
    design a solution, 72
    develop a presentation, 239
    evaluate and choose solutions, 57,
      58

    identify and recommend a solution,
      120
    identify the need, 54, 58
    identify the problem, 55
    precise statement of the problem,
      56
    prototype, 57
    redefine of the problem, 56
    solution development and testing,
      56
    use in mitigating natural hazards,
      53, 65
Engineer It, 16, 71–72, 134, 161
    Determine a Safe Building Site, 31
    Evaluate Solutions for Climate
      Change, 240
    Evaluate Trade-Offs, 189
    Identify the Effects of an
      Engineering Solution, 90
    Reduce Erosion, 106
Enhanced Fujita Scale, *19*
environment, 153
    case study: The Elwha River, 157,
      157
    changes in, 183
    consequences of use of natural
      resources, 88–90, 95, 150–153
    developing a method to monitor
      human impact on, 201–214
    human activity related to, 183, *183*
    human impact on, 180, 182–194
    impact of dams, 157
    impact of human use of land,
      158–159
    impact of human use of resources,
      164
    impact of human use of water,
      154–156
    impact of power plant, 215
    living things dependence upon, 162
    methods to reduce human impact
      on, 202–206, 214
    monitoring human impact on,
      202–205, 206, *206,* 217
    pollution of, 88, 89, 112
    reducing human impact on,
      200–223
    scale of human impacts, 190–194
    wildfires in, 4

Environmental Protection Agency (EPA), 205

erosion
cause of, 8, 106, *106*, 161, 187, 213, *213*
clear-cutting and, 150
climate change and, 227
during the Dust Bowl, 214
prevention of, 105, 157
redistribution of resources, 98
of soil, 99

eruption cloud, *13*

eruption column, *13*

ethanol, 92

evacuation plan, *60*

evaporation, 102, 108

evaporite deposits, *119*

Evidence Notebook, 5, 9, 14, 18, 23, 27, 29, 35, 45, 49, 52, 60, 63, *77*, 83, 87, 93, 97, 103, 108, 113, 127, 134, 140, 145, 149, 153, 156, 167, 187, 182, 186, 193, 197, 201, 206 215, 221, 225, 233, 237, 239, 243

explanation, 23, 45, 63, 93,113, 121, 127, 145, 167, 197, 221, 236

Exploration
Analyze Human Population Data, 128–132
Analyze the Impact of Human Use of Land Resources, 157–161
Analyzing Per Capita Consumption, 137–142
Analyzing Recent Climate Change, 234–237
Analyzing the Impact of Human Use of Plants and animals, 162–164
Analyzing the Impact of Human Use of Water, 154–156
Analyzing the Scale of Human Impacts on the Environment, 190–194
Comparing Renewable and Nonrenewable Resources, 84–87
Describing Methods for Monitoring Human Impacts on the Environment, 202–206
Describing Methods to Reduce Human Impacts on the Environment, 211–215

Describing Natural Hazard Mitigation, 50–53
Describing Natural Hazards and Natural Disasters, 6–10
Developing a Method to Monitor a Human Impact on the Environment, 207–210
Developing a Method to Reduce a Human Impact on the Environment, 216–218
Developing a Natural Hazard Mitigation Plan, 54–60
Evaluating the Effects of Using Natural Resources, 88–90
Explaining Human Impact on Natural Resource Distribution, 105–110
Explaining Patterns in Natural Resource Distribution, 98–104
Exploring Earth's Climate, 226–229
Exploring the Environment, 182–184
Exploring the Ways We Use Natural Resources, 78–83
Identifying Global Climate Change Factors, 230–233
Interpreting Patterns in Tornado Data, 18–20
Interpreting Patterns in Volcanic Data, 12–17
Investigating Rates of Resource Use, 133–136
Predicting Geologic Hazards, 32–36
Predicting Natural Hazards, 28–31
Predicting Weather and Climate Hazards, 37–42
Reducing the Effects of Climate Change, 238–240
Relating Human Activity to the Environment, 185–189
Relating Rates of Resource Use to Impacts on Earth's Systems, 150–153

Explore ONLINE!, 12, 52, 234,

extinct, **187**

extinction, *85*, 163, *163*, 164, *164*

extinct volcano, 12

extreme temperature, 8, 11

F

fertilizer, 157, *157*

firefighters, *52*

fish, *78*, 88
consumption rate, *140*
as natural resource, 79
as potentially renewable resource, 85

fishing, *162*, 187

flash flood, 41

flood, 6, 8, 9, 26
of 1913, 66, *66*
cause of, 35, 41
effects of, 1, 41, 49, *49*, 50, 63, 64
from hurricanes, 7
number of occurrences, 8
number of people affected by, *11*
predicting, 41
prevention of, 190
risk in New York City, *42*
from tropical cyclones, 21, *21*
types of, 41
worldwide locate of, *41*

flood-risk map, *42*, *42*

food supply, 131

forest fire, 1, *1*, 3, *3*, 66, 183

fossil fuels
consequences of use of, 89
formation of, 98, 136
greenhouse gas from burning of, 233, *233*
impact of use on climate, 177
impact of use on environment, 177
location of, *100*
mining of, 157
as natural resource, 79, 81
as nonrenewable resource, 85, 100, 134
paleoclimate data in, 218, *218*
percentage of energy sources used, 82, *82*
pollution by, 158, 159, *159*, 187, 188, 237

Franz Josef Glacier, 241, *241*

freeze, 22

freshwater, 103–104, *103*, *104*, 108

frog, 170, *170*

G

geologic hazard, 9, 9, 20, 47
  cause of earthquakes, 9, 14
  cause of tsunami, 9, 35, 59
  causes of landslides, 8, 14, 30
  earthquake frequency on Mauna
    Loa, 35
  earthquake locations, 10, 29, 32
  earthquake mitigation solution, 53,
    54
  earthquake occurrences, 8
  earthquake risk map, 35
  effects of earthquake, 1, 12, 32, 35,
    50
  effects of tsunamis, 9, 9, 12, 59
  hazards of volcanic eruptions, 14, 25
  historic volcanic eruptions, 13
  human effects on landslides, 167
  landslide, 9
  landslide in Pineville area, 31
  location of landslides, 29, 32
  location of tsunamis, 27, 46
  monitoring earthquakes, 59
  number of people affected by
    landslide, 11
  occurrence of landslides, 8
  patterns in volcanic eruption data,
    12–14
  predicting, 32–36
  predicting landslides, 30–31
  probability of 7.0 earthquake near
    Yellowstone National Park, 36
  risk of earthquakes in U.S., 6, 10
  tsunami warnings, 29
  types of, 32
  volcanic eruption frequency and
    size, 17
  Volcanic Explosivity Index (VEI), 13
geologic process, 9
  changes in materials, 98, 103
  distribution of resources, 73
  formation of fossil fuels, 79, 100
  formation of minerals, 98
  impact on resource distribution, 108
geosphere, 150
  effect on climate, 227
  human impact on, 152, 185, 187,
    187

impact of human use of land,
  157–161, 174
impact of human use of plants and
  animals, 162
land use for agriculture, 162, 162
REEs in, 112
as source of natural resources, 78
world population and arable land,
  159
geotechnical engineer, 61–62
geothermal energy
  as energy resource, 81
  percentage of energy sources used,
    82
glacier
  evidence of climate change, 230
  freshwater in, 103
  impact of climate change, 177, 177,
    239
global climate, 226, 230–233
global paper consumption, 171
Global Warming Potential (GWP),
  250
gold
  formation of deposits, 98, 102, 102
  location of, 97, 113, 114
  mining of, 107, 157
  uses for, 97
government
  preparation for hazards, 51
  recovery from hazards, 52
  response to hazards, 52
GPS, 34, 35
graph
  of adoptions and temperature, 236
  atmospheric carbon dioxide, 244
  average number of tornadoes per
    month in U.S., 19
  birth rate, death rate, population
    size, 130
  of carbon dioxide levels in
    atmosphere, 236
  carbon dioxide levels near Mauna
    Loa, 159
  changes on Mauna Loa, 35
  cod population, 194
  of consumption of yogurt, 146
  of deforestation, 168

of Earth's average temperature, 231
electricity use at school, 218
of emissions and cost of drive
  system designs, 189
of energy consumption, 161
of forest fires, 3
of frequency of earthquakes on
  Mauna Loa, 35
of global rubber consumption, 173
global temperature change, 231
of human population, 128
human population and extinction,
  164
of ice cream sales and temperature,
  235
of impact of dam removal, 156
number of tornadoes in North
  Carolina, 39
of passenger pigeon population,
  163
population by world region, 131
rate of use of natural resources, 151
of sunspot activity, 232
of trends in timber consumption,
  136
of types of biofuels, 92
of world population, 128
of world population and arable land,
  161
of world rice production, 171
Great Flood of 1913, 66, 66
Greener Skies Initiative, 251, 251
greenhouse effect, 227
greenhouse gas
  in atmosphere, 89, 158, 159, 161,
    207, 213, 227, 230, 231, 233
  climate change and, 234, 237
  emissions during food production
    vs. car miles driven, 250
  human activity producing, 227
Grinnell Glacier, Montana, 232
groundwater, 9, 103, 104, 104, 110,
  185, 203, 207
growth rate of population, 128
gypsum, 136

H

habitat, 3, 66, 152, 153, 154, 155, 157, 158, 163, **182**, 187, 188, 238
habitat destruction, 154, 158, 164
halite, 102
Halls Bayou Flood Map, 71
Hands-On Lab
  Analyze Your Impact, 160
  Assess Building Sites Near a Volcano, 15–16
  Design a Method to Monitor Solid Waste form a School, 209–210
  Develop and Evaluate a Flood Solution, 58–59
  Evaluate a Method to Reduce the Impact of Solid Waste on the Environment, 217–218
  Explore Replacement of a Natural Resource, 86–87
  Model Factors in Resource Use, 138
  Model Ocean Pollution from Land, 186
  Model Recharge and Withdrawal in an Aquifer, 109–110
  Model Resource Use, 135
  Model the Greenhouse Effect, 228–229
  Predict a Landslide, 30–31
Health Connection
  Natural Disasters and Disease, 66
  Vaccination and Population Growth, 170
historical data, 29, 39, 42
human population
  analyze data, 128–132
  by country in 2015, 129
  deforestation and, 183
  extinction and, 162
  in North Africa, 127
  number of cars and, 168
  resource use and, 126–142
  world population, 128
  world population by age, 129
  by world region, 131
humans
  developing a method to monitor impact on environment, 207–210
  impact of human use of water, 154–156
  impact of use of coal, 158, 158
  impact of use of land, 157–161
  impact of use of plants and animals, 162–164
  impact of use of resources, 164
  impact on atmosphere, 187, 187
  impact on biosphere, 187, 187
  impact on climate, 238–240
  impact on Florida panther, 188, 188
  impact on geosphere, 187
  impact on hydrosphere, 185
  impact on Mississippi River, 190–193, 193
  impact on natural resource distribution, 105–108
  methods to reduce human impacts on environment, 211–215
  monitoring impact on environment, 207–210
  number affected by weather and climate hazards, 11
  reducing impact on environment, 211–215
  reliance on fossil fuels, 157
  scale of impact on environment, 190–193
  use of natural resources, 78, 79, 88–90,
  use of resources, 133
  use of water, 154–156
  world population and arable land, 161
hurricane, 9
  damage from, 1, 7, 41
  historical paths, 29
  reducing the effects of, 48, 48
  risk in U.S., 6
  time and location of, 29
  as tropical cyclone, 21
hydroelectric energy
  location of, 101
  percentage of energy sources used, 82
  as renewable resource, 85
  world consumption of, 161
hydrosphere, 150
  effect on climate, 227
  human impact on, 185, 185
  impact of human use of fossil fuels, 156, 161
  impact of human use of water, 154–156
  as source of natural resources, 78

I

icecaps, 103
ice cores, 230
impermeable rock, 104, 104
Industrial Revolution, 158
infrared radiation, 227, 227
inorganic material, 207
Interactive Review, 25, 47, 65, 95, 115, 169, 174, 199, 223, 245
iron ore, 102, 102, 121

J

Japan, 175–176

K

Katmai volcano, 17
Kilauea volcano, HI, 15, 17
Krakatau volcano, 17

L

Ladybower Reservoir, England, 96
lahar, 12, 14, 51
land
  human impact on, 187, 187
  impact of human use of, 157–161
  use for agriculture, 164, 164
  world population and arable land, 161
landfill, 207, 207
landforms, 103
landslide, 8
  in area of Pineville, 31
  cause of, 8, 14, 30
  impact of human use of, 167
  location of, 29
  number of occurrences, 8
  number of people affected by, 11
  predicting, 30–31

Language SmArts, 55
  Analyze Energy Usage, 82
  Analyze Extinctions and Land Use, 164, *164*
  Choose a Promising Solution, 209
  Compare Tornado Data, *20*
  Explain Temperature Ranges on Earth and the Moon, 229
  Identify Facts, 184
  Rate Per-Capita Consumption and Population Size, 142
  Use Flood Maps, 42
lava flow, 12, *14, 15, 16, 33*
Lesson Self-Check, 23–25, 45–47, 63–65, 93–95, 113–115, 145–147, 167–169, 197–199, 221–223, 243–245
levee, 190, *191, 192*
Life Science Connection
  Ecological Succession, 66
  Frogs and Pollution, 170
line graph, 35, *128, 130, 136, 140, 151, 156,159, 161, 164, 179, 194, 204, 231, 232, 236*
Literature Connection
  The Great Flood of 1913, 66,
living resources, 162–164, *162*
lock and dam system, 191, *191*
Long Valley Caldera, *13*

M

magma, 12, *13, 33, 34, 102*
material
  inorganic and organic, 207, *207*
  for natural hazard mitigation, 60
material resource, 79–80, *79, 80,* 83, 85
Matto Grosso, Brazil, *163*
Mauna Loa volcano
  carbon dioxide levels near, *159*
  distance across summit crater, *35*
  eruption data, *34*
  frequency of earthquakes on, *35*
methane
  as greenhouse gas, 207, 227, 234
  produced by livestock, 250

minerals, 79, *79*
  deposits in North America, *102*
  human impact on distribution, 107
  as nonrenewable resource, 85, *85,* 134
  uses of, 102
mining
  of asteroids, 116, *116*
  impact on geosphere, 157, 187, *187*
  mountaintop removal mining, *90, 188*
  reduction of pollution from, 212
  release of greenhouse gases, 233
Mississippi River, 190–193, *190*
mitigation, 50–53, **50**
models/modeling
  computer modeling of hazards, 53
  hazard areas, 53
  ocean pollution, 180
  resource use, 131
  resource use for each individual, 134
moon
  distance from the sun, *226*
  surface of, *78*
  temperature range on, 226, 229
mountaintop removal mining, *90, 182*
Mount St. Helens, 66
mudflow, 51
Music Connection
  Songs about Saving Earth, 246

N

NASA (National Aeronautics and Space Administration), 43
National Oceanic and Atmospheric Association (NOAA), 38
National Weather Service (NWS), 38
natural changes, 183
natural disaster, 7, 19, 25
  cost of, 21–22
  disease associated with, 66
  earthquakes, 35
  interpret, 11
  prevention of, 28
  volcanic eruption, 12, 33

natural gas
  location of, *100*
  as natural resource, 79, 81
  as nonrenewable resource, 85, *100,* 134
  percentage of energy sources used, 82, *82*
  world consumption of, *161*
natural hazard, 1, **6,** 25
  data on, 10–11, *10–11*
  describing natural hazard mitigation, 50–53
  describing natural hazards and natural disasters, 6–10
  development of a mitigation plan, 54–60
  flood, *49*
  interpreting patterns in tornado data, 18–20
  interpreting patterns in volcanic data, 12–14
  prediction of climate and weather hazards, 37–38
  reducing the effects of, 65, 238
  risk in U.S., 6
  types of, 6, 8
  volcanoes, 5
natural hazard prediction, 26, 32–36, 47
  asteroid impacts, 43–44, *43*
  natural hazards, 28–29
  weather and climate hazards, 37–41
natural processes, 232, 233
natural resource, 78
  availability of, 84, 105
  careful use of, 211
  develop more efficient types, 159
  distribution of, 96–110
  Earth's system and use of, 146–164
  effects of using, 88–90
  energy resource, 81–83
  evaluating effects of using, 88–90
  exploring the ways we use natural resources, 78–83
  freshwater, 103–104, *103, 104*
  human impact on distribution, 105–108
  impact of human use of land, 157–161

impact of human use of water, 154–156

management of, 88

material resources, 79–80, *80*, 83

monitoring human use of, 202, *202*

nonrenewable resource, 100, *100*, 133, 136

nonrenewable resource compared to renewable resource, 84–87, 95

patterns of distribution, 75, *75*, 98–104

per capita consumption, 137, 139, 140, *140*

potentially renewable resource, 85

quality of, 198, 207

rate of use, 133–136, 149

relating rates of use to impacts on Earth's systems, 150–153

renewable resource, 101, *101*, 133, 136

resource depletion, 183

reuse and recycling, 212

use and population growth over time, 131–132

uses of, 136

near-surface air temperature, 226

NOAA (National Oceanic and Atmospheric Association), 38

NOAA Storm Prediction Center Outlooks and Confirmed Tornado Tracks, *40*

nonpoint-source pollution, 185

nonrenewable resource, 85

coal, 77, *77*

consumption of, 105

fossil fuels, 136

human reliance on, 143

oil, 100, *100*

renewable resources compared to, 84–85

types of, 98

North Africa, 127, *141*

Novarupta volcano, *13*

nuclear energy, 81, *82*, 89, *161*

NWS (National Weather Service), 38

O

oasis, *103*

ocean

absorption of greenhouse gases, 239

absorption of solar energy, 227, 232

acidity of, 190

impact of climate change, 227, *227*

natural resource in, 78

oil

formation of, *100*

human impact on distribution, 107

locations of, 98, *100*

as nonrenewable resource, *100*

offshore drilling for, *88*

products made from, *98*

oil spills, *90*

olive oil production, *125*

online activites, EXPLORE online! 6, 12, 34, 52, 109, 226

ore, 107, *107*

ore deposits, 107

organic material, 207, *207*

overbank flood, *41*

overfishing, 162, 163, 198

overharvesting, 162

oxygen, 79, 100, 155, 157, 163, 192

ozone layer, *179*

P

Pacific Remote Islands Marine National Monument, *88*

paleoclimate data, 230, *231*

paper consumption, *171*

passenger pigeon, *85*, *163*

pattern

in earthquake locations, *10*

of natural changes in environment, 177

in natural resource distribution, 75, *75*, 98–104

of population density in North Africa, *127*

in tornado data, 18–20, *18*, *19*, *20*

per capita consumption, 139, *139*, 140, *140*

effect on resource use, 150, *150*

of fish and shellfish in U.S., *140*

of land, 153

reduction of, 153

of water, 156

Performance Task. *see* Unit Performance Task

permafrost, *103*, 225, 234, *239*

permeable rock, 104, *104*

Persad, Geeta G., 241–242

pesticide, 105

petroleum

as natural resource, 79, 81, 83

as nonrenewable resource, 85, 133

percentage of energy sources used, *82*

PHA (potentially hazardous asteroid), 43

Physical Science Connection

Seabed Mining, 116

Pinatubo, Mount, 13, *13*, *17*, *32*, *33*

plants

as energy resource, 101

impact of climate change, 226

impact of human use of, 162–164

loss due to human use of land, 157

as natural resource, 79, *79*

needs of, 78

as renewable resource, 85, 161

plastic usage, *249*

point-source pollution, 185

polar area, *75*

pollution, 88, 89, **158**

amphibian sensitivity to, 170, *170*

concentrations, 198, 204

effects on organisms, 162

filtration of, 176

from fossil fuels, 158, 187, 207

by humans, 183

impact of, 198

from landfills, 207

monitoring, 206

nonpoint-source, **185**

point-source, **185**

reduction of, 207

by removal of trees, 161

of water, 185

polymetallic nodules, 116
population, 128
    change in Japan, *175*
    by country in 2015, *129*
    deforestation and, *183*
    density in New York and Tokyo, *219*
    density of in North Africa, *131*
    extinction and, *164*
    growth and resource use, 136
    growth rate, 130–132, *132*
    number of cars and, *168*
    per capita consumption and, 142
    world population and arable land,
      161
    world population by age, *129*
    world population over time, *128*
    by world region, *131*
population growth, 130
postdoctoral research scientist,
    241–242
potentially hazardous asteroid
    (PHA), 43
potentially renewable resource, 85
power plant, 215, *215*
prediction
    of earthquakes, 35
    of floods, 41
    of geologic hazards, 32–36
    of natural hazards, 10, 28–29
    of population changes, 128, 132
    of resource use, 136
    of tornadoes, 38, 54
    of tsunamis, 60
    of volcanic eruptions, 33
    of weather and climate hazards,
      37–42
preparation for hazards, 50, 51, *51*
problem
    definition of, 55, 58
    identification of, 53
    precise statement of, 56
process
    dissolution, 102
    engineering design process, 53–59,
      208, *208*, 216,
    evaporation, 102
    geologic, 9, 73, 79, 98, 100, 102
    harvesting plants and animals, 162

impact on climate, 232, 233
impact on resource distribution, 115
mineral formation, 102
of mining, 157
of obtaining water, 154
pyroclastic flow, 12, *14*

Q

Qingdao Haiwan Bridge, *62*

R

rain, 8
rainforest, *150*
Raleigh Weather Forecasts, *40*
rare Earth elements (REEs),
    111–112, *111*
recovery from hazards, 52, *52*, 55, 65
recycling, 107, 112, *185*, 212, 216, *216*
REEs (rare Earth elements),
    111–112, *111*
renewable resource, 85
    distribution of solar energy, *101*
    humans' reliance on, 143
    locations of, 99
    management of, 105
    nonrenewable resources compared
      to, 84–85
    solar energy, 136
    trees, 77, 93
    types of, 101, 133
research scientist, 241–242
reservoir, 107, 154
resource depletion, 183
reuse, 212
rice production, *171*
rock
    absorption of solar energy, 232
    as natural resource, 79, *79*
    as nonrenewable resource, 85, *85*
    paleoclimate data in, 231, *231*
    permeable and impermeable, 104,
      104
    as source of minerals, 102
    weathering of, 98, 99
rubber consumption, *167*
runoff, 197

S

salmon, 155, *156*
sanitation, 131, *131*
satellite imaging, 246, *246*
satellites, 40, 205, 230
scale of human impacts, 190–193
scientific knowledge, 53
seabed mining, 116
sea surface temperature, 226
sediment, 98, 99, 155, *155*, *156*, 190
seismograph, 35, *60*
severe storms, 9, 18, 41
    damage from, *26*
    effects of, 50
    mitigation of damage, 50
    number and cost, *22*
shield volcano, 34
Shishmaref, Alaska, 225, *225*, *233*
shooting stars, 43
silver, 102
sinkhole, *9*
Social Studies Connection
    Economic Geologists, 116
    Science and Activism, 246
    Technological Ages, 170
soil
    absorption of greenhouse gases,
      227
    degradation of, 187
    erosion of, 106
    formation of, *99*
    human impact on distribution, 105
    as natural resource, 79, *79*
    pollution of, 198
    role in Earth's system, 99
solar energy
    in Earth's system, 227, *227*, 232
    locations for use of, *101*
solid waste, 207, *207*
    disposal of, *210*, 211–218
    monitoring, 203–204
solution
    brainstorming solutions, 56, 58
    choose and test, 59
    evaluation and selection of, 57
    testing of, 55

soybean, 83, 91, *91, 92*
steam engine, 158
St. Helens, Mount, *13, 17, 66*
storm
    effects of, *50*
    number of occurrences, *8*
    number of people affected by, *11*
subway system, *219*
sulfur dioxide, 188
sun
    distance of Earth from, 226, *226*
    energy from, 233
sunlight
    effect on climate, 227
    as energy resource, 82, 101, *101,*
      133, 136
    as inexhaustible renewable
      resource, 134
    as natural resource, 78, 81
    percentage of energy sources used,
      82
sunspot, 232
supercell, 18, 38, 40
surface water, 104, *104,* 185

T

table
    of billion dollar weather disasters,
      22
    of cause and effect, patterns,
      stability, and change, *248*
    of causes of climate change, *232*
    of consumption rates, *137, 141*
    of criteria, *235*
    of criterion and constraints, *203, 211*
    of deforestation and population
      growth, *168*
    of diamond production, *114*
    effects of weather and climate
      hazards, *11*
    Enhanced Fujita Scale, *19*
    of eruptions of Mt. Etna, *46*
    ideas for reducing carbon dioxide
      emissions, *240*
    of impact of change in fishing
      harvest, *162*
    of impacts of coal use, *156*
    of landslide model data, *31*

    of observations, *86, 109*
    of per capital consumption of fish
      and shellfish, *140*
    of population growth and car
      ownership, *168*
    of questions and notes, *74, 122, 178*
    Raleigh weather forecasts, *40*
    ranking criteria and constraints, *57*
    of renewable and nonrenewable
      resources, *133, 172*
    of technologies for natural hazard
      mitigation, *60*
    of tornado engineering problems,
      55
    of types of energy resources, *81*
    of types of resources, *118*
    volcanic eruption frequency and
      size, *17*
    Volcanic Explosivity Index, *13*
    worldwide natural disasters, *8*
    of your impact on Earth's system,
      160
table salt, *102*
Take It Further
    The Atmosphere as a Resource,
      165–166
    Careers in Engineering:
      Geotechnical Engineer, 61–62
    Careers in Science: Biomass
      Engineer, 91–92
    Careers in Science: Conservation
      Scientist, 143–144, *143*
    Careers in Science: Postdoctoral
      Research Scientist, 241–242
    Chernobyl Nuclear Disaster,
      195–196
    The Cost of Natural Disasters, 21–22
    Predicting Asteroid Impacts, 43–44
    Rare Earth Elements and
      Technology, 111–112
    Urban Planning to Reduce Impact,
      219–220
Tambora volcano, *17*
technological ages, 170
technology
    automated systems, 43
    for climate data collection, 218
    computer, 7, 55
    computer modeling of weather, 38
    conversion of biomass, 91

    development and use, 207
    Doppler radar, 40
    evaluation of technology for natural
      hazard mitigation, 60
    GPS, 34, 35
    for hazard mitigation, 55
    mapping technology, 52, 55
    for monitoring hazard areas, 1, 29,
      34, 35
    for monitoring human impact on
      environment, 202, 206
    natural resource use and, 136
    phone, 52
    portable medical equipment, 52
    for predicting natural hazards, 28
    radar, 7
    radio, 52
    for reducing human impact on
      environment, 205, 207
    reducing impact of resource usage,
      153
    role in natural hazard mitigation, 60
    role in population growth, 127
    satellites, 7, 40
    seismograph, 35
    seismometer, 34
    sensors, 206
    solar power, 89
    telescope, 43
    temporary shelters, 52
    thermal imaging sensors, 34
    tiltmeter, 34
    use in disaster response, 52
    weather balloons, 38
    weather satellites, 38
    wind power, 89
Technology Connection
    Asteroid Mining, 116
tectonic plate boundaries
    earthquakes at, 10, *10, 32*
    uplift at, 102
    volcanoes at, *32*
temperature, 226
terraced farming, *106*
thermal pollution, 215
Three Gorge Dam, China, *120,* 184
thunderstorms, 8, 9, 18, *22, 26, 41*
timber, 132, *150*

Toba volcano, *13, 17*

tornado, 9
- average annual number in U.S., *19*
- average number per month in U.S., *20*
- classification and hazards, 19
- damage from, *1, 20, 25, 38, 47, 54*
- effects of, *54*
- Enhanced Fujita Scale, *19–20*
- formation of, 18, 38
- frequency and location of, 18
- historic data on, *39*
- interpreting data patterns, 18–20, *18, 19*
- mitigation plan, 53
- NOAA Storm Prediction Center Outlooks and Confirmed Tornado Tracks, *40*
- number in North Carolina, *39*
- number of EF-1 or larger in U.S., *24*
- path of, *177*
- predicting, 38–39, 53
- risk in U.S., *6*
- time and location of, 29
- tracks in U.S., *39*
- worldwide risk, *37*

Tornado Alley, 18

tornado season, 18

tree rings, 230, *230*

trees, 132
- ash trees, 144
- clear-cutting, *152, 152*
- impact of human use of, 190
- interaction of Earth's subsystems and, 150
- management of, 153
- as natural resource, 77
- as potentially renewable resource, 133
- rate of renewal, 87
- as renewable resource, *93, 94*
- replacement of, 105
- replanting, 205, *205*

tropical area, 75

tropical cyclone, 21, *22, 29*

tropical storm, 8

tsunami
- cause of, *8, 9, 35, 59*
- damage from, *1, 12, 59*
- location of, *27, 46*
- warning for, 29

typhoon, 21

U

Unit Connections, 66, 116, 170, 246

United States
- average annual number of tornadoes in, *19*
- average number of tornadoes per month in, *20*
- carbon dioxide emissions, *240*
- earthquake locations and risk, *10*
- energy consumption, *82*
- location of earthquakes in, *10*
- location of fossil fuel deposits, *100*
- natural disasters in, 21, *21*
- natural hazard risk, *6*
- number and cost of natural disasters, *22*
- number of EF-1 or larger tornadoes in, *24*
- tornado tracks, *39*

Unit Performance Task
- How can air travel be improved to reduce impacts on Earth systems? 251–252
- How does population change affect energy consumption in Japan? 175–176
- What is the best plan to improve a park? 71–72
- Which iron ore mine location is a better investment? 121–122

Unit Project
- Community Climate Change, 179
- Natural Hazard Planning, 3
- Natural Resource Distribution, 75
- Natural Resources and Earth Systems, 125

Unit Review, 67–70, 115–118, 171–174, 243–245

Unit Starter
- Analyzing Frequency of Wildfires, 3
- Analyzing Patterns in Resource Distribution, 75
- Interpreting Ozone Layer Data, 179
- Olive Oil Production and Consumption, 125

uranium, 85

urban planning, 219–220

USGS (United States Geologic Survey), 202

V

vaccination, 170

VEI (Volcanic Explosivity Index), *13*

Vesuvius, Mount, *17*

volcanic eruption
- damage from, *23, 24*
- hazards of, *14*
- historic eruptions, 6, *13, 23*
- impact on climate, 219
- location of, *29*
- occurrences of, *8*
- patterns in data, 12–14
- predicting, 33
- Volcanic Explosivity Index, *13*

Volcanic Explosivity Index (VEI), *13*

volcanic mudflow, *51*

volcano
- active, 12
- dormant, 12
- extinct, 12
- location of, *32*
- number of eruptions, *8*
- pyroclastic flow, 12
- shield volcano, 34
- types of, 12

W

water
- absorption of solar energy, 227, 232
- erosion by, 102
- filtration of, *89, 153,* 157
- human impact on distribution, 108
- impact of human use of, 154–156, 167

locations for use of, 101

as natural resource, 78, 79, *79*

pollution of, 198, 207

as potentially renewable resource, 85, 133

quality of, 202, *202*

regulation of use, 202

storage of, *96*

usage over time, 132, *132*

use and replacement, 86–87

water cycle, 104

water pollution, 185, *185*

watershed, *193*

water table, *104*

weather, 37, 214

weather forecast, 37

weather hazard, 8, 9, 37–41

blizzard, 9, *9*

causes of floods, *7*, 21, 35, 41

climate change and, 227

damage from hurricanes, *1*, *7*, 41

drought, 8, *8*, 9, *9*, *11*, 22

effect of floods, *1*, *11*, 41, 49, *49*, 50, 63, 64

flood, 8, 9, *26*, 41, 66, *66*

flood occurrences, *8*

flood risk in New York City, *42*

historical path of hurricanes, *29*

hurricane, 9

hurricane risk in U.S., *6*

locations of floods, *41*

number of people affected by, *11*

patterns in tornado data, 18–20, *18*, *19*, *20*

predicting, 37–42

predicting floods, 41

predicting tornadoes, 38–39

prevention of floods, 190

reducing the effects of hurricanes, 48

severe thunderstorms, 8, 9, 18, 22, *26*, 41, 50

time and location of hurricanes, *29*

tornadoes, 25, *47*

tropical cyclone, 21

winter storm, *22*

worldwide tornado risk, *37*

weathering, 98, 99, *114*

weather prediction, 40

weather stations, 35, 40

well, 108, 154, 179, 197, *198*

wetlands, 89, *155*, 188, 239

Why It Matters, 2, 74, 124, 178

wildfire, 4, 8, *52*

causes of, 12, 35

number and cost, *22*

number of occurrences, *8*

number of people affected by, *11*

Wilson Butte Inyo Crater, CA, *13*

wind, 163–164

as energy resource, 81, 89

erosion by, 102

from hurricanes, *7*

as inexhaustible renewable resource, 85, 101

locations for use of, 98, 101

percentage of energy sources used, 82, *82*

from tropical cyclones, 21

wind farms, 165–166, *165*,

wind turbines, 165–166, *165*

winter storm, *22*

wood

as biomass, 91

consumption of, 132, *132*

as potentially renewable resource, *94*, 133

world energy consumption, *159*

world population, *128*

world rice production, *171*

Write, 132, 156, 214

Y

Yellowstone Huckleberry Ridge volcano, *13*

Yellowstone Lava Creek volcano, *13*

Yellowstone Mesa Falls volcano, *13*

Yellowstone National Park

eruption frequency, *17*

probability of 7.0 earthquake near, *36*